LINCOLN CHRISTIAN

P9-CRQ-988

AUTHENTIC
TRANSFORMATION

AUTHENTIC TRANSFORMATION

A New Vision of Christ and Culture

Glen H. Stassen

D. M. Yeager

and

John Howard Yoder

With a Previously Unpublished Essay
by H. Richard Niebuhr

ABINGDON PRESS
Nashville

AUTHENTIC TRANSFORMATION:
A NEW VISION OF CHRIST AND CULTURE

Copyright © 1996 by Abingdon Press

All rights reserved.

No part of this work may be reproduced or transmitted in any form or by any means, electronic or mechanical, including photocopying and recording, or by any information storage or retrieval system, except as may be expressly permitted by the 1976 Copyright Act or in writing from the publisher. Requests for permission should be addressed in writing to Abingdon Press, 201 Eighth Avenue South, P. O. Box 801, Nashville, TN 37202, U.S.A.

This book is printed on acid-free, recycled paper.

Library of Congress Cataloging-in-Publication Data

Stassen, Glen Harold, 1936-
  Authentic transformation : a new vision of Christ and culture / Glen H. Stassen, D. M. Yeager, and John Howard Yoder ; with a previously unpublished essay by H. Richard Niebuhr.
        p.   cm.
  Includes bibliographical references (pp.)
  ISBN 0-687-02273-8 (alk. paper)
  1. Niebuhr, H. Richard (Helmut Richard), 1894-1962. Christ and culture. 2. Christianity and culture. 3. Christianity and culture—United States 4. Sociology, Christian. 5. Christian ethics. I. Yeager, D. M. II. Yoder, John Howard. III. Niebuhr, H. Richard (Helmut Richard), 1894-1962. Types of Christian ethics. IV. Title.
  BR115.C8S72   1996   96-18575
  261—dc20   CIP

Unless otherwise noted, all scripture quotations are from The New Revised Standard Version Bible, copyright © 1989 by the the Division of Christian Education of the National Council of the Churches of Christ in the USA. Used by permission.

"Types of Christian Ethics" copyright © 1996 Richard R. Niebuhr. Used by permission.

Selected quotes from *Christ and Culture* by H. Richard Niebuhr copyright © 1951 by Harper and Row, Publishers, Inc. Reprinted by permission of HarperCollins Publishers, Inc.

96 97 98 99 00 01 02 03 04 05 — 10 9 8 7 6 5 4 3 2

MANUFACTURED IN THE UNITED STATES OF AMERICA

CONTENTS

93759

Guide to abbreviated titles of works by H. Richard Niebuhr:

C&C   *Christ and Culture*

Faith   *Faith on Earth: An Inquiry into the Structure of Human Faith* (ed. by Richard R. Niebuhr)

KGA   *The Kingdom of God in America*

MR   *The Meaning of Revelation*

PCM   *The Purpose of the Church and its Ministry: Reflections on the Aims of Theological Education* (in collaboration with Daniel Day Williams and James M. Gustafson)

RS   *The Responsible Self: An Essay in Christian Moral Philosophy*

SSD   *The Social Sources of Denominationalism*

Since 1994 marked the one hundredth anniversary of the birth of H. Richard Niebuhr, it seemed an apt occasion for focused reflection on the most widely used of his books, *Christ and Culture*. This text is studied in graduate and undergraduate classes; it is required reading in courses in colleges, universities, and seminaries. It is used primarily not to introduce the theology of H. Richard Niebuhr, but to introduce a systematized representation of the various dominant forms of Christian belief. Often it serves as a basic text in the systematic study of Christian ethics, but probably just as frequently as an orientation to Christian theology more generally.

If sales are a reliable guide to the influence of a theological text, *Christ and Culture* must be regarded as the most influential of Niebuhr's theological arguments; Richard R. Niebuhr reports that *Christ and Culture* "has consistently been the top-selling book" among those written by his father. At the same time, it has been subjected to the least critical scrutiny of all his books. To imagine reasons for this critical neglect is not difficult. Descriptive typologies differ from arguments in that they are not subject to the same sort of objection and exchange that are inevitably provoked by a lively conceptual thesis. Moreover, the primary test of a typological study is its success in effectively simplifying some welter of possibilities and in packaging that "booming, buzzing confusion" in a pedagogically attractive way. People do not commonly argue about the theoretical merits of an existing typology; a new and more adequate typology simply displaces its predecessors because it organizes more information, and does so more effectively. What makes *Christ and Culture* such an interesting book is that it is not only a typology but also an argument. It not only clusters and compares options, it argues normatively and theologically for the superiority of one of the types. For this reason, it deserves critical scrutiny of the same kind that has been accorded Niebuhr's other works. The set of reflections collected here is designed to open the long-delayed conversation about the defensibility and reliability of this value-laden typological portrait of Christian attitudes which has, for forty years now, shaped the theological consciousness of rising generations of students.

The extensive use of *Christ and Culture* as a textbook is surely due not solely to its apparent usefulness as a clear and accessible schematization of the varieties of Christian faith. It continues to command attention because what Niebuhr's first chapter names as "the enduring problem" that he grapples with is so important, and even more so in our time of pluralism, postmodernism, global encounter of multiple cultures, and culture wars. The problem is involved in relations between loyalties to Christ and culture, church and state, faith and reason, and Christian discipleship in secular society. It is the problem of how to be in but not of the world; how to be a Jew to the Jews and a Gentile to the Gentiles (I Cor. 9:19ff.); how not to be conformed to this world, but transformed by the renewing of our minds (Romans 12). It is fundamental for every ethical issue, for theology, for hermeneutics, for missions, and for Christian philosophy. It is about how the assumptions, values, perceptions, and understandings of society (culture) penetrate us and influence our understanding of who Christ is, what it means to follow him, and what the mission of the church is. Conversely, it is about how Christians are called to withdraw from, or compromise with, or selectively affirm and reject, or transform, society and culture. It is about the consequences of the bedrock belief of Christians that this Christ, known only through all our conditioned interpretations of his presence, is the means by which the Lord of all becomes known to us and judges all cultural wisdom and aspiration. Niebuhr argues that the answer is transformation, conversion, "Christ transforming culture." In our essays and the book's conclusion we shall try to develop our understanding of what authentic transformation implies and what shape it takes when it is embodied.

We begin with Niebuhr's original sketch of "Christ and Culture,"

10

written nine years before the book was published, but itself never published until now. Diane Yeager served as editor of the essay. We include it both for its intrinsic interest and because it will introduce readers to, or refresh their memory of, the basic perspectives in the book. Furthermore, it provides interesting clues to the context and original intentions behind the book. The original essay turned out to be remarkably accurate in laying out the more fully developed argument, nine years ahead of its full fruition. We are deeply grateful to Richard R. Niebuhr for granting us permission to publish his father's essay for the first time.

The three present contributors come from quite different perspectives and locations. John Howard Yoder comes from a Mennonite/Anabaptist background, training in the history of Christian thought, and a lifetime of very extensive discussion in ecumenical circles as well as widespread addresses to lay audiences. His published works have been based, not on his denominational background, but on a biblical realism with claims on all Christians of whatever denomination who respect the biblical faith. He is author of *The Politics of Jesus* (Eerdmans, 1972; revised edition 1994), and many other books. In these books Yoder argues persuasively that mainstream ethics has neglected the alternative community-based political ethic of Jesus, and thus has evaded the concrete criteria of authentic Christian discipleship. He develops a highly influential corrective. He is Professor of Theology in a Roman Catholic university, Notre Dame.

His essay, "How H. Richard Niebuhr Reasoned: A Critique of *Christ and Culture*," is based on a close analysis of Niebuhr's book *Christ and Culture*, and does not claim to interpret the full scope of Niebuhr's historical development. Yoder has been known more as a critic of Niebuhr than as a sympathetic expositor of Niebuhr's contribution, and the most notable exception to the meek acceptance of Niebuhr's typology was Yoder's very critical essay attacking the book, an essay which was originally written in 1958 and which has remained unpublished until now. His extended and brilliant criticism of Niebuhr's classic *Christ and Culture* has been not-yet-published almost as long as the Dead Sea Scrolls, held in private and circulated for decades only in mimeographed form.

Diane M. Yeager comes from a background in the Evangelical Lutheran Church in America, and training in Christian ethics. Her essay for this book, "The Social Self in the Pilgrim Church," and much else she has written, is based on her scholarly study and appreciation of H. Richard Niebuhr. She is Associate Professor at Georgetown University—a Catholic university—and General Editor of the *Journal of Religious Ethics*.

Yeager seeks to answer the question posed by Raymond Whitehead: since *Christ and Culture* neglects the question of power, does not Niebuhr fail to distinguish between cultural thought forms and structures of political and economic power, and fail to name ways that culture often masks or justifies oppressive power? And does Niebuhr not then understate the need for followers of the Christ—who opposes oppression—to oppose oppressive forms of culture? This question is closely related to Yoder's work reinvigorating the biblical theme of the powers and authorities, and to his argument that some forms of culture must be opposed or rejected while others may be used or transformed. Yeager wrestles similarly with the question posed by Charles Scriven: since one cannot convert culture by capitulating to it, does not Niebuhr neglect the Christian community's need to develop an alternative culture? Is not Yoder right that Anabaptist witness and alternative community are not a withdrawal from culture, but a direct challenge to the powers and authorities, and the only project by means of which the program of transformation can be achieved? Her answer affirms the import of the questions, and especially Scriven's, but argues forcefully that Niebuhr develops a more profound, insightful, and subtle answer in his writings on the church than has been previously recognized. The answer involves the conversion of faith, the dynamic presence of God, and the church as apostle, pastor, pioneer, and pilgrim.

Glen H. Stassen comes from a background in several different Baptist denominations and training in Christian ethics and the history of Christian thought. He is the author of *Just Peacemaking: Transforming Initiatives for Justice and Peace* (Westminster/John Knox, 1992), which advances a grace-based interpretation of the Sermon on the Mount and proposes a just peacemaking theory. He is Professor of Christian Ethics at the Southern Baptist Theological Seminary.

In his essay, "Concrete Christological Norms for Transformation," Stassen intends to set *Christ and Culture* in the wider sweep of Niebuhr's lifelong wrestle with historical relativism and the sovereignty of God. He takes up Yoder's questions concerning Niebuhr's appeal to the Trinity as his normative basis for evaluating types of Christian ethics, and Yoder's criticism that Niebuhr lacks concrete criteria for faithful discipleship, especially in Niebuhr's description of transformationism. Stassen argues for the importance of Niebuhr's "historical realism" as a response to Yoder's criticisms that affirms both Yoder's constructive argument and Niebuhr's transformationist intent. Based on this method of historical realism and Niebuhr's emphasis on the sovereignty of God, he proposes seven historically concrete Christological norms for measuring authentic transformation.

In the book's concluding essay, Glen Stassen builds on the critical analyses of the three preceding essays, and on dialogue among the three authors, to offer a constructive proposal for relating Christ and culture. The three critical essays evidence some discernible tensions. Together, however, they point in mutually complementary directions for the church in our multipolar society.

In the mobility of our shrinking global context, the presence of persons from many faiths and many cultural backgrounds, the experience of the interweaving of multiple cultures, and the polarization of society, the question of how to relate Christ to culture grows increasingly intense and urgent. The question for Christians who would be loyal to Christ is not only how to relate to competing faiths or loyalties, but how to shape faithful embodiment in community in our complex society. The constructive proposal argues for the church as Apostle, Pioneer, and Pastor, embodying authentic transformation in faithful communities of discipleship. It then sketches a typology of ways churches and Christians avoid authentic transformation—ways they conform to society's polarization between laissez-faire individualism and authoritarian reaction. And it points in a direction of repentance, conversion, and faithfulness.

Types of Christian Ethics[1]

H. Richard Niebuhr

1. The Typological Method

The modern turn to typological method in the social sciences or *Geisteswissenschaften,* including ethics, represents, in part, an effort to overcome some of the limitations of the genetic method as a way of understanding individual events. Using the latter method, we tend to assume that a single idea or principle is exhibited in various degrees of maturity or clarity in the individual phenomena we have selected. So in Christian ethics we may endeavor to understand how teleological striving after vision or kingdom of God comes to expression in individual men, groups, or movements. The genetic scale, not as a scale of the earlier and later but rather of the less and the more evolved, then becomes a value scale by means of which we seek to determine the worth of individual events. The inadequacy of the method appears when we note that the principle which we have chosen as central may not be important in the view of an individual we are seeking to understand, or that its significance in this individual is dependent on its relation to other factors, so that he must be understood not as a variant form of one principle but as a unique concretion of a number of principles, each of which derives its particular meaning from its place in the whole. With the recognition of this fact, however, we seem to be left with a confusing pluralism of principles and an even greater multiplicity of historic individuals. Typology is the effort to order these many elements into families in such a way that some of the characteristic combinations of principles may be understood. On the one hand, then, typology, in ethics as in psychology (I am here paraphrasing Jung), challenges the assumption that there is only one ethics or one ethical principle; in our particular field it denies the assumption that there is a single Christian ethics or a single Christian ethical principle. It assumes, on the contrary, that there are multiple principles and a large number of creative individual concretions of the Christian life. On the other hand, typology seeks to understand these unique individuals with the aid of ideal figures or types, that is, of relatively concrete models of combinations of interests or convictions.

The method is helpful but has definite limitations which need to be kept in mind. First of all, a type is a mental construct to which no individual wholly conforms. It must be used, therefore, only as a means toward understanding the individual and not as a statement of necessary connections, so that the rational is given precedence over the empirical. Secondly, these mental constructs, if they are to be useful toward understanding, must be of one sort—that is to say: among the many variable factors which may be discerned in any concrete, historical event, only one set can be chosen at a time to furnish material for the mental model. Psychological or sociological or anthropological or theological models may be constructed, but only confusion results if these categories are mixed. Further, the prejudice in favor of the fundamental character of the category which is being employed must be guarded against. It is one thing to distinguish psychological types of religious or moral life, but quite another thing to ascribe primary importance to the psychological factors. It is one thing to distinguish sociological types of Christian ethics, but another to claim that the kind of sociological organization which prevails in a group determines its ethical character. Correlations, not determinations, can be dealt with by typology. Again, the typologist needs to remember that he is not constructing a value scale. His enterprise is directed neither toward explanation nor evaluation, but toward understanding and appreciation. If his types are well constructed and, so, empirically relevant, he will belong to one of the types himself and will have a preference for it; but one purpose of typology is that of helping him understand his own type as one of many and so to achieve some measure of disinterestedness.

2. The Various Ways of Typing Christian Ethics

No absolute types of Christian morality can be discerned, but there are various points of view from which the individual historical phenomena may be analyzed and classified. A psychological method, made popular by William James, distinguishes "once-born" and "twice-born," or "healthy minded" and "sick soul," types of religious experience and expression.[2] These types may be used to distinguish the ethical convictions and attitudes of Christians also. For the "once born," moral values seem to be directly realizable and moral imperatives immediately fulfillable. The "twice-born" type approaches such values and laws indirectly, using them first of all not as guides to action but as criticisms of the self, which by means of them must be reduced to a state of receptivity and brought into dependence on God before it can employ them as guides to action. The distinction between the extroverted and introverted types corresponds in part with the former classification; in part, however, it cuts across that division, since the introverted type of Christian ethics may employ either the direct or indirect approach and the extroverted may be similarly divided into meliorists and revolutionaries. Another typology which has been very useful in the understanding of different Christian groups with their varying approaches to the social problem is the Weber-Troeltsch distinction between churches and sects, with the addition of a third, heterogeneous class of mystics. To what an extent the types are mental constructs to which no historic individuals conform completely becomes evident in any effort to classify the historic Christian groups into churches and sects. On the other hand, it has also become fairly certain that a positive correlation exists between ethics and type of social organization, so that this sociological typing has been very helpful in the effort to understand the various groups. Again, it is possible to classify the Christian ethical organizations of thought and practice by reference to cultural types represented in them. There are Hebraic, Hellenistic, Latin, Medieval, Byzantine, and modern Christian ethics. Each of these has an apparently distinct character which must be appreciated in itself

17

and not only by comparison with one of the other cultural types. If any scale of worth is to be erected, it must be done within the scope of the cultural type by reference to the degree of typical purity or integrity exhibited in the individual. A fourth principle of classification is the socio-economic, for which the mode of economic production is taken as the key to character; hence pastoral, agricultural, and early and late industrial types may be distinguished. In this case a correlation between the system of ethical values and imperatives and the system of production is sought. In the contemporary situation, for instance, an ethics of rural Christianity may be opposed to the ethics of urban, industrial Christianity. The philosophical point of view allows us to make a distinction between the teleological and deontological types of Christian ethics, in accordance with the primacy in the system of thought and conduct of the conception of the good or of the right. Early Christian, Calvinist, and most sectarian ethics will be seen to represent, in general, the deontological type of ethics, while Roman Catholicism, both in its Augustinian and Thomistic forms, and modern liberal Christianity will be classified as teleological. Subtypes in each case need, then, to be distinguished in accordance with, on the one hand, the priority of the objective or subjective good (God or salvation) and, on the other hand, the objective or subjective law (Biblicism, inner light).

It may be that laborious, detailed historical study of, as well as analytic clarifying inquiry into, the nature of these various systems of classification may reveal correlations between sociological and psychological, or philosophical and socio-economic, types. Hence there is a possibility that more inclusive mental models may be possible, but for the present, the task of typology would appear to lie elsewhere—in the more precise definition of each group of types and in the use of such limited models for the understanding, not for the explanation, of historical actualities.

3. The Theological Types of Christian Ethics

If it is possible to construct models in which ethical convictions are correlated with sociological or psychological variables, it is no less possible, and for the theological moralist it is more enlightening, to discover or construct types in which the variable is Christian faith.

18

Hence we raise the questions, whether there is in the gospel itself a source of the infinite variety of Christian moral forms; whether the differences in the ways in which Christians conceive their duty and understand good and evil are simply correlated with the variety of cultural, psychological, and sociological patterns evident in their lives; or whether they may be related to variations in the Christian situation before God. Is Christianity, as gospel, a simple thing which enters into relation with other simple elements, or with compounds, being modified by them, or is it itself a compound so that issues would need to arise within it and differentiations would need to take place on the basis of Christian convictions alone? The ancient church raised the question in terms of Jesus Christ's unity or duality and needed to decide for the latter, for there was an evident polarity between the Jesus of history and the Christ of faith which could not be resolved by the absorption of one into the other. Similarly, the question was raised in Trinitarianism.

The nature and, in general, the character of the most important theological types of Christians have been discerned by Gilson, who, in his *Reason and Revelation in the Middle Ages*, characterizes "the main spiritual families which were responsible for the copious philosophical and theological literature of the Middle Ages."[3] They are the Tertullian family, for whom revelation, opposed to reason, is the source of all saving knowledge and who are "partisans of exclusive otherworldliness" (14); the Augustinian family, which proceeds from revelation to reason, believing in order that it may know, transfiguring rather than rejecting cultural wisdom ("you cannot fail to know an Augustinian when you meet one in history, but it is not an easy thing to guess what he is going to say" [21]); the family of Latin Averroists with their doctrine of twofold truth (the skeptical branch of this family which denies revelation in fact though not in word has really left the clan completely); the Thomist family, which synthesizes faith and reason; and finally, the family of Modern Devotion, which rejects the whole problem, seeking a "straight practical Christian life, and nothing else" (90). It is questionable whether, as Gilson describes them, the members of the latter group constitute a family; mere dissent does not constitute a type. A group such as the latter represents a stage of reflection rather than a theological type, and in it all the other types are likely to be represented, though not in developed form.

Gilson's differentiation of the spiritual families with respect to their use of revelation and reason points a promising direction in which to move in seeking to distinguish the Christian ethical types theologically. The Christian life moves between the poles of God in Christ as known through faith and the Bible and God in nature as known through reason in culture. If it be regarded as a life directed toward the good, it is, on the one hand, directed toward the attainment of the vision of God through Jesus Christ and, on the other, through creation; if it be regarded as a life under obligation, then it is under the obligation of obedience to Christ on the one hand, of obedience to the demands of nature on the other. But neither Christ nor nature is directly present to the Christian; as the former is mediated by the church and the Bible, so the latter is mediated by the cultural community and its wisdom. The variability in Christian ethics appears, then, to be analyzable by noting the manner in which the two strains of the Christian life are united. (It may, however, be said that this classification of types is not an a priori deduction of categories, since the result has been gained only after various hypothetical schemes have been applied to the historical individualities and rejected, while this scheme has been found close enough to the historical facts to render them intelligible.)

The main types of Christian ethics, from this theological point of view, are then (1) the new law, (2) the natural law, (3) the synthetic or architectonic, (4) the dualistic or oscillatory, and (5) the conversionist types. The use of the term "law" in designating the first and second types does not mean that these groups are particularly legalist in character. So far as I can see, any one of the five types may appear in primarily teleological or primarily deontological form, but the kinship between teleologists and deontologists within a type is greater than the kinship between formalists or teleologists of all types.

4. The New Law Type [Christ Against Culture]

New law Christianity is represented in the New Testament by the first gospel. A characteristic feature of its presentation of Christian morality is the sharp antithesis between the law of God as known through Jewish culture and the law declared through Jesus Christ. The latter really supplants the former, though, as is inevitable, some regard must be given the former as possessing a validity that cannot be ignored. ("Think not that I am come to destroy the law" [Matt. 5:17].) The values with which Matthew is concerned are almost wholly the values of life in the Christian spiritual community, as is indicated particularly

20

by his form of the Beatitudes. He also illustrates the general tendency of the new law group to mark off the Christian community with its standard of value and its imperatives from the cultural community in which it lives.

The type is represented in more developed form in the second century in such writings as the *Didache*, the *Epistle of Barnabas*, the *Epistle to Diognetus*, and similar documents. Tertullian is evidently a member of the family. A fundamental idea of these early Christians (who, significantly, are regarded by modern representatives of the types as representing primitive Christianity) is the conception that Christians are a new people with a new law. The primary source of the law is Jesus Christ, though it is inevitable that in the development of the content to meet increasingly complex conditions, ideas and precepts are drawn from the cultural environment, especially from a popular Stoicism; but such interpretation of the law by the use of principles drawn from culture is scarcely noticed. The keynote of the ethics seems to be holiness. So Harnack describes this Christianity as one in which "no point of dogma is more emphatically brought forward than the duty of a holy life, by means of which Christians are to shine as lights amid a crooked and corrupt generation. . . . Every sphere of life, down to the most intimate and trivial, was put under the Spirit and rearranged."

Not all members of the type, however, are spiritualists. The epistemological principle varies so that Biblicists find a place beside spiritualists in this family as in all the others. In any case the content of the moral law is drawn from Christ; the revelation of values in Jesus Christ is the only valid one; separation of the community with this ethics from the world with a false ethics is sought; the direction of life is otherworldly. The close correlation of this type with the sect type of sociological analysis is apparent.

Other representatives of the "new law" abound in Christian history, each one reflecting, of course, the peculiar conditions of his time and place, his background, and his problems. Benedictine monasticism clearly belongs to this family, and in modern times Leo Tolstoy appears to be one of its foremost representatives. The latter, however, reminds us that there is a certain meeting of extremes and that a dependence on the revelation of Jesus Christ as the exclusive source of knowledge of good and right may regard itself as eminently reasonable. "Christ's teaching," Tolstoy writes, "is the teaching about the son of man, common to all men, . . . which enlightens man in this striving."[4] But in Tolstoy's case, as in that of inner light Quakers, it appears that, whatever be the way Christians believe they have arrived at knowledge of the new law, its content is stated in terms drawn from the gospels, and the role which secular culture has played in the selection and interpretation of this teaching is denied.

5. The Natural Law Type
[Christ of Culture; The Accommodationist Type]

At the opposite extreme from the new law type, yet remarkably akin to it in some ways, is the natural law type. Perhaps this type ought to be called the cultural type, since nature is known only through culture and since the members of this family tend to interpret and seek good and right as members of the cultural society. If they do so without reference to Christ, the church, and the Bible, they do not, of course, represent a Christian type. As Christians they are characterized by the fact that they tend to interpret the revelation of values and imperatives through Christ from the standpoint of the common reason of their culture. They assimilate the church to culture, identify cultural good and law with Christian good and law, yet seek also to interpret the cultural ends and imperatives in Christian fashion. Members of this family seem akin to members of the new law family because they apparently live under one set of imperatives and are directed toward a single end; by contrast, all the median types find an element of discontinuity in their morality. Though the members of the new law type are, in general, sectarians and though the members of the natural law type are Christians who are at home in their culture, still both are members of only one society and hear the word of God in only one language. If the natural law Christians are once-born, the second birth of new law Christians lies in the past. By contrast, all the median types are tormented by the problems of rebirth.

To describe the natural law type in more detail:

1. It seeks to assimilate the injunctions and values of the gospel to those of the society at large. The imperatives of Jesus are regarded as republications of the law of reason or nature; the values of the Christian life are religious formulations of the values of natural and social existence as understood by culture at its best.

2. This process involves the interpretation of gospel values and demands through culture. The gospel is dealt with very selectively. Those elements in it which are most intelligible to culture are taken as primary, and they are understood in the context of

the culture. Thus John Stuart Mill finds good, Anglo-Saxon, bourgeois utilitarianism in the Sermon on the Mount. "In the golden rule of Jesus of Nazareth, we read the complete spirit of the ethics of utility. 'To do as you would be done by,' and 'to love your neighbor as yourself,' constitute the ideal perfection of utilitarian morality."[5] Thomas Jefferson's use of the New Testament indicates a similar spirit. Whether Mill and Jefferson wanted to be regarded as Christians is doubtful, but John Locke surely did, and as his *The Reasonableness of Christianity* shows, the assimilation of the New Testament to prevailing common sense morality is well-nigh complete in him.

3. This assimilation does not truly represent the type unless the complementary statement is made; those elements in cultural ethics are selected as normative which are most in agreement with the New Testament. Hence this type does not simply sanction prevailing culture with its natural law or common sense ethics; it emphasizes the "ideal" in that morality. Between this ideal and essential Christianity it finds no real distinction.

4. The type is marked by a sense of harmony; its strategy is melioristic rather than separatist or revolutionary; it does not abandon the idea of another world but makes it an extension of the best parts of this aeon.

Among the representatives of this family, James, the brother of the Lord, may be mentioned; the fact that the ethics of the Judaism to which he tended to assimilate Christianity regarded itself as based on revelation need not confuse us. Christianity for him apparently was a kind of party of progress in Judaism, and its ethics was that of a serious yet liberal Judaism. In the setting of Hellenistic culture, Clement of Alexandria is an illustrious member of the family. His ideal Christian gnostic is a combination of saint and philosopher; the education of young Christians is as much an instruction in the polite manners of Alexandrian society as in Christian virtue; the salvation of the rich is accomplished without the perilous passage through a needle's eye, though with less than Aristotelian ease. No genuine revolution occurs in the life of the Christian as he passes from philosophic to Christian spirituality, or from this world to the deification of the next. Hellenistic idealism and Christian love of God are parts of one continuous life. The spirit and content of Clement's ethics seem wholly derived from his culture rather than from the church, yet the content has been selected by the use of the culturally interpreted gospel. It is true that the two elements in Clement's ethics do not always fit together, but of this he seems unconscious. In the medieval period Abelard is typical. For him the natural law known by reason is basic; in content it is, of course, the law known by cultural reason. The ethics of the gospel is the republication of the law of nature. The most evident example of this ethics is modern liberal Christianity in its various sub-forms—the liberal German, liberal English, liberal American, etc. In liberalism, characteristically, ethics is really made the basis for theology, so that even Schleiermacher begins his *Glaubenslehre* with assumptions taken over from the former science. Ritschl, then, marks the full development of a synthesis of Christian and cultural ethics. The dominant tendency is to regard the moral consciousness as independent of religion and as prior to revelation or faith. The fact that this consciousness is, at least in its content, historically and socially relative, is ignored. A basis for ethics is found by inquiry into the first principles of the moral consciousness, and these are then used for the interpretation of the demands and values of the gospel. In its teleological form, liberal Christian ethics defines the end of the Christian as the kingdom of God on earth, which again is defined in terms of the dominant cultural ideal as a kingdom of ends, that is, an association of intrinsically valuable individuals, or as the reign of "liberty, equality, and fraternity." In its deontological form, liberalism chooses the imperative of love as the essential commandment in the gospel but interprets it perfectionistically; slurring over the end-terms of the gospel imperative—God and neighbor—it tends to regard the virtue of love as the required thing. In its value theory, this ethics tends to adopt the value judgment of modern society, according to which the *individual* is the supreme value; hence gospel statements about the value of life or the soul are reinterpreted in this sense. Christian liberalism, however, like other representatives of the type, not only interprets the ethics of the gospel from the point of view of culture but also selects those elements in cultural ethics which appear ideal from a Christian point of view. In the synthesis which is so achieved, a certain hiatus remains discernible, though there is a tendency among liberals to ignore it.

6. The Median Types

Many of the most important men and movements in Christian

history cannot be interpreted adequately with the use of the models described above. Moreover, an analysis of their methods of dealing with gospel and nature reveals that they do not belong together in one family. Hence we cannot distinguish one median type but must recognize several groups, which, however, have the following features in common:

1. They are, if not trinitarian, at least bi-nitarian, whereas the new law and natural law types are essentially unitarian, Jesus Christ being essentially God for the former and the Almighty Father the single God of the latter.

2. The median types recognize that divine values are apprehended in two situations or from two points of view, in the church and in culture, sub *specie aeternitatis* and *sub specie temporis*, and that divine imperatives come through two mediators, Christ (Bible, church) and nature (reason, culture).

3. They find it impossible to reconcile the two sets of values or imperatives by interpreting the one through the other (thereby absorbing one in the other) or to achieve peace by eliminating one set. In short, these types are two-worldly whereas the other types are one-worldly, though the one world of the new law is not the one world of natural law.

The distinction between the median types arises from the variations in their methods of combining the disparate elements in Christian ethics. Three main groups seem distinguishable— the synthesists, the dualists, and the conversionists; but since "synthesis" and "dualism" are big words, we may indicate the types more accurately by naming them architectonic, oscillatory, and conversionist.

A. *The Architectonic Type [Christ Above Culture]*

There is, so far as I can see, no true representative of this type in early Christianity. Its great individual representative in Christian history is Thomas Aquinas, and its great social representative, the modern Roman Catholic Church. The nature of the synthesis which Thomas achieves between natural law and new law, between this-worldly and other-worldly values, between the claims of culture and those of the gospel, is too well known to require extended comment. These points only need to be noted in order that the type may be defined:

1. Both the imperatives of nature and those of the gospel are

recognized as divine imperatives, yet a partial and genuine discontinuity between them is also acknowledged; though the divine law is in part republication of the natural law, there are in it some things which cannot be apprehended by reason.

2. The discontinuity involves no real antithesis. In fact, the values and imperatives of nature known through culture prepare for the reception of the values and imperatives of the gospel, though they do not mediate them.

3. In view of the fact that the values and imperatives of nature-reason are realizable by human effort and have a preparatory function, the practical emphasis falls upon them. Hence this type is confused sometimes with the natural law type, but it is genuinely different.

4. The type is "architectonic" in the sense that it recognizes that the two sets of values and of imperatives do not really lie on the same level, that the imperatives of the gospel do not adequately supply directives for the life of men in culture, and that the imperatives of nature do not supply adequate motivation or guidance for the life of man in spiritual relations to God and fellow-men.

B. The Oscillatory Type [Christ and Culture in Paradox]

If the parable to be employed for the previous type is that of the Gothic cathedral, the symbol which indicates the second type is that of the pendulum; each movement in the direction of one pole is modified by a pull in the opposite direction lest it proceed too far. The figure may be extended slightly; the energy for the movement in both directions is due neither to the power of attraction of opposed goods nor to the repulsive power of the imperative "Thou shalt not," but to a hidden spring or moving weight, an energy, whether vital or spiritual, which forces action. This point, I believe, is often ignored when representatives of other types seek to understand the oscillatory dualist.

This type may be briefly characterized as follows:

1. It accepts the gospel ethics in radical form, not attempting to re-interpret it so as to make it seem reasonable to the "natural" mind. It also protests sharply against any effort to qualify this ethics by making it applicable only to the future or to a spiritual

aristocracy or to a spiritual level of existence, as the architectonic type tends to do.

2. It accepts the demands of nature and culture as inescapable and as divine demands. Procreation, self-preservation, the maintenance of order in a wicked world, the coercive protection of the just against oppressions by the unjust are demands of God. There is no escape from these.

3. As the values and imperatives of the gospel cannot be translated into the values and imperatives of culture, so also the latter cannot be translated into the former.

4. The demands of God in the gospel convict man of sin in his fulfillment of the demands of God in nature. The demands of God in nature and culture convict man of sin when he seeks simply to fulfill the demands of the gospel and abandons nature and culture. This conviction of sin operates so as to modify each movement, toward this world or the other world, and prevent it from becoming exceedingly sinful.

5. Peace and righteousness are therefore impossible, save as they exist in faith and hope, by a kind of anticipation. The moral life of oscillation not only receives its energy from outside itself but also its meaningfulness from beyond itself.

6. Various explanations of the situation are offered: *(a)* Man is a *homo duplex*: as spirit and body, as transcendent person and as empirical individual, as man in God and man in society, as essence and existence, as man in revolt against himself. *(b)* God is *deus duplex*: grace and mercy in Jesus Christ, wrath and darkness in the world. *(c)* The world is *mundus duplex*: created and fallen, good and corrupted. These explanations may be variously combined.

The type is represented in contemporary thought, with many variations of course, by Nikolai Berdyaev, Ernst Troeltsch, Reinhold Niebuhr, Gogarten (the earlier), Emil Brunner, and perhaps Karl Barth. A great representative in the past was Martin Luther.

In Luther's case, as in that of the others, individual features occur which, while not atypical, are strictly individual. But it seems more or less typical that he does not conceive of the gospel as a law at all, for its injunctions and values lie on a different plane, have different functions, from those of the moral and social law as usually regarded.

27

The gospel offers no real alternative to natural law, and certainly the latter is in no sense a substitute for the former. The imperatives of the cultural-natural world are not so much corrupted orders of creation as orders for a corrupted creation. The gospel applies to man's inner being, not to his works in society, but the being of man modifies the works he does in society without taking him out of cultural society at any point or permitting him to regard any work of his as good.

C. The Conversionist Type [Christ Transforming Culture]

The third of the median types resembles the other two in its recognition of a dual mediation of divine values and imperatives but has these distinctive features:

1. The natural law, apprehended by reason, is not the true law of God mediated by nature, but the law as apprehended by a corrupted reason—hence the distinction from the Thomistic type. Yet the imperatives are not imperatives for a corrupted order, but corrupted imperatives issuing from a true order—hence the distinction from the oscillatory type.

2. The values recognized by reason in the world apart from Christ are true values for God and not merely relative to the world; the values are, however, disordered by reason and culture, being detached from God and attached to the self or to some temporal final end.

3. The imperatives issuing from the gospel and Christ do not take the place of the imperatives issuing from nature and reason, nor are the values apprehended in the gospel values of the same order as those apprehended by reason. They are truly final imperatives, final values.

4. The vision of the good in Christ and the reception of the final commandment through him are to be used for the restoration of the corrupted order in nature-culture, for the reinterpretation of the natural imperatives. As, in the case of knowledge, revelation does not take the place of reason but restores it, so in the moral life the vision of eternal good in the gospel does not take the place of temporal good but puts this in its proper place and leads to restoration of the true order of values in the world—though the power of sin is so great and the corruption of the moral as

28

of the rational life so deep-seated that no easy transvaluation is possible.

The type is allied with the new law type in that it makes the gospel its point of departure, but the function of the gospel is not conceived to be the establishing of a new society so much as the conversion of existent society. This conversion implies a radical revolution, ultimately metaphysical as well as moral in character—hence the distinction of the type from the natural law type.

Paul appears to me to be truly representative of this type, both in the way he deals with Hellenistic culture and the natural knowledge of God's law and in the way he understands eschatology. ("We shall not all sleep, but we shall all be changed" [1 Cor. 15:51].) In later history Augustine is the great representative of the type, though occasionally, as in parts of the *City of God*, he approaches the Thomistic and again the Lutheran types. However, his theory of good—which is not a theory of temporal and eternal good, or of relative good in a corrupt world and absolute good in the incorruptible, but rather of divine goods whose order is corrupted in culture and restored by Christ—makes him evidently a member of the conversionist type. So, also, his theory of virtues is conversionist; practices that are vices in the context of worldly ambition become expressions of love of God when apprehended and practiced in the context of the gospel.

I am inclined to regard Calvin as a member of this family, with the proviso that he belongs to the deontological subtype while Augustine is primarily a teleologist. Jonathan Edwards and his colleague Samuel Hopkins in the Great Awakening exhibit the dominant features of the ethical type mentioned, and among contemporaries, Karl Barth, despite his occasional tendencies toward the second mediating type, appears to me to be dominantly a conversionist.

The last example, however, as well as recollection of previous ones, impels me to conclude with the repetition of two observations: typology helps us to understand the infinite variety of creative morality in Christianity, but every individual man or movement has a unique character which is inexplicable in terms of type alone; further, the types of Christian morality are not measures of value.

29

CHAPTER 1

How H. Richard Niebuhr Reasoned: A Critique of *Christ and Culture*

John Howard Yoder

Few single works of contemporary theology could compare to H. Richard Niebuhr's *Christ and Culture*[1] for popularity going beyond theological circles, for enormous formative impact upon the way other people think, and for great "holding power." Within just a few years following the appearance of this book, the terms it suggested, and the classification of various typical positions which it proposed, had become the common coin of contemporary thought, not only among specialists in Christian ethics but in many other circles as well.

In the context of Christian ethics we have special reason to give attention to this work because of the implications which Niebuhr's arguments have for our understanding of the church, of its place in society, and of its social faithfulness.

It continues to be worthwhile to read Niebuhr carefully, even a near half-century after he wrote. Niebuhr taught more than a generation of mainstream American ethical thinkers. His kind of apology for pluralism was the stance of many others in his time who would not have stated it as well. His categories have been borrowed consciously by many,[2] unconsciously by many more. His pupils have led the Christian social ethics guild in North America ever since. His book has

31

continued to be assigned for reading in college and seminary classes, and to be reprinted.

Being careful about how we read Niebuhr is therefore our task. The more a text is treated as a "classic," the more it matters that we be critically aware of its unspoken axioms, its tacit biases and lacunae, and the way it directs and diverts attention. The more self-evident an authoritative writer's categories seem, the greater the need to test them critically.

The first outline of the present study was drafted a generation ago for a campus ministries study setting, one of several series on "how to read a book"[3] It was circulated only informally. Since *Christ and Culture* has continued to be found useful and to be reprinted as a classic, I have agreed with my colleagues Yeager and Stassen that bringing this conversation to print may be worthwhile, and am grateful for their encouragement and collaboration, and that of the press, in bringing our common project to this point. This basic outline of my part of the collection has undergone only minor expansions, with the addition of a slight amount of annotation to cross-reference to other works by and about H. R. Niebuhr,[4] but most readers should need few footnotes to follow.

One last disclaimer; this critique is addressed to the argument of the book *Christ and Culture* in its status as a classic; not to the man Helmut Richard Niebuhr nor to all of his thought.[5] The man was a sensitive and changing person, as my co-authors Yeager and Stassen know better than most people.[6] Others of his works would not be subject to the same challenges I have to address to C&C. Not all of the developments of his thought went in what an outside observer would consider a straight line. Only rarely therefore shall I suggest cross-references to his other writings.

1. A Question and Two Answers: The Problem Stated

The book *Christ and Culture* (henceforth C&C) is organized along a roughly historical outline. It surveys five different ways in which Christians in the past have attempted to resolve the problem of "Christ and Culture," which is for H. Richard Niebuhr the basic moral issue. Its powerful impact is derived from the way in which this typology has convinced people. The book must begin, of course, by defining its two operational terms. The author titles the definitional chapter, "The Enduring Problem."

"*Culture*" is according to one early definition (p. 32) everything which people do. Far from being limited to that narrow realm of the arts to which the word refers in some other contexts, the term "culture" points for Niebuhr to every realm of human creative behavior, and especially to those points at which we may observe in human experience certain kinds of continuity in this world. The State, the economy, the family, and the arts are all samples of the great world of culture. Each one of these realms possesses its own coherence and its own set of values.

It is this entire realm of cultural endeavor and cultural values which is challenged by *the radical demands of Jesus*, which are what "Christ" must mean for the thesis of the book to proceed. Although not systematically analyzed by Niebuhr, Jesus' critique is sweeping. It would seem to have several dimensions. On the one hand Jesus calls into question the values of culture because they are not ultimately important. Some see this as dictated by Jesus' expectation of an early end to the world;[7] for others the same depreciation follows rather from the absolute priority of spiritual realities over this-worldly values.[8] Yet others would hold that it is the uniqueness of God as the sole proper object of devotion which condemns preoccupation with culture.[9]

As Son of God he [i.e. the Jesus of Niebuhr's particular reading just here] points away from the many values of man's social life to the One who alone is good; from the many powers which men use and on which they depend to the One who alone is powerful; from the many times and seasons of history with their hopes and fears to the One who is Lord of all times and is alone to be feared and hoped for; he points away from all that is conditioned to the Unconditioned. He does not direct attention away from this world to another; but from all worlds, present and future, material and spiritual, to the One who creates all worlds, who is the Other of all worlds (p. 28).

But not only are the values of culture to be challenged or at least to be relegated to second place; the means of cultural creation are themselves also morally dubious. Jesus calls his disciples to a life of poverty, whereas the accumulation and use of wealth is a major cultural tool. Beyond this he calls his disciples to be itinerant preachers and to be nonresistant to evil, thus striking at the roots of all stable society.[10] After having thus by definition set the stage for the Christ/Culture conflict, Niebuhr then can devote the rest of the book to sifting and sorting down through the history of Christian ethical thought for the last two millenia. He interprets that history as a series of efforts to define the relationship between C&C, as defined above. He willingly recognizes that the "types" he uses do not fully represent some of the individuals he will be describing, but he does hold that each "type" represents a distinct logical possibility. In the rest of this chapter we shall pursue the simplest alternatives.

"Christ Against Culture": Radical Tension

> "Do not love the world nor the things in the world. If anyone loves the world, love for the Father is not in him." (I John 2:15)

If as Niebuhr indicates at one point, "culture" is what the New Testament refers to as "the world," then it becomes obvious that one of the "types" of answer to the question we are studying will be to expect a clear and abiding conflict between Christ and culture. This position Niebuhr finds represented in history especially by the church father Tertullian and by the Russian novelist Tolstoy. Between the third century and the nineteenth Niebuhr devotes a single sentence to Mennonites[11] (in a way which indicates that Niebuhr actually must be thinking of the Old Order Amish) as apparently also belonging in this category.

The strengths of this position, which Niebuhr does not hesitate to honor, lie in its radical consistency and the striking parallelism with what Jesus and the apostles said about "the World." Yet this self-evident strength is seriously compromised by a number of weaknesses which Niebuhr then catalogues. First, this kind of social critique is not effective in changing society. Social reform is brought about not by those who radically reject every compromise,[12] but those who humbly continue the search for the best possible balance between the unavoidable evils of the situation and their ultimate ideals. (67ff) The "Christ against culture" radicals tend almost to forget that man is a natural and not only a spiritual animal; they fail to recognize the element of nature both in the individual and in society, and therefore are unable to struggle effectively against it.[13]

Beyond this, the "against" position is refuted by the obvious fact that although talking as if they rejected all culture in principle, the "radicals" continue to use its benefits. Tertullian, although radically condemning pagan philosophy, used its vocabulary with great freedom.[14] Leo Tolstoy, condemning every kind of power even on the level of property ownership, still lived from the profits of his family's landholdings and from the labor of his serfs.[15]

The radical position must further be challenged because of its superficial view of the meaning of sin. By locating human sinfulness in culture rather than in the human heart, it tends to assume, mistakenly, that some sort of moral purity can be attained by withdrawal from culture; the experience of sectarian groups through the centuries demonstrates how serious this misconception can be.[16]

The last and most powerful of the arguments against the radicals is of quite another kind; Niebuhr clothes this argument in the language of high orthodox theology. Those who reject culture fail to understand adequately the meaning of the Christian doctrine of the *Trinity*.[17] They are guilty of what Niebuhr calls *"Unitarianism of the Son"* in their unique attention to the teachings of Jesus. They thereby fail to understand the full meaning of the confession of orthodox Christian faith that God is also the Father and Creator of the world (and thereby of culture) and that through the ages God sustains the world and the church by the Holy Spirit, in such a way that the decisions and compromises to which Christians have come, and the cultures which they have thereby created, must be spoken of as works of the Spirit of God. As Niebuhr had already argued in a 1948 article on his understanding of the ethical meaning of the doctrine of the Trinity, to which we shall return,[18] a proper Trinitarian understanding will keep these various dimensions of Divine concern in constant balance; the Father and the Spirit, each in some sense on the side of culture, must not be forgotten in unique concentration upon the (anti-cultural) demands of the Son.

"The Christ of Culture": Accommodation

Just as Niebuhr had found in the Epistle of John an ancient expression of the opposition between Christ and culture, so it is the gnostics, against whom John was arguing, who provide the first historical example of the alternate position, namely, that Christ is seen as merged with the best available human insights and the already acknowledged values of civilization. This, too, is a theme which can be traced down through the history of Christian thought, with special significance during the Renaissance, with its revival of concern for the

35

noble pre-Christian pagans. We find it again in modern protestantism, in which there is no fundamental distinction between the worship of God in Jesus Christ and the best of our own intentions and insights.

Although present in many ages of history, this position can hardly be considered adequate. Pagans and Christians alike will call it inconsistent for its failure to recognize that biblical faith and general human wisdom are not identical (p. 108). Usually it leads to sifting out certain biblical materials which it judges to be incompatible with the best contemporary knowledge. Niebuhr is aware that if Christ is to be anything at all for us He must be more than simply the equivalent of our own best ideas. He gives this option the least attention.

In most of the following resume, as hitherto, I shall be seeking to play back as simply as possible Niebuhr's analysis of earlier patterns of Christian thought, without questioning much the accuracy of his description. This is proper as a general approach, since Niebuhr's intention is not really to educate his readers very accurately in the details of the history of very early Christian thought. His intention is rather to draw from past experience models which may give some depth to his typological categories.

Nonetheless something of the credibility of the total analytical system does have to depend on whether in real history it did in fact happen that way. Are the historical samples of prototypical ways to reason in fact representative of the ways people's minds really did work? In this connection I must note for the present just one specimen of the kind of doubt which a more thorough reading of the history for its own sake would need to raise at other points as well.

The adversaries of the John of the epistles, i.e. the people whom Niebuhr identifies as the "Christ-of-Culture" people of the first century, were not, as far as we can tell, really sweepingly affirmative about culture in general or "as such." They did want to incorporate the truths revealed by or through Jesus Christ into a larger body of "truths," which they held to be broader or deeper or prior to the particulary Christian insights, and of which they claimed already to have knowledge by other means. But that "wider insight" which they claimed, and to which John refuses to let Jesus be subjugated,[19] was by no means simply "culture." *Gnosis*, the special "knowledge" the "Gnostics" claimed, was one very specific, in fact very narrow, even secretive body of privileged insight. It was derived from a few elite individuals' special authority, received through special initiation or through mystical or cultic experiences. The privilege of knowledge separated the "knowing ones" or gnostics from ordinary mortals. The substance of their knowledge separated the world that really matters in the mind of God and in religious experience, from the world of mundane human concerns: from the body, the family, fruitful labor, and social communication.

In other words, the real historical gnosticism was against culture, if we take the word "culture" in the general senses in which Niebuhr at the outset said he was interested. Thus the shape of the larger problem which Niebuhr comes to later is significantly skewed by his choice of this illustration. The problem he proposes to talk about in modern terms is important, namely subjugating or submerging Christian convictions within a wider or prior frame of reference. But a better early Christian specimen would have been the Saducees or Josephus, who made peace with the Roman presence, or Philo, who fused the Mosaic heritage with hellenistic philosophy.

This must raise further questions about the aptness of Niebuhr's categories for the purpose he wants them to serve. Can his categories render appropriately a sense of what perennial issues must be dealt with, and of what the standard answers are? If the typical way to affirm the "Christ of Culture" in the first century was to subjugate Jesus to an *ahistorical* and in fact anticultural gnosticism, this is not an example that proves Niebuhr's point. This case certainly does not show us that there is such a possibility as affirming culture *in general*. It may be beginning to make us suspect that the concept "culture" itself, as denoting something homogeneous, is undefinable.

The problem which the subjugation of Christ to culture raises might well have been rendered better if Niebuhr's account had waited a few generations in order to use as an example the response of Christians to Constantine as a political power, or neoplatonism as a cultural power, or antijudaism as a social force. Each of these phenomena did arise within Christian history, and each did represent something of the "Christ of Culture" temptation, by absorbing the meaning of Jesus into something "bigger" which overruled him. In fact it is because of the relevance of such dimensions that so many people like to borrow Niebuhr's categories. But then his exposition could not have used the artifice of beginning with instances from the New Testament, and would have had to be much more complicated.

Where does this leave us? Two polar alternatives, as described and evaluated by Niebuhr, both seem too simple. Our minds reach out for something in between. To those possibilities we next turn.

37

2. Better Answers

"Christ Above Culture": Synthesis

The first two "typical" positions we have described were in a sense self-evident. One stands simply on the basis of what Jesus himself seemed to be saying; the other is the logical opposite extreme. The remaining three "types" to which we now turn will all be in some sense efforts to mediate between the two poles. This mediation is worked through, in Niebuhr's narration, in three significantly different ways.

The third position, to which we now turn, "Christ above culture," represents (as Niebuhr tells it)[20] a careful and self-conscious effort to find a "both-and" solution to the problem. It has been represented down through the centuries, Niebuhr says, by the "mainstream" of the "catholic" Christian tradition, ever since there was such a thing. Its starting point, though, as Niebuhr characterizes it, was not a new social phenomenon but an idea, namely the recognition of the universality of human sin (pp. 118f.). Once the radical sinfulness of human nature is clear, it will follow automatically, as all serious theologians of this position since Augustine have seen, that all human works are dependent upon the grace of God. Because of this need for divine grace, human works cannot be glorified as was done by the accomodators.[21] Yet neither have we any grounds for proud separation from human culture, as in the position of the "radicals."

What has just been said thus far characterizes all of the last three types to which we shall now turn. The first of these types is the mode of *synthesis*, best represented by Thomas Aquinas, though the "apologetic" writers of the earlier centuries had begun in this key. Here we have a confident intermingling of the two realms. The priority of Christ is affirmed; the synthesists do not reduce "Christ" to the best in culture. Culture can not do the work of grace for salvation and faith. Yet for other important purposes human understandings of truth and value are reliable. The synthesists choose one human vision, like that of Aristotle, or modern visions of human rights, and forge a synthesis between that and the Christian faith. There is no great difficulty in holding at one and the same time to the substantial reliability of most human understandings of truth and value, and the normativeness of Christ.

The major shortcoming of this position for Niebuhr would seem to be that it may lose its critical vigor, and thereby tie the church to the world views and the philosophy of a given age. There is nothing much wrong with Thomas Aquinas "baptizing" *for his time*; the mistake is giving the impression that we should be Thomists in ours.[22]

Paradox

The continuing critical tension which was insufficiently present in the "synthesis" position is according to Niebuhr more successfully maintained in the protestant position, as represented by Martin Luther (leaning on the Apostle Paul), arguing from the paradoxical intermingling of Law and Grace. Although the Law's demand upon human performance is somehow "overcome" by the Grace of God, when we are concerned for our justification as sinners, Law still retains its reliable knowability and its bindingness for culture. Law is not the last word, yet grace does not swallow it up or replace it.

Thus culture is an indispensable yet not "religious" backdrop for preaching the Gospel.[23] Since it is socially indispensable, it has an authority of its own in spite of the critique of "Christ." Yet this critique expresses itself by proclaiming the "culture" to be insufficient or inadequate for justification, rather than by calling it sinful.[24]

The obvious shortcoming of this approach, according to Niebuhr, is that the lack of any constitutive link between Law and Grace, since they do not operate on the same level, means that there can be no clear way of guiding the Christian's discriminating choices about action on the level of culture. One form which this gap may take, and has taken, is antinomianism, i.e. the denial of any binding Christian obligation in the cultural and ethical realm. A more common effect is political conservatism, since the present order is understood to be indispensable and not subject to any specific criticism. It was perhaps a distortion of this attitude which permitted some Lutheran "German Christians"[25] to accept the guidance of Adolf Hitler as given them by providence; but it was a possible distortion,[26] which this understanding of the relationship of law and grace did not exclude.

Christ Transforming Culture: The Synthesis of Syntheses

Each of the two previous positions (i.e. "above" and "paradox") represents a sort of melding of the "radical" and the "gnostic" posi-

39

tions. Similarly, the "transformationist" type will be in its turn a synthesis between these mediating views. The theme of this type in Niebuhr's formulation is "conversion," a term which through much of Christian history had been understood with special reference to the experiences and decisions of individuals, but which Niebuhr proposes to apply to entire cultures, or at least to sets of cultural values.

Like the radicals and the Lutherans, Niebuhr is aware of the profound effect of sin and of our dependence upon grace; but like the accommodators and Thomas Aquinas, his attitude toward creation is positive. Since the "fall" into sin is a human action, a product of the creature's will and not of nature, nature is still usable. Therefore the values of culture can be "converted" or "transformed" for Christian purposes.

Thus "transformation" affirms "nature" as God's good Creation; it also affirms more positively than would Luther the action of God (and of people) in history. Niebuhr characterizes the Christian under-standing of history with the phrase, "the eschatological future has become the eschatological present"; i.e., God is now active within time, achieving his purposes by transforming human experience.[27] This double affirmation of nature and of history, which we may note is cognate to the earlier discussion of the work of the Father and of the Holy Spirit, explains the claim that the "transformationist" position is more complete and balanced than any of the others. This position, Niebuhr says, was held in ancient times especially by Augustine of Hippo, and more recently by F. D. Maurice. Niebuhr describes it in the kind of sympathetic tones which indicate that it is also his own preference.[28]

If there had been a section critiquing the fifth strategy, it could well have called for Niebuhr to give attention to concrete criteria and cases. To "transform" must mean to change the form of something according to some standard. We should have had to be shown "before" and "after" pictures of how the impact of Christ can be expected to modify cultural values, or how it has in fact done so in history.[29] We would have expected to see by what criteria adequate and less adequate "transformations" would be discerned. Yet Niebuhr identifies no such cases or criteria. The "transformation" chapter proceeds on a higher level of abstraction than the others (192–229). There is no specification of Augustine's views on marriage or on commerce or on Caesar's wars, in order to illustrate how transformation "works," nor of the social thought of F. D. Maurice.[30]

40

3. How Does Niebuhr Evaluate These Five Strategies?

Niebuhr affirms that each of these five positions, especially each of the last three, has its strong points and that each is needed on the Christian scene. Each (except for the last) has certain weaknesses and should therefore not be taken alone. We should thus not seek to choose from among the five alternative possibilities only one which we hold to be right, but should rather rejoice (pp. 230ff.) that all five continue to be alive in the church. One reason for this "pluralistic" or "equiprobabilist" attitude toward the question of truth[31] is Niebuhr's understanding of the unity of the church as being precisely the product of the interplay of all the positions which are present on the scene.[32] Diversity is a characteristic of true unity rather than a shortcoming, even if the diversity is such that the positions held by various Christians seem to be mutually exclusive.

There is a second reason for Niebuhr's pluralism. His own sensitivity toward the limitations of all human wisdom and the destructive effect of pride leads him to consider humility as the chief of all virtues.[33] It is this humility which keeps him from pronouncing a final judgment on the worth of any human conviction, even though he will of course list strengths and weaknesses. This reticence to express a value judgment results in Niebuhr's transforming the field of ethics from a "normative" to a "descriptive" science.[34] A "normative" discipline is one which claims to have a way of determining truth and falsehood or right and wrong, and concludes with judgments of value. Most thinking and teaching in the field of ethics in the past has assumed that this was its purpose. At some point hard decisions must be made. For H. Richard Niebuhr, however, the prior concern is to portray with historical faithfulness and with respect the various positions which it has been possible for Christians to take. Since each stance is reported in the C&C survey with a view to noting its strength and weaknesses, a sort of value judgment scale is implicit, but this is not supposed to be the last word.[35]

Yet behind this posture of humble non-normative objectivity, it will become clear to any careful reader that Niebuhr has so organized his presentation as to indicate a definite preference for "transformation." We see this preference in the fact that in the structure of his presentation each position is the synthesis of those that went before. "Transformation" takes into itself all the values of its predecessor types and corrects most of their shortcomings. As already noted, for Niebuhr unity in diversity is itself one weighty standard of value; therefore a presentation following the pattern of thesis, antithesis and synthesis constitutes an implicit argument in favor of the last position reported. This preference is very clearly reflected as well in the literary form of *Christ and Culture*; "transformation" is the only strategy whose description is not accompanied by a list of shortcomings. It is also as we saw the only one devoid of illustrative ethical detail whereby its meaning might be clarified or its adequacy might be tested. Niebuhr is satisfied in this section with abstractions about sin and hope. The reader who does not already know it would not learn from Niebuhr's account that (or why) Augustine urged for war against the Arians, that (or why) Calvin opposed religious liberty, or that (or why) F. D. Maurice was a socialist.

This vacuity about moral substance[36] is especially odd because of the choice of the terms "transform" and "convert" to label it. Those words for change would ordinarily, one should think, call for someone to define with some substantial clarity one's criteria or lines of direction for change. This same analysis of the implicit argument of the book, in favor of the fifth option as preferable within the pluralism, is confirmed by the use of the typology by many who find it illuminating in their own thinking on social ethics; all of these interpreters come out in favor of "Christ transforming culture," whatever be their theological heritage.[37]

Not only is it clear to which of the five types of thought Richard Niebuhr is himself inclined; it also becomes increasingly evident that only one of the other positions needs radically to be challenged. It is only the first position, the "radical" one, which Niebuhr makes the object of serious negative arguments. The negative critique at this point is longer and more fundamental than for the other three strategies. It is the only section in which the critical argument resorts to general theological considerations and weighty traditional language like the appeal to the doctrine of the Trinity or the nature of human sinfulness.

At the same time, this "radical" position is the one which comes closest to what the introductory chapter had told us about the teachings and nature of Jesus.[38]

Thus to summarize the core argument of the book, Niebuhr is saying, with careful refinement and pluralistic respect, "Jesus would have us turn away from all culture, but we prefer not to do this because of our more balanced vision of the values of nature and history. Yet in our affirmative attitude to 'culture' we do want to continue to show some respect for the criticism (or the 'transformation') which flows from Christ's critical attitude toward it."

Jesus has become in sum one of the poles of a dualism. It is we, the modern practitioners of Christian ethics, who shall judge to what extent we give our allegiance to him and to what extent we let his critical claims be conditioned by our acceptance of other values, within the culture, which He in principle calls us to turn away from. We also are in charge of defining the other pole of the dualism. We manage our epistemology. We are the moderators in charge of the balancing process. We want to be be modest and gentle about this, but (according to Niebuhr) we still have the last word; Christ does not. Jesus is very important; Lord he is not, if "Lord" denotes an ultimate claim.

This makes clear in turn why the dialogue with Niebuhr is important for continuing Christian moral discourse. What is at stake is the whether and the how of Christ's being Lord.

4. Beginning Critique: How Do "Types" Work?

At this point, as we move from description to evaluation, we cannot responsibly evade a somewhat technical excursion into the question of intellectual method raised by the use of ideal types. We need a critical analysis of how "types" work. Niebuhr recognizes (pp. 43f.) that types are unfair to history, but he claims that nonetheless they "call to attention the continuity and significance of the great *motifs* that appear and reappear in the long wrestling of Christians with their enduring problem."

We need to work at being more clear about what is going on when the teller of a story claims to discern within it "motifs" which are not identical with what the people in the story themselves thought they were doing. It would seem obvious that the prior intellectual commitments and categories of the narrator the history help to the determine what will be recognized as a "motif." This is quite openly the case for Ernst Troeltsch, from whom Niebuhr borrows many of the first elements of his approach. Certainly there is nothing wrong with simplifying and classifying, as we seek to understand real history, especially real intellectual history in its diversity and originality. The story of the past, and especially the story of our mental past, would be chaos, if we were limited to listing names and statements without analyzing and grouping them. Naming "types" and "schools" helps us to do that. Yet certainly there must be some discipline in the ways we classify and collocate. There must be better and worse ways, more or less helpful, and more or less fair ways of understanding what various minds and schools of thought have had in common over the centuries. As he continues, Niebuhr recognizes with growing openness that his "pure" categories do not fit the people to whom he applies them; this recognition is signalled by his move from the term "type," which does involve some claim to intrinsic coherence and inner logic, to the much looser label "motif," which does not in the same sense project the assumption that consistency is a virtue. Yet Niebuhr's students and those who borrow from him regularly make more of the typology than he claims to do when he is thinking self-critically. In fact he himself makes more of it when he is using it to describe and critique people,[39] than when he is explaining his method's limited claims.

Any interpreter seeking to find a way through the history of thought, and specifically the history of Christian thought, in which matters of fidelity and truth are important, will as I said make *some* use of "type" language. Then instead of criticizing the instrument I should ask what are the disciplines to which it ought to be subject. What are the claims which the historian or teacher makes in suggesting a typology? To what tests should such claims be subjected?

Any teaching tool as impressive and as widely used as Niebuhr's typology deserves that we devote serious analysis to the spoken and unspoken underpinnings which make it so popular. The analysis would be most fruitful if on closer attention we should perceive that it is more effective for understanding fairly some phenomena than for some others. If on the other hand there should be some data which this pattern of interpretation is not able to handle fairly, then our learning that may also be significant.

It will therefore be fitting that at the end of the pilgrimage the reader should ask at what points the critique to which we have been led would call for the use of an alternative grid, what that alternative might look like, and how it might more adequately deal with the same subjects.

In seeking to be fair to Niebuhr's intention, certainly one question demanding direct attention is the relative weight which he himself meant to assign to the use of types. The ordinary historical meaning of the word "type" presupposes a degree of normativeness and rigidity in determining the possible forms which reality, by its own deep nature, can take. In ancient philosophy and early Christian exegesis, the "archetype" and the "type" stood in a very firm determining relation-ship.[40]

A typology is therefore in normal usage not an arbitrary, impres-sionistic, or whimsical principle of classification, nor a mere set of suggestive analogies to provoke interesting insights. A typology is offered as a serious aid in establishing a classification of entities or events, which will throw some needed light on the very nature of those things classified, or on the logic of how they "work" in the mind or in cultures.

Certainly something of this typological solidity is assumed in certain portions of *Christ and Culture*. The types, especially the first two, are projected with sufficient clarity that they can be used from then on as a basis for judging the degree to which particular persons fit them. Failing to fit them comes across to the ordinary reader as a weakness or inconsistency on the part of the thinker being described, and not of the type. Niebuhr does not say that it is to Tertullian's credit that he sometimes does and sometimes does not fit the "radical" model. It is rather a weakness of Tertullian himself, at least an intellectual weakness if not a moral one, that he fails to be consistent. Niebuhr is thus assuming that a type is firm, so that there is more logical (or perhaps even moral) integrity to be recognized in a person who consistently lives up to the criteria of the given type, than in one who would "waffle" or mix the types.

When I make these observations concerning the built-in logic of the presentation of *Christ and Culture,* I am not suggesting that this built-in logic *has to be* a fault on the part of Niebuhr. I am rather saying that his assumption of the relative solidity of the types is built into any serious use of typological reasoning. Yet when commentators point out, as many do, that no major thinker covered by Niebuhr's survey really fits the types, we are then tempted to say in Niebuhr's defense that he did not mean these outlines to be taken that seriously. Later in the book he tends, as we saw, to use more the term *motif*, as does his pupil James Gustafson.[41] A *motif*, as distinguished from a type, is a theme or an accent which is never complete or self-sufficient. It can with no inconsistency stand side by side with other motifs.

Certainly it must be granted that the power and popularity of *Christ and Culture* comes from the fact that the "types" have been taken seriously in the strong logical sense by most readers. They are used as aids in making choices or even as support for arguments like "you cannot have it both ways: you must either be dualist or accommodationist, synthesist or transformationist." The outline has been used especially to put people called "radical" in a box in which they do not recognize themselves, by dictating what conclusions, implementations, or implications would logically have to follow from their being initially identified as radical or as critical of culture.[42]

I am accustomed to making generous use of typologies in ecumenical conversation, in analyzing difficult problems of a difficult debate, in reading history, and in teaching. I have used typological analysis especially frequently in teaching the history of Christian attitudes to war, peace, and revolution,[43] in analyzing the varieties of Christian pacifism,[44] and in interpreting within the field of radical reformation history the dynamics and structures of church renewal.[45] I therefore do not at all intend to fault Niebuhr for developing an illuminating typology. Yet my experience does drive me to be self-conscious and self-critical, more than *Christ and Culture* indicates Niebuhr was trying to be, about how properly to use typology as an intellectual instrument. Rather than letting the typology determine which events or people are recognizable, I have sought as historian to try to let the realities remodel my tools of interpretation.[46] One must somehow or other make the claim that the principles of classification one is laying out are "really there in the nature of things," and are not merely impressionistic insights which one may knock around "for whatever they may be worth." A typology which on closer analysis can be seen to be less able to deal fairly with persons or events or schools of thought in their own inner consistency would seem then not to be the best typology.

To question the use of typologizing methods is thus not at all to say that the whole idea is wrong. Any way of analyzing experience, even a whimsical or arbitrary one, may possibly offer something by way of new light. The question is whether *just this* way of identifying the motifs really does identify the differences that matter most, rather than differences that are less important. If we fix our gaze on motifs which are far from the heart of the problem, and thereby fail to see others that would make more difference, then the categories themselves stand in the way of clarification. Although Niebuhr himself is explicitly humble about the historical appropriateness of the categories, we have seen that a striking number of followers have picked up the typology and made more use of it, as if it were a very objective and helpful tool for almost any kind of question. So let us state the method question bluntly: Is there a difference between a good and a bad typology? Can a typology be somehow "true"? Can it be shown to be deceptive? A deceptive typology would be one which would confuse rather than clarifying. It would project inappropriate assumptions into the effort to explain. Some subjective biases about what the possible phenomena are which one can respect and recognize would get in the facts' way. It would therefore constitute the intrusion of bias into telling the story, and a falsifiable limitation of the spectrum of the possible. The thesis which underlies my present critique is the growing impression that *Christ and Culture* has regularly led its readers to make too much of the normative rigidity of the five-type model. A typology which is more convincing to the naive than it is true when examined therefore becomes in the technical sense demonic, a structure which gets in the way of wholeness and understanding rather than serving those goals.

One way to face the challenge of verifying the usefulness of a typology is to try to show, on the level of logic, that if one thinks more carefully one will increasingly find the available logical options to be limited. For example, concerning the morality of killing people in war, you can either say that there is no warrant for such killing or you can say that there is. There does not seem to be middle ground between those two statements. Thus "pacifism" is one type of moral judgment about war, whose definition becomes more solid with increasing analysis.[47] On the other hand, when one says that there may be moral warrants for taking human life in war, we do learn with closer attention that those warrants are of different kinds, so that, as one watches real debates and analyzes possible debates, one finds differences coming to the fore such as are labeled by the distinction between the "just war" and the "holy war," and between both of them and "Machiavellianism" or "realism," and between all of the above and pop machismo. As you think more clearly, or apply your logic to more cases, the adequacy of this further distinction grows on you. Thus the heuristic utility of these types is confirmed in the practice of using them to interpret real decisions and debates, thereby demonstrating the inherent logic of the structural options which distinguish among the types. It can be said of these views on the morality of war that if you think carefully you will have to think in one of these five ways.[48] If people's thought is guided by the canons of coherence and noncontradiction, if they face the challenge of adversaries, of arbiters and Socrateses, then increasingly they will face the need to make certain fundamental logical decisions. This is the kind of claim that can now be made by developing a typology of various possible ways to deal with the question of war.

a) There is the doctrine of the "just war," which promises to subject the use of violence to careful casuistic discipline, considering it as always an evil, usually morally wrong, but sometimes justifiable.

b) There is "pacifism," which says it is never justified.

c) There is the "holy" war which says that it may be divinely mandated without need for careful casuistry.

d) There is the blind obedience to the sovereign which asks no questions at all.

e) Finally, there is hysteria or insanity, or pure passion for killing, or the celebration of one's manhood through killing. This is not a type of accountable moral reasoning at all, although it is a kind of war which really happens. It may in fact be a truer description of real wars than are the others.

The longer we watch the debate about the morality of violence, the more clearly we see those people who debate self-consciously,[49] and who give a rational accounting for their reasons, moving toward one of these five types.

Even people who begin by reasoning in two ways at once, for instance mixing the "just war" and the "holy war" models, as many Christians did in the Middle Ages, will increasingly be driven by careful analysis to separate those intrinsically incompatible ways of reasoning.

Thus in this application the claim can be seriously sustained that a typology, when properly discerned, lies in the logic of a problem, and is not imported arbitrarily by the historian. In deciding what to think about the morality of violence, you ultimately cannot have it both ways. In the concreteness of citizenship these four ways of reasoning (or the fifth path, the refusal to be accountable) will take us along different paths. There are, as far as one can see, no more than four basic moral options, although in particular situations there may be mixed or mediating efforts, or more than one of them may coincide in approving the same action. Failing to be consistent in such a case is a mental flaw if not a moral one.

Certainly Niebuhr does not formally make this kind of case for his typology. He does not seriously, formally claim that there are five and only five ways to solve the Christ/Culture problem. He does not deliver an argument to the effect that it is an imperative of logic to become more clearly committed to one type or the other as each is subjected to more analysis. Yet he does use against people his accusation that they are inconsistent; the point I shall return to later under the heading "monolithic." Especially is such inconsistency counted against Tertullian and Tolstoy.

Another use of typological analysis is to seek to clarify more and more dimensions of diversity, by identifying more and more ways in which people differ, bending the type labels to fit really different cases. Here, instead of telling people they cannot have it more than one way but must choose among a limited number of logical possibilities, we seek to flex our categories to fit their realities, and seek to be as differentiated as possible in affirming differences. That makes for recognizing more types, and not objecting if they overlap. Thus in my pamphlet *Nevertheless*,[50] after having begun with four major models, I was driven by the facts to expand the list. I had to recognize real differences in reasoning styles which separate seventeen major consistent approaches (leaving the door open for another twelve distinguishable sub-types). Of none of these can one say, "you can't have it that way. You must either . . ." The closer one looks at the facts, the more types one has to recognize, letting the system of analysis be bent and stretched to fit the phenomena. The longer I looked, the more visible it became that the different phenomena refuse to be grouped under only a few common headings. In this frame of reference one cannot accuse someone of inconsistency, as Niebuhr does Tertullian and Tolstoy.

Yet such itemization, even with great openness to recognizing differences, is far more than a simple listing. By asking "typing questions," one perceives similarities and differences that the actors themselves had not noticed. One can simplify helpfully at some points the ways people have perceived their identities and their differences, and complexify wholesomely at other points. One can perceive that people who think they differ deeply are still reasoning within the same thought model, by showing for example that to each kind of pacifism there corresponds also a kind of militarism, which reasons in the same key.[51] This mode of analysis will then be very different from that of Niebuhr. It will not reproach any of the actors in its history for failure to be true to type. A third way to test and verify the adequacy of a typology is to discern some kind of mental or logical relations connecting the various phenomena. It can be suggested that certain rules of debate lead people's thought to evolve in one direction or another.

Still another sort of type analysis is the claim to have identified an imperative not in logic but in history. As real life goes on, we can say that those who hold to a certain position will have to face inevitable new choices. Christians who begin as a minority "sect," excluded from social respectability and power, may very well with the passage of time be numerically and economically stronger, may find themselves tolerated or even favored by the authorities, and will thereby be evolving into a different kind of social status. They cannot simply refuse that change, since the authorities no longer respond to them in the same way. The "sect" will tend to become a "church" (or some sub-type thereof), and the pacifist will have a chance to become "socially responsible." Or if the "sectarian" tries to refuse that accommodation, this very resistance will also be a change from the earlier separate stance.[52] This is a realm in which H. Richard Niebuhr made a very important contribution to the sociology of religion in America. As his *Christ and Culture* moved from the categories of Troeltsch into systematic ethics, so his earlier *Social Sources Of Denominationalism*[53] had built the same kind of concepts into a notion of organic evolution which leads a group from one identity to another with the passage of time. American sociologists of religion have for two generations now been seeking to develop further, into a science, a near-mechanistic notion of a "sect cycle" which moves any dissenting group necessarily from separation through toleration to accommodation. Here the sociologists' interest is not in telling the types apart but in linking each to another with a pattern of nearly necessary organic development. This alternative way of relating types also opens an alternative means of verifying or falsifying a typology. If groups do not evolve in that way, then the analysis needs correction (although sometimes the sociologist who is more committed to the typology will criticize the phenomena rather than the categories). If a religious pacifist can become powerful and still remain pacifist, or if the protagonist of what was thought to be a minority ethic can still hold to the same standards in a position of social responsibility, then something about the evolutionary hypothesis has become questionable. The notion of the "sect cycle" continues to be used by sociologists, but increasingly they are abandoning the notion that there is only one pattern of evolution, or that it is necessary.

Even if it were demonstrated that some groups or all groups or many groups tend to evolve in a certain direction, namely from separatism to inclusivism, this would not yet have decided whether that evolution constitutes faithfulness to their mission or betrayal of their identity. In any case, H. Richard Niebuhr does not correlate his Christ/Culture typology and his sect cycle pattern, in such a way as to claim that the way groups evolve from separateness to establishment would correlate with the five types of attitude to culture. Neither system should be used to verify or falsify the other.

We see thus that there might be several approaches to verifying the adequacy of a typology. To say "verify" means also to open the door for falsification. Could a typology ever in some sense be "wrong"? The classic charm of *Christ and Culture* on the superficial level is its flaw on the fundamental level: it can hardly be falsified by any kind of test which Niebuhr could suggest. Thereby its power to convince by seeming to project great clarity is revealed as spurious.

One way to test would be to see whether Niebuhr's five categories actually "work" to sift out various persons or schools of thought, in the face of certain specific challenges. Yet as the book is put together, almost all the readers decide that "transformation" is what they believe in.

Another test would be to ask whether the parties used as samples of the various views, or competent interpreters of those parties, would believe that they are adequately portrayed by the way in which they are described. With the exception perhaps of Thomas Aquinas' being taken as the interpreter of "Christ above Culture," that does not seem to be the case. Interpeters of Martin Luther do not feel that that section adequately represents him, and interpreters of Tertullian or Tolstoy or the Anabaptists would say the same.

The point of this detour into self-consciousness about method has been to sustain the testimony that when I object to the typology of Niebuhr, the issue is not the *fact* that it is a typology, but rather the fact that in doing the work of a typology it has not been tested and proven to be an apt instrument.

One last kind of test would be simply to ask whether the user of such an instrument has openly given an accounting for the assumptions which he makes. Our inductive reading of *Christ and Culture* above has made clear that the reasoning of the book cannot stand up unless one makes the assumption which I have already alluded to, and shall describe below more fully as "monolithic." Yet Niebuhr did not himself state that assumption or justify it. Awareness of that axiom arises out of careful reading of his text, but he did not acknowledge the way its presence predisposed matters, and did not seek to justify it.

Another such axiom is the assumption that the state, or even the violence of the state, is pre-eminently representative of culture, so that pacifists who reject that are described as being against culture "as such"

51

or as a whole (even though they are in fact affirmative about agriculture, the arts, marriage, communication, and social justice).[54] H. Richard Niebuhr does not make the state (or war) nearly as important for his whole system as does his brother Reinhold to whom he dedicated C&C,[55] yet in his portrayal of both Tolstoy and Tertullian it is their challenging the Empire (Roman or Russian) and its wars which best exemplify the "against culture" posture. These are specimen points at which our author fails fully to take responsibility for justifying his own operative axioms.

5. The Inner Structure of *Christ and Culture*

H. Richard Niebuhr was beyond any reasonable doubt a most wise, tolerant, sensitive interpreter and teacher. As I move beyond reporting to commenting on the logical and theological validity of the analysis he has so creatively put together, I intend in no way to question the hermeneutic helpfulness of his contribution to Christian thought in our generation nor the generosity of his intentions. I owe him special thanks for the provocative impact of the project I now need to proceed to challenge.

The first observation must be that although Niebuhr writes in a tone of lofty and widely informed objectivity, his position is clearly partisan, clothed in and carried by the pluralism of his presentation. He speaks with enormous authority, giving grades to every figure of church history with an air of great clarity and certainty, and thereby impresses his readers as enormously competent. Yet in making "humility" the prime virtue he rejects as naive any conviction that truth can be clearly known and can lay upon us definite claims which we must unequivocally obey. Thus paradoxically, as with the moralists and psychiatrists who condemn all "judgmental" positions without recognizing that this is itself a judgment, the claim to treat the field of ethics in an humbly "descriptive" or equiprobabilist way, and humbly to avoid being one-sided, because it is bad to be biased, comes out as a strong partisan argument in favor of the "transformationist" position' as the only one which is correctly balanced in its weighing one side against another. The claim is heightened when we are told that only this view rightly weighs "creation and history" against the New Testament.

One of the ways in which it becomes clear that the entire presentation is set up so as to predispose the reader to see the superiority of the fifth position is the response of readers who have borrowed the scheme for all kinds of applications.[56] Routinely the borrower is convinced of the superiority of the fifth postion. Paul Ramsey said this in the simplest way in his observation on the basis of his use of the text in college classes:

> It is difficult to speak with sobriety about "Christ transforming culture" and converting the works of men. This I have learned from attempting these last several years to teach H. Richard Niebuhr's C&C to my students: they can never quite understand why Augustine and Calvin belong under the type "Christ transforming culture." That this is not simply a function of their lack of information or their immaturity, or their teacher's lack of aptitude, seems to me to be indicated by the fact that when Richard Niebuhr's book first appeared almost everyone in American Christendom rushed to locate hmself among the "transformists": naturalists, process theologians, personalists, idealists, Lutherans and Anglicans who were sometimes Thomists, as well as those you would have expected. It was as if the "typology" or clustering of Christian approaches to man's work in culture and history had suddenly collapsed in 1951, so universal was the conviction that, of course, the Christian always joins in the transformation of the world whenever this is proposed.[57]

Professor Ramsey's concern in the context just cited was not first of all or merely to make an observation about the bias in the Niebuhr outline. He was making a more substantial and deeper point. For one thing he was concerned to notice that what H. Richard Niebuhr meant by "transformation" is so inadequately defined that its popularity with the readers seems to correlate with an assumption that it is more or less indistinguishable from our western doctrine of progress: i.e. that society moves forward from one transformation to the next, always getting better by coming nearer to what "culture" was intended to be. This is one possible way to read modern western history; but as Ramsey makes clear, it is a serious redefinition or foreshortening of what is meant by the major "conversionist" thinkers like Augustine (who was very pessimistic about any kind of forward movement in the "earthly city") or F. D. Maurice. For Augustine, the locus of the newness which faith in Christ brings is not easily verifiable in the objective world, and does not lend itself to being built upon by succeeding higher levels of achievement as other generations in their turn find yet other conversions in the face of yet other challenges.

H. Richard Niebuhr himself may very well be closer to the

Augustinian understanding than to the modern doctrine of progress; but the reason his fifth model is popular, Ramsey suggests, is that his readers do not perceive that distinction.

We shall need now to examine with greater care some of the arguments for this position which *Christ and Culture* thus refinedly argues for. We first had to recognize that the book does advocate a particular position, broadly correlated with the Reformed tradition. We now move on to evaluate the normative claims underlying its descriptive treatment.

Defining "Culture" in the Light of the Argument

To begin with let us look back over the course of the exposition in order to ascertain with greater precision than before the definition of "culture" in Niebuhr's argument. We noted at the outset that "culture" can mean everything people do, every realm of human creative behavior. As we look back over the course of the argument, it has become clear that Niebuhr is committed to some further characteristics of this phenomenon he calls "culture," which are especially important in understanding how he thinks. His concern is not simply with the fact that there is such a thing as human effort or an accumulation of values created by human effort. These further assumptions about how the concept must operate can be most clearly characterized by the use of two adjectives. Culture for Niebuhr is first of all *monolithic*. In the course of the argument, we observed that each position was measured by Niebuhr according to the *consistency* with which a thinker responds to the entire realm of values called "the world" or "culture." Should anyone not have the same attitude toward every part of culture, this is itself evidence of inconsistency. Tertullian was a radical critic of culture, and yet he "could not extricate" himself from it (p. 55) but in fact used Latin philosophical terms in his writing. This is clearly reported as a limitation, not of the validity of H. Richard Niebuhr's concept, but of Tertullian's intelligence or integrity. The early church at the same time tried to be separate from the world and yet borrowed non-Christian ethical concepts (p. 69). Tolstoy is subjected to the same critique.

For this inconsistency to be a logical or moral flaw, as it is reported to be, "culture" must be assumed to be a single bloc, which an honest and consistent approach would either reject entirely or accept without qualification; you must either withdraw from it *all*, transform it *all*, or keep it *all* in paradox. Niebuhr cannot conceive of, much less respect, a position which would not make a virtue of such consistency. In my presentation of a positive alternative, I shall seek to illustrate how inappropriate this assumption is, by demonstrating that every morally accountable affirmation of culture discriminates.

In the later portion of Niebuhr's argument it further becomes clear that culture is also *autonomous*. It is a necessary presupposition of the entire argument that the value of culture is not derived from Jesus Christ but stands somehow independently of him. It is independent of Jesus Christ in the orders of both being and knowing.[58] Such rightness or wrongness of things is based not on their relationship to Christ but on some other grounds. Christ can critique or "convert" those values, but their validity stands prior to his criticism of it. Once this axiom is (tacitly) established, then the question will be simply to what extent in particular cases this autonomy is allowed to remain standing over against the call of Jesus, or how it may be qualified.

I noted above a further mark; namely that the state is prototypical, if not pre-eminent, as representative of "culture." To that we shall need to return separately. It is less pre-eminent for Niebuhr than for his brother Reinhold, or for classical Lutherans or Calvinists, but it is present.

Now we go back to the introductory chapter to check. It is striking to note that neither of these logically fundamental characteristics of culture, without which Niebuhr's argument would make no sense, had been described with any clarity in his setting up the problem (pp. 1–44). At that point there was no advance warning that this would in fact be the shape of the problem. Most other authors would probably say that the trait of "autonomy" is characteristic of culture, but that the monolithic character which Niebuhr attributes to it is not necessary to the concept. He has let his argument depend quite strongly, in fact completely, upon a set of assumptions which at the outset were neither stated nor argued.

"Monolithic" Culture as Seen in the "Radical" Mirror

I noted previously that the one passing reference to the entire Free Church tradition made on p. 56 is both unfair and illogical.

> The Mennonites have come to represent the attitude most purely, since they not only renounce all participation in politics and refuse

to be drawn into military service, but follow their own distinctive customs and regulations in economics and education.

This characterization is unfair because it misrepresents the intention and the practice of most Mennonite groups, taking the Old Order Amish or the Bruderhof (which alone organize an independent economy) as representative, ignoring most other radical reformation communities (Friends are said to be less consistent). The argument is inconsistent because the criticism directed toward this minority group is precisely that it has a culture of its own, namely its own "economics and education." When free-church Christians are culturally productive (agriculture, family, schools, literature, trade) this is taken to mean they are "against culture" as Niebuhr sees it. The only way to ascribe any logic to Niebuhr's position at this point is to assume that the word "culture" now means not what he had previously defined it to mean, namely everything people do together, but rather "a given non-Christian civilization to the exclusion of the cultural productivity of Christians." Such a redefinition is not prepared for by anything else in the book.

If at that point on page 56 Niebuhr had been obliged to heed our reminder about the cultural affirmativeness of the Mennonites,[59] his answer might have been to say that by "culture" he *now* means the *majority* position of a given society. That would be an alternative premise under which his statement might stand. Yet that too would be a new definition, without explanation anywhere else in the text, and counter to his logic with its call for transformation.

The objection to the way Mennonites are treated in passing would be just as applicable to the way Tertullian is dealt with. The prominent Lutheran ethicist, George Forrell, after having once quoted this section from Niebuhr in a text of his own,[60] later went back to read Tertullian for himself, and discovered a very different picture. Tertullian was very critical of idolatry and of the sword and the violence of war. Yet he was very affirmative about human intelligence, despite the fallenness of human nature. He was even positive about the moral and orderly qualities of the Roman empire as an intelligent organization, which when not taken in by idolatry is sober about its own finitude, and committed to doing justice.

In other words Tertullian discriminated very concretely, even casuistically, between those aspects of the life of the Roman empire which were evil, and the proper self-understanding and performance of the empire which despite human fallenness, even outside the church, was still seen as morally acceptable. Tertullian even affirmed that there had been prior to his time good emperors, who had been protectors of Christianity. This striking pro-Roman historical construction, with little basis in actual history, demonstrates how far Tertullian was willing to go give the benefit of the doubt to the civil order.

Even where Niebuhr was able to quote Tertullian as being critical of the artifice and hypocrisy of professional rhetoric, this is hardly a case of his rejecting his own profession or his prior education. Such polemic against sophism and against people who play with words in a frivolous way was itself a regular part of the tradition of pagan rhetoric. Forrell concluded "there may be indeed a Christ against culture pattern, but it is a result of this investigation that Tertullian is hardly an example of it."[61]

Another point where Niebuhr has to argue hard to defend his categories against the facts is where he drives a wedge between the founders of new movements, who he says were against culture, and their successors who changed culture by being in favor of it (pp. 66–68). The wedge between Tertullian as a lawyer and Origen with his rejection of sexuality is surprising. The division proposed between Benedict, who created model productive communities, and St. Francis, who called people away from their work and families to beg, also fails to convince. No more can one accurately call John Woolman an affirmer of culture as over against George Fox, who especially in his earliest days seemed to be proposing a way whereby all England could actually be saved. The historical fact that movements which at the outset use anti-culture rhetoric turn out to be very culturally creative[62] must for Niebuhr be a vice of the movements described, rather than indicating a possible flaw in his categories, or in his assumptions about sociology.

A Test Case

One quite appropriate way of clarifying the impact of Niebuhr's analysis, into which my last comments just began to move, will be to ask how his typology will handle the issue of violence and the historic peace church attitude toward society. If pacifists take a position of "absolute" rejection of war, they can rejoice that Niebuhr will courteously acknowledge the validity of their position as the clearest reflection of the teaching of Jesus;[63] this position is necessary but it is not for everyone. Most people are not so heroic; society needs as well the compromising contribution of those who, by not aiming at the moon, keep the world afloat.

The effect of this chain of thought, especially upon peace church young people in the college generation, has usually been to make them ashamed of the over-emphasis of their elders on faithfulness to Jesus as a moral style, and on thorough pacifism as a moral commitment. They do not want to be self-righteous, and they have can no longer be naive about discipleship because they have gone to college.[64] Then it is the crowning blow to be told that this position of "withdrawal" is in fact a theological sin against the ancient and honorable doctrine of the Trinity.[65] It would seem to many of them that the best compromise, which would represent within the peace church tradition the "Christ transforming culture" perspective, would be a kind of *relative* pacifism. Instead of being negative toward the world, such a view would have hopes for civil rights and for the United Nations and would be critical of exaggerated nationalism, but it would accept necessary violent social power and military national defense. Those young pacifists who in response to the critique of pacifism by the Niebuhrs come out at this position are not aware that it is in the mind of both Niebuhrs the least respectable option of all; for it still dodges full cultural responsibility, and is the most naive in its optimism about the effects of human sinfulness.[66] The relative, humanistic pacifist, who claims to be socially responsible without accepting ultimate loyalty to his nation, combines the vices and rejects the virtues of both the radical and the accommodationist postures.

6. The Meaning of "Christ"

Testing how Niebuhr defines "culture" led us on a long path of testing, since behind that set of definitions, at once self-evident in his mind and yet covertly tilted, we could see an entire system of assumptions at work.

In a similar inductive way, yet in contact with a different set of test questions, we should now do the same with the other concept in the pair, asking what is the picture of Jesus Christ which is left with us by the way in which Niebuhr first portrays and then transcends Jesus' critique of culture. Part of this understanding of Christ is found in the opening chapters; other dimensions have to be filled in from later arguments.

Jesus is first of all seen as a *moralist*. He is a teacher of human values who affirms the transcendence of the spiritual and therefore condemns concern for this world. One of the ways he teaches is by being an exemplary human being, but this is true more about his thought (about God) than about his social behavior.[67] He "points away" both from the world and from himself to his Father who alone is worthy of loyalty (p. 28). To use a phrase from Niebuhr's own later work, Jesus is a "radical monotheist." He does not condemn culture because it is particularly sinful, nor does he condemn aspects of culture because these portions of it are more sinful than others; in fact he does not condemn it at all. He simply "points away from" it towards something else incomparably more important. "In his single-minded direction toward God, Christ leads men away from the temporality and the pluralism of culture." (p. 39).

Niebuhr cites with apparent approval the Jewish historian Klausner who had said that Jesus came to abolish culture, ignoring everything concerned with material civilization. He seems almost to accept the characterization of Gibbon who says that Christians are "animated by a contempt for present existence and by confidence in immortality" (page 5). Niebuhr challenges neither the accuracy of this description of the early Christians nor the assumption that they were properly understanding something they had heard from Jesus.[68]

Nowhere in *Christ and Culture* does it become clear that this understanding of the meaning of Jesus[69] might be less than fully acceptable to the great body of Christian thinkers. Yet if we step back for perspective and compare this portrait of Jesus with portraits drawn by other Christian thinkers, it is striking in its onesidedness. The main stream of Christian tradition has said concerning Jesus (a) that he was the Son of God incarnate, his teaching authoritative and his person unique; and (b) that his death is the atonement for human sin, following which his resurrection is the guarantee of a new living power in human experience.[70] Niebuhr does not name or reject any of these themes; he never disavows the tradition they have dominated. Yet they are markedly absent from his description. The implications which would flow from them for the discipline of Christian ethics are manifold, so that their absence is significant.

If we test this picture of Jesus, not in comparison to traditional Christian thought but by the New Testament itself, we find there two additional themes of central importance. One is (a) that Jesus is in his life and death an exemplary human; not only a teacher whose instructions are authoritative but a person whom his disciples are to imitate, not in slavish mimicry but in free discipleship.[71] Christ further (b) is affirmed to be Lord both over nature and over all human history by virtue of his resurrection and ascension.[72] Thus the New Testament writers could not say with Niebuhr that nature or creation is the domain of the Father and history that of the Spirit, and therefore not subject to the Son. Nor could the New Testament writers agree in contrasting the will of the Father or of the Spirit with the teaching and example of the Son.[73] Yet further: in a few New Testament texts (c) Jesus is described as uniquely identified both with "The Father" (John 14:6ff) and with "The Spirit" (Chapters 14–16).

As we compare the Jesus of Richard Niebuhr's description to the Jesus of the New Testament and of the history of Christian thought, it becomes evident that Niebuhr has so set up the question as to make it clear from the outset that Jesus must be *by definition* inadequate. To do this, he has excised from his picture of Jesus precisely those dimensions, clearly present in the biblical witness and in classical theology, which would have made impossible the interpretation of Jesus as "pointing away" from the realm of culture, and thereby as needing the corrective of a "more balanced" position.

That the "Christ" who is "against culture" has been defined as a straw man, and not as a serious historical possibility for real living people, is evident in the way this position is arbitrarily distilled out of the New Testament. It is a position which Niebuhr recognizes is not present in this pure form in the New Testament.[74]

It is furthermore a position whose consistent application is impossible (pp. 69–72) because the person who holds it can only communicate it or stay alive by sinning against it. Thus failure to apply consistently the "radical" position is not due to the degeneration of the original vision, nor to the undesirability of the goals it sets, nor to the intellectual or moral weakness of the Christians holding it. It rather follows automatically, as the position is defined, from the the way it must necessarily collide with the nature of historical existence.

Yet on the other hand this "radical" position is the only real ethical challenge which gives the entire book its meaning. All the other serious positions (synthesis, paradox, transformation) are merely refinements of the one "mixed" answer to the abiding challenge which the "against" posture poses. The "radical" position is, according to Niebuhr's own account, the only one with an intrinsic connection to the Jesus of history and of the New Testament.[75] It is the only one whose structure is consistent with the definition of "the enduring problem" furnished at the beginning of the book. It is the position which is given the most extended refutation (pp. 67- 82); it is the one position to which the reporting is the least fair historically[76] and the only one to which reference is constantly made in the course of the later discussion.

7. Father, Son, and Spirit

We have noted more than once the appeal made by Niebuhr to the doctrine of the Trinity. It is his rhetorically most powerful way of arguing that the teachings and example of Christ need to be "corrected" or brought into balance by appeal to nature and to history (81f, 114). This argument was stated at greater length in his 1946 article "The Doctrine of the Trinity and the Unity of the Church."[77] God the Father is appealed to there as both the Creator of nature and the Governor of history. Nature and history are therefore channels of revelation from God the Father. What they have to say about "culture" is of course largely affirmative,[78] and thereby stands in tension, as we saw above, with the authority of "Christ."

God the Spirit, in Niebuhr's understanding, is active in the life of the Christian community and therefore in the decisions made by the churches down through the years. The Spirit is active as well in the "leading" by which decisions are made from one situation to another.[79] Thus the term "Spirit" can serve as a general code label for a number of not further specified sources of valid moral insights, which can be complementary to (or prima facie contradictory to) the revelation received in the teaching and example of Christ.

This understanding of the doctrine of the Trinity needs to be tested first of all biblically. Is it the teaching of the New Testament that Jesus Christ and the Father are distinguishable from one another as regards moral obligations? Can we thus distinguish between the teaching and example of the Son and the will of the Father? Can we distinguish between creation as the work of the Father on one hand, and radical discipleship or redemption on the other, as the work of the Son? Is any independence of a parallel sort ascribed to the Spirit over against the Son?

To turn in a merely exploratory way to the New Testament is

already to come to a negative answer. The work of the Son and that of the Father are uniformly affirmed to be identical. The Son is confessed as the agent of creation (Col. 1:16, I Cor. 8:6; Heb. 1:10; John 1:3). It is Jesus Christ who is the Lord of history (I Cor. 15:24). God as Father is identified in the New Testament most precisely as the one whose will the Son did, as the Father of Jesus, and as the One who raised Jesus from the dead. The Holy Spirit in the life of the church is definitely affirmed by the New Testament not to be another source of conflicting or even complementary insight but a confirmation of the meaning of Jesus (John 14:26). The early church is warned that whatever is spoken to the church by "spirits" is to be tested by the standards of the Incarnation (I Cor. 12, John 4).

But the doctrine of the Trinity is after all not primarily a biblical theme. It developed in the later history of the church in response to certain serious intellectual challenges which Christian thought needed to meet. We must therefore also ask, as a second test, what the later doctrine of the Trinity meant creedally. Might it be that Niebuhr's understanding of the Trinity, while not faithful to the New Testament, has justification in the later history of Christian dogma?

Once again the answer is clear. The intention of the post-Nicene doctrine of the Trinity was precisely **not** that through Father, Son, and Spirit differing revelations come to us. The entire point of the debate around the nature of the Trinity was the concern of the church to say just the opposite, namely that in the Incarnation and in the continuing life of the church under the Spirit there is but one God. The point of the doctrine of the Trinity is not to affirm distinctions or even complementary differentiations between Father, Son, and Spirit, but rather to safeguard the unity of these three ways in which we know of God. It was not to relativize Jesus or to cut the later church loose from his normativeness.

The doctrine according to which Father, Son, and Spirit, as separate sources, revealed different moral insights at different times and in different ways, was rejected by the early church under the name of "modalism" or "Sabellianism." This was the heresy which centered its attention on the differences between Father, Son, and Spirit, with the idea that each was revealed at a different time and in a different place saying different things. Over against this "distributive" or modalist tendency, the concern behind the development of the mainline doctrine of the Trinity was the intent to reaffirm the centrality and the normative uniqueness of the revelation in Jesus Christ.

It can hardly be assumed that H. Richard Niebuhr was ignorant of the real historic meaning of the doctrine of the Trinity. Did he really mean his appeal to the Trinity to count as a theological argument?

I have put this question to several former students and friendly interpreters of H. Richard Niebuhr.[80] None of them seem to believe that he meant seriously to claim that the distributive or modalist use which he makes of the doctrine of the Trinity, for purposes of a corrective polemic against one-sidedness in modern ethics, should be taken as real appeal to what was at stake in Nicea. Yet the more refined and sophisticated a theologian is, the less we should let him get away with this kind of creative distortion of the real meaning of historically derived norms. Within historic Christianity, the classical rightness of being trinitarian, as correcting for the symbolic inadequacy of anything more simple, is a powerful indirect value claim. If Niebuhr really meant only to be using the metaphor of the unity of the Godhead as shorthand for the idea of keeping several things in balance, and not to be claiming the momentum of canonical orthodoxy in favor of his preference, it is regrettable that he reached so high for a so powerful figure of speech. Certainly many who in his train have used the notion that an ethic must be trinitarian have given it the weight of such a truth claim.[81]

The reference to the Trinity seems therefore rather to be a slogan, symbolizing in a superficial way our author's urbane, pluralistic concern for a balance between Christ and other moral authorities. If we want accurately to undererstand the Niebuhr argument we must therefore pare off this deceptive Trinitarian clothing and state it in a more logical form, and then evaluate it on its own grounds, not granting that the allusion to the Trinity accredits it. The outline would then need to read somewhat like the following:

A. H. Richard Niebuhr is committed, in addition to his sincere loyalty to the Jesus Christ of the New Testament, to the independent value of certain "other sources" of moral judgment. They are not autonomous over against God, but they are independent of Jesus. He need not spell out in detail just what those other sources are, or just what they tell us to do (which Jesus would not), in order to make us face the problem thus posed.

B. Jesus Christ in the New Testament, like the prophets of the Old Testament, like the authors of the NT and the Christian prophets through whom the Holy Spirit has since spoken in the history of the church, condemned the claims to autonomy of other moral authorities, on the grounds that JHWH alone or Christ alone is Savior and Lord. This creates the conflict which the book seeks to resolve.

C. Niebuhr's first step must therefore be to shift the meaning of Jesus' criticism of creaturely rebelliousness within culture, so that Jesus' call is not itself a real option within history and culture but rather a direction, "pointing away" from the world, and therefore by definition incapable of standing alone, incapable of faithful Incarnation.[82] The New Testament's critical judgment on creaturely rebellion must be redefined so that it need not be taken seriously as an alternative but only as one perspective among several.[83]

D. Similarly Niebuhr must proceed to shift the definition of those claimants to cultural values which Jesus judges: the state, money, the arts, the clan, sex. Instead of recognizing the idolatrous rebelliousness of their claim to autonomy, he ascribes this independence of the creatures to a divine mandate, which he ascribes to the Father and/or the Holy Spirit. He thereby confuses in the reader's mind the createdness and the fallenness of the world. He puts the goodness of nature as the work of God and the destructiveness of the sword as man's rebelliousness all in one sack.[84]

E. The sum total of these redefinitions means that whereas in biblical faith the coming of God to humankind, in the prophet's word and in Jesus, places before people a judgment and a call to obedience which is itself relevant within history and culture, in C&C the prophetic impact of God's speaking into history has now been so reformulated that it cannot be taken seriously as able to be obeyed. Thus what for the Bible is a pair of alternatives, a summons to choose, becomes with Niebuhr a challenge to synthesize.

We noted Niebuhr's recognition that the "types" he was using are admittedly not always descriptively fair to the personages or movements which he is interpreting. His acknowledging this may be sufficient to excuse him for not being fully accurate as an historian. The fact that the types chosen do violence to the real historical and logical options presented by biblical faith, does not however in the same way excuse him as an ethicist.

How seriously should we take this argument? It is too easy to let Niebuhr off with the excuse that he was only being playful or modern in reaching for trinity language. This is the way *Christ and Culture*, alone, might be read: yet the 1946 article claims a rootage in the early history of Christian thought, quoting for instance the standard historical study of McGiffert.[85]

At the first place where this trinitarian reference arose, pp. 80ff., Niebuhr did seem to be claiming an orthodox base. He said that "some exponents of radical Christianity . . . regard the doctrine of the Trinity as having no ethical meaning, and as the corrupt invention of a corrupt church. But they cannot escape the problem with which it deals, and they try to solve it in their own way."[86] At this point he names no such "exponent of radical Christianity."[87] Then he goes on to admit that Tertullian was one of the creators of the doctrine of the Trinity. "Trinitarianism is by no means a speculative position and as unimportant for conduct as is often maintained." Here the claim to some kind of "orthodox" validation still seems to be strong.[88]

Then the argument is stood on its head with the claim that "the radicals" frequently fall into spiritualism and Manichaeanism, denying both the goodness of the natural world and the humanity of Christ pp. 81f.). It is not clear whether this tendency to anticultural "spiritualism" is supposed to be proving that Christ as norm is not sufficient, (so that the addition of the spirit which relativizes Christ would be a corrective, parallel to what Niebuhr himself wants)[89] or that spiritualism is a mistake (since he seems to be talking about it pejoratively at the same time). Is it a corrective which people are somehow driven to in order to be practical or sober, to keep from being too dominated by Jesus? Or is it a further degeneration into which they fall because of the wrongness of narrowing loyalty upon Jesus?

"Perhaps it is indicated that Christ cannot be followed alone, as he cannot be worshiped alone. . . ."[90] This would seem to be taking the development toward spiritualism, which he claims to discern in history, as evidencing the recognition by others of a truth to which Niebuhr also holds. Yet he had not described the "spiritualists" sympathetically.

We need to be open to the other valid reasons which may call us to relativize over-simple visions of the call of Jesus; but our conclusion must not be that we shall be doing this most fairly if we free Niebuhr from the question of whether he really meant the appeal to the language of ancient dogma to be a warrant for loosening Jesus' claims.

8. The Standards of the Ethicist's Judgment in *Christ and Culture* and in the New Testament Worldview

The Implicit Standards

We have observed with what arguments Niebuhr has made room for his freedom to follow other standards of ethical decision than "Christ." It has become clear that his claim for the authority of those other standards is not really a trinitarian argument even though clothed in those terms. Now we are ready to ask what are really in his own argument those standards, for which he needs thus to make room.

The first and perhaps the most basic implicit assumption, all the more important because it is never really brought to the surface consciously, is that it is the responsibility of the ethicist to stand within the "main stream" of his own religious civilization. This is exemplified superficially by Niebuhr's lack of any serious attention to free church strategies within Christendom since the Reformation or to dissenters since Tertullian.[91] It is said more deeply in his unargued assumption of the necessity of managing society from the top and his identification of political control with "culture." Tolstoy was in favor of story-telling, the novel, the folk tale, the arts, the family, the village, the school, the restoration of peasant crafts, and heavy labor in the fields, but because he rejected the *sword* and criticized the Tsar he is pigeonholed as a radical anticulturist. Thus government becomes exemplary for all of culture.[92]

A further standard, one which is stated clearly and sincerely, is that of humility. Humility means for Richard Niebuhr not simple subjection to Divine command[93] but rather the recognition that for many questions there is no answer or no one right answer, so that we are left to our own resources, with none of us having any right to impose his convictions on anyone else. It also issues in the ultimate authority of the teacher or reporter over his data. It winds up setting ourselves in judgment on what sounds like a divine command. No divine word can come up out of the subject matter and judge the ethicist; no creaturely value threatens to become his idol. Thereby the responsible self has become (in the order of knowing, and despite verbal professions to the contrary) its own God.

Still another standard is clearly that of consistency. We observed this before in Niebuhr's assumption that "culture" is by definition "monolithic" and that each position may be judged by how uniformly it responds to the various challenges of culture. It follows in practice that the logic with which a scholar analyzes human efforts is the ultimate criterion of integrity.

The Christ of the New Testament: Authentic Transformation

Niebuhr's recognition that the "Christ against culture" position is not *clearly* represented in the New Testament should send us back to the original documents to attempt to describe a "type" which would be more faithfully descriptive of the truly "enduring problem." What does the New Testament itself say to our theme? Can its message be disengaged from the texts in a way less slanted by Niebuhr's agenda? Can our awareness of the tilt in Niebuhr's categories aid us toward a more balanced reading of the same sources, an alternative formulation?

Many readers of C&C have taken at face value the notion that one could and should choose one of the "types" as one's own preference. It would in fact sometimes seem that one *must* so choose, because these five types seem to be mutually exclusive and to exhaust the possibilities. This impression we have seen to be deceptive. They are not mutually exclusive for Niebuhr after all, since the "unity of the church" should mix and match them. Neither could we cleave to just one, since the first four types are caricatures, "pure types" in the logical sense, which no one has to be true to and perhaps no one has been true to in history. The book C&C is thus an intentional mix of two modes of approach to the experiences it reviews:

a) Partly it exemplifies a "tolerant" or "pluralist/descriptive" style according to which all five "types" are in some sense "right," all are needed, the interaction of them all being truer than any one standing alone; and no one view should claim to be right; yet

b) Partly it represents a "directional" or "dialectical" view, according to which the fifth pattern ("transforming") is truer than the others, because it takes all of the others into account. As we have seen, the book as a whole tilts this way.

Our appropriate response to the book as a whole will then not be to choose one of the other "type" postures,[94] as Niebuhr had set them up, and to argue for its being right. Our response should rather be to ask how the preferred but insufficiently defined notion of "transformation" should in its turn be transformed, so as to take account adequately rather than inadequately of the element which Niebuhr's last and best position (as synthesis of syntheses) claims to have included.[95] We therefore need to ask what would be the criteria and the prerequisites, if Christ were authentically to transform culture. Without making these criteria substantially clear, to talk of "transformation" is not so much wrong as empty.

There is today no serious challenge, from the point of view of biblical scholarship, to the conclusion reached by textual studies that the central affirmation of New Testament faith is that "Jesus Christ is Lord." It is therefore the fuller meaning of this confession of faith which I should seek to explicate, as criteria of authentic transformation. How does Christ's Lordship relate itself to the claims of those activities and the institutions which H. Richard Niebuhr calls "culture"? I here seek to formulate a broad consensus of what New Testament interpreters are finding.

A. Because the Christ who is Lord is inseparable from the man Jesus of Nazareth, neither who he was nor what he was, nor what he did nor what he taught, nor his "Lordship" as the holistic claim he made on his disciples or makes on us now, is properly understood if thought of as "pointing us away from" full and genuine human and historical existence. The humanity of Jesus of Nazareth was a cultural reality. To confess him as "Christ" makes that no less the case. Then those disciples who follow him faithfully are also within culture, not by accident or compromise, or out of weakness or inconsistnecy or in spite of themselves, but *by virtue* of their being his disciples. Any way of setting up the problem as if a priori Christ were alien to "culture" as a whole, or on another level or wave length, is therefore sure to distort.

B. The church of the New Testament confessed that Jesus was Lord over the "principalities and powers." Outside the circle of the Christian church, within which disciples, members of the body of Christ, share in willing (cultural) obedience to Him, it is in terms of "principalities, powers, thrones, angels, dominions," etc. that New Testament thought, especially in the vocabulary of the Apostle Paul, spoke of the tendency of human civilizations toward claiming *autonomy* and *unity*.[96] The *autonomy* claimed by the powers of this world is not only independence of any higher will such as that of the Creator God, but also the claim to exercise dominion over men and women, who thereby become slaves of the law, of idols, or of other powers. The *unity* which these "powers" claim lies precisely in their pretention that independently of the will of the Creator God they are able to provide to a person and to society a full, integrated, genuine existence.[97] The reader will have recognized in these two themes counterparts of the two characteristics of "culture" which we have found to be latent in the logic of Niebuhr; its autonomy[98] and its homogeneous or monolithic unity. Now what the New Testament affirms in claiming that Christ is Lord is precisely that these structures of creaturely unity and meaningfulness have no such autonomy, but have rather been brought into subjection under the feet of our Lord. They have in their rebellion against him no unity, since rebellion is not a principle of unity. What for H. R. Niebuhr is the definition of "culture" in its essence is for the New Testament the definition of perdition and demonic self-glorification, from which the "powers" need to be, and can be, saved in order to be brought under the Lordship of God in Christ.

C. The cultural stance of the Christian church according to the New Testament will therefore not be a matter of seeking for a strategy to be applied uniformly, either accepting or rejecting (or paradoxing or transforming) all of "culture" in the same way. It will and should proceed precisely by denying such a global character to culture, and will move rather by *discrimination*. Some elements of culture the church categorically rejects (pornography, tyranny, cultic idolatry). Other dimensions of culture it accepts within clear limits (economic production, commerce, the graphic arts, paying taxes for peacetime civil government). To still other dimensions of culture Christian faith gives a new motivation and coherence (agriculture, family life, literacy, conflict resolution, empowerment). Still others it strips of their claims to possess autonomous truth and value, and uses them as vehicles of communication (philosophy, language, Old Testament ritual, music). Still other forms of culture are *created* by the Christian churches (hospitals, service of the poor, generalized education, egalitarianism, abolitionism, feminism). Some have been created with special effectiveness by the Peace Churches (prison reform, war sufferers' relief, international conciliation).

Therefore our need is precisely *not* to get the kind of total formal answer around which the entire Niebuhr treatment is oriented, namely, the call for a global classification of all of culture in one category. Our need, one with which Niebuhr gives us no assistance, is precisely to find categories of *discernment* by virtue of which the several value dimensions of cultural creativeness can be distinguished.

D. Where there is opposition between the claims of Christ and the claim to autonomy of a given cultural value—i.e., when it claims our ultimate loyalty, making itself an idol—then the Christian church and the individual disciple must reject that claim, even at the cost of some sacrifices. It is important that Jesus does say this not only about wealth or war but also about the family. At these points, whether the idol be Mammon, the State, or the family, the New Testament-oriented Christian will follow Christ in taking the kind of position which Niebuhr calls "radical" and "sectarian." But by no means need it be assumed that this choice is always necessary. Even when it is, those who take that position are not leaving the world, but influencing it. To assume that the imperative of negation is *regularly* the case would be to accept the prior dualistic philosophical commitments of Niebuhr or of a Tolstoy (as seen by Niebuhr[99]), which find no basis in the New Testament. For when the New Testament speaks of "world"[100] it precisely does not mean, as Niebuhr says (pp. 45–48), all of culture. It means rather culture *as self-glorifying* or culture *as autonomous* and rebellious and oppressive, opposed to authentic human flourishing.

E. Where there is rebellion of some segment of "culture" against God and authentic human well-being, so that Christians are called to withdraw from certain dimensions of the larger society and civilization, the New Testament still affirms that the world continues to be under the Lordship of Christ. Paul said even of pagan Rome that its power was exercised subject to Divine Providence (Rom. 13). There is no need for the church to be running the Roman Empire, for Christ to be Lord over it. The task of the church is, it follows, not to try to seek to take over the rebellious world on its own terms through shrewd scheming or naive compromise, nor are Christians reduced to the position of the irrelevant "gadfly" or "prophetic minority" resigned to getting no hearing. The believing community's assignment is rather to represent within society, through and in spite of withdrawal from certain of its activities, as well as through and in spite of involvement in others, a real judgment upon the rebelliousness of culture and a real possibility of reconciliation for all.

F. Where the rebelliousness of a given element of culture can be overcome, where its tools can be used Christianly, it should and will in fact be the Christian whom we should expect to find being most creative. This was true of the "radical" Tertullian who had a major part in the creation of the whole vocabulary of ecclesiastical Latin. It has largely been true as well of the radical reformation traditions, whose proportional cultural creativity over the centuries has been greater per capita than that of the conservative established churches. It is precisely the "radical," because of his or her capacity for discrimination (which is the only assurance that there is a criterion by which to evaluate culture), who can effectively be "conversionist." Those who seek to modify society by taking "more positive" attitudes toward it are actually rendered unable to do so, when by "positive attitude" they mean abandoning an independent standpoint.

9. The Social Shape of Moral Judgment in the Church[101]

Having examined critically some of the arguments made or presupposed in *Christ and Culture*,[102] I should conclude this analysis by suggesting an alternative set of assumptions on the level not so much of ethical notions as of social forms and processes.[103] These have obtained generally in the Christian church. In the previous section I described the early Christians' world view. Now I turn to what taking that orientation seriously would mean for our doing ethics. The assumptions or implications to which I now turn are by no means "sectarian" or "radical," either in logic or in provenance. Now I am in a position to formulate them with a view to their functioning as criteria to evaluate the authenticity of the call to transformation. I owe to Niebuhr a debt of gratitude for the provocation whereby C&C has helped to clarify them.

The Church Assumes That the Will of God May Be Known

It is frequently characteristic of Niebuhr's way of arguing, that it seems that the consistency and clarity of anyone's position can be measured in purely logical terms by clarifying how terms are defined

71

and how people reason. The historian of ethics works from his office: there is no need for attention to social process for us to know what issues count in a concrete decision process and to know how people come to conclusions. Positions can be described as they stand in the pure mental integrity of the thinker being interpreted.[104] For us on the other hand stating such generalities is only the beginning of the job.

The vocation of the scholar within the church is to clarify the knowability of the will of God. "Transformation" can be spoken of accountably only if criteria can be applied which are trans-subjectively knowable. If the total effect of the scholar's reasoning and research, even under the pretentious headings of "objectivity" and "humility," is to make it impossible to know clearly what God wills, then a Christian scholar has either not been faithful or not been competent in the exercise of that ministry, or has not yet finished the job.[105] Certainly the awareness of complexities and difficulties is a part of the theologian's responsibility; but unless coming to grips with such difficulties leads the moral theologian to a more precise and faithful definition of the meaning of obedience, her/his task is incomplete and her/his results are not yet ready to be shared with the church.

The task of the intellectual in the faith community is then not to prove the superior adequacy of her/his general categories by showing that no one can be consistent with them, but to analyze the communal quality of obedience, so as to demonstrate the difference between wholesomely complementary diversity and counter-productive contradiction. This might mean demonstrating that it is not contradictory or inconsistent that on one cultural theme (e.g. education or agriculture) or in one realm a Christian as thinker or actor should be more optimistic about the possibilities of active Christian involvement than he/she would be in some other realm, or than yet another brother or sister on another question or in yet another realm. This gives the lie to the "monolith" axiom. Or in the same "realm" (e.g. nuclear politics in the 1970's) a nonelectoral activity like SANE/FREEZE might have been more a fitting tactic than supporting a particular presidential candidate, not because it would be a form of withdrawal but because it would be a stronger mode of responsible participation.

The Church Assumes That the Will of God Can Be Done

Faithful "transformation" is not an unreachable ideal. Many argue that the very fact that a command is given implies that it must be possible to obey. Certainly commands were given in the Bible; therefore faithful compliance must be a possibility. This logic is surely too simple. It can be argued, against it, that the impossibility of doing God's Will perfectly teaches us something which we could learn in no other way. This is the element of truth in the view of Law underlying the "paradox" model.

The more profound and correct rootage for the assumption that the will of God can be done is not the logic of command but the fact of the Incarnation of Jesus Christ. That obedience is not impossible is a statement not about us but about him. The New Testament church confesses that in Jesus human history knew a fully obedient human being. He was not simply a Divine figure masquerading as a man, whose apparent obedience was therefore irrelevant to the rest of us, unattainable by definition. He was the true human being.[106] This is not a "liberal" or "humanistic" but a classical Christian affirmation. Faith in Jesus Christ is not an arbitrary or magical notation on the heavenly ledgers; faith is rather a participation in the Being of God, by way of incorporation into the body of Christ. The possibility of obedience is therefore a statement not about our own human capabilities, but about the fullness of the humanity of Jesus and the believers' identity with Him through the Spirit in the church.

To bring this axiom to bear on real decisions will mean the opposite of naive optimism or simplicity. It will mean readiness to face in every possible situation the need (and the promised enablement) to discover something do-able, which will constitute a confession of faith responding to the claims of Christ. This "something do-able" need not be perfection. Sometimes it will be the cross. Other times, it will be the same kind of commonsensically sane deed that any reasonable neighbor would choose. But we have not adequately described it if the best we can do is to avow that our faith makes no difference in what we are called to, or that nothing is possible which can be called obedient.

The Church's Consistency Is its Being a Fellowship Under Christ's Lordship

The standard of consistency by which we test whether various positions taken by various Christians, or by one Christian at different times, are consistent, is not ultimately the abstract logic with which the historian or the ethical analyst at his desk reviewing the classics distills out of any given set of decisions some general principles which seem logically to underlie them all. The consistency which counts is not trueness to an abstract type, as if (to use Tertullian again as whipping boy) emperor worship were an instance of the same principle as writing in the Latin language. The consistency which counts is the concrete community process of discernment, as that community converses, in the light of the confession "Christ is Lord," about particular hard choices.[107] Accountable discernment may be compatible with considerable fuzziness as to language and logic, or with seeming contradictions like those of which the major "radicals" are accused in the narrative of C&C.[108] It is the actual functioning fellowship of the church within human experience which validates claims to have known the will of God.[109] When the intellectual's measures of integrity are such as to proclaim that everyone in the past was rather stupidly inconsistent, it is the standards of consistency and not the pilgrim church of history which must stand challenged.

This consciousness of the importance of the church as a body will not do away with tensions, but it will define and locate them more properly. The tension will not be between a global reality called "culture" on one side and an absolute spiritual distance called "Christ" (or "monotheism") on the other side, but rather between a group of people defined by a commitment to Christ seeking cultural expression of that commitment (on one hand) and (on the other) a group or groups of other people expressing culturally other values which are independent of or contradictory to such a confession. This latter group is what the New Testament calls "the world." To say that these are two different stances is not to deny interest in both of them, but to define the specific quality of each. "Transformation" is meaningful and accountable only when those who call for it have a place to stand.

The Church Is the Locus of the Process of Decision

It is normally to the Christian fellowship that the command of God comes. It is normally in this Christian fellowship that the speaking of the Spirit is tested. Niebuhr's treatment in C&C is striking by the absence of any reference to the place of the Christian community in the process of decision. His other writings make much of the church as social reality, and of the self as socially defined. His theoretical view of human nature, his historical studies of denominationalism, and his practical studies of the ministry could have led the reader to expect some attention to the way general ideas about cultural value are mediated through concrete group process.[110] But (to our surprise) all that Niebuhr says in C&C about cultural discernment can be exhaustively understood in terms of the mental processes of solitary individuals.

The Church Functioning Within Society Is a New Cultural Option

Not only does Niebuhr fail to recognize the church as part of the process of decision; he indicates in *Christ and Culture* no interest in the Christian community as a sociological entity in its own right. This certainly can not mean that he had no interest in the sociology of the church's existence; his other studies certainly indicate a deep sensitivity at this point. He does not, however, work into the present book his awareness (or that of his teacher Troeltsch) that the Christian church as a sociological unit is distinguishable from the rest of culture and thereby constitutes a new cultural option.[111]

This distinctness of the church from the rest of society means that Christians will be making their moral decisions on grounds which not all men and women will apply. The appeal to Christ which gives form to their decisions must then not be measured by whether all will follow it, or by projecting what would happen if they did. Suffering love can be seen as the way to which Christians are called, without our expecting the rest of society all to share in a radical obedience for which it is not prepared.[112]

It is this specificity[113] of the church as a new phenomenon within history, sharing the uniqueness of the Incarnation as humanly possible obedience, which seals the impossibility of reasoning as if "culture" were a "monolithic" unity. The call to "transformation" can only have substance if there has already been some modeling of that to which the hearers are called.

The New Form of Culture Is Concrete

What needs to be transformed is actual ways of living, working, relating, and not merely our ways of thinking about them. The farther Niebuhr's treatment went up the scale of syntheses from "against" to "transforming," the less concrete substance we saw he gave to the motifs he described, and the more he was satisfied with a general rationale. I have already alluded to Paul Ramsey's report that "transformation" is favored by practically all readers of C&C, by virtue of the tacit tilt of the text. That report indicated that Niebuhr's pose of "objective" descriptive pluralism was unauthentic. I now come back to the same observation affirmatively, as our point of entry into our further considerations. One reason the vision of "transformation" is convincing prima facie to almost every unsuspecting reader is that Niebuhr provides no reality test. The "paradox" of Luther is shown to have been inadequate by observing the social conformism of German Christians, and by the general lack of normative substance which can get through the Law/Gospel filter. The Thomistic Synthesis is shown to be unconvincing because of its tacit espousal of present structures and assumptions under the headings of "reason" and "nature." How then will authentic "transformation" be recognized as avoiding those mistakes?

The Lordship of Christ Must Be Proclaimed as Judgment on Idolatry

The double-edged reality which in Niebuhr's portrayal we identified as "monolithic autonomy" is what must be broken down under Christ's sovereignty. Niebuhr's own narration gives the reader no chance to test how the preferred fifth strategy would work. Now we are in a position to offer clear criteria. The judgment of God on that Lordship which the Powers claim is not destructive but merciful. It redeems ("transforms") the Principalities and Powers[114] by rescinding their claimed autonomy. It transforms them by denying their monolithic unity in favor of discerning discrimination. Naming and denouncing the Powers' rebellion is prerequisite to becoming able to project the direction in which restoration would lie.[115]

The Church-Specific Structures for Decision Making

The alternative to seeing moral discernment as embodied only in the spirit of a scholar like Calvin or Niebuhr, or in a writing clergy like Augustine or Maurice, is to attend to how the community as organism makes decisions. Normatively and normally, the body of Christ actualizes the plurality of members and charisms, thereby attaining a credibility such as cannot be claimed for the "established" traditions where a ruler, a professor, or a priest makes decisions for the community by virtue of his office.[116]

The Church Needs a Canonical Foundation

Not only do believers need a place to stand if they are to move the environing culture; they need a bar and a fulcrum not of their own making. The course of events cannot be self-validating, as some dialectical visions of history, or some older Catholic visions of the magisterium, have seemed to claim.

This is a functional need, not a conservative reflex. Protestant liberalism in the age of Niebuhr's teaching ministry could afford to avoid facing the question of authority, as long as Fundamentalism on its right guaranteed both (directly) that one could affirm one's identity by eschewing obsurantism and (indirectly) that Jesus and the Bible would not be forgotten. That allowed Niebuhr to evade any critical accounting for what makes a position specifiably Christian,[117] or for the place of the Bible, and to appeal to some larger unspecifiable "universal community."[118] That explains in turn the vagueness of the notion of "transformation" at the point of specific moral content.

The concept of "canon" does not assume any special view of how to read the scriptures, or how to construct behind the scriptures one's notion of "Christ." The issue at stake is not a doctrine of Scripture but the principle of accountability.[119]

10. Issues of Method Remaining After the Conversation

The Classical Issue of "Autonomy" in Context

It is correct when Niebuhr indicates that for Martin Luther the concept of "vocation" can stand in almost without change for Niebuhr's concept of "culture" in its moral autonomy (174f). "Vocation" is one of the best classical labels for that "other" standard of moral behavior with which the guidance of Jesus needs to be complemented or by which it even sometimes needs to be corrected or replaced.[120]

The traditional notion of "vocation" or "station" in Lutheranism does in fact have many of the logical characteristics which Niebuhr gives to "culture." It is assumed about the "vocation" that anyone knows clearly what action it calls for, even though as a matter of fact not every butcher, not every weaver, not every prince has exactly the same understanding of how God wants him to serve his neighbor in his "station."

It is also assumed that the content of the moral obligation derived from the vocation is a part of revelation: i.e., although we know it by looking at the social order, the authority by which we know it is that of creation as revelatory.[121] This is the case even though at the same time the social order in which we can find the vocations at work is fallen, and no longer reflects everything of the divine intention.

Underlying the two characteristics cited above is a third assumption, perfectly self-evident, and naturally so, for Martin Luther and his medieval predecessors, but hardly for us, namely that the moral content of the vocation's call is stable, since society itself was assumed to be stable. Our sense of the plurality and the fluidity of history will never permit us to forget that all such structures are in flux.

Beyond the shortcoming of the notion of "vocation" understood as revealing God's will for people in particular stations in society, it needs to be remembered that vocation also means division in society. It puts people in fundamentally different social categories, so that what separates them from one another is held to be more important for their social behavior than what they have in common in Christ.

The critical Christian perspective which should be articulated at this point would not reject *wholly* the idea that one's social location can be a moral guide. Such a rejection could be argued on the grounds that the Christian is committed to some *other* moral "absolutes," which the imperatives of vocation would *necessarily* cause one to sin against. This might be the argument if we said that the soldier *has* to kill, the capitalist *has* to exploit, the diplomat *has* to lie, the mother *has* to smother, etc. . . . That is already an important argument, and it represents a *kind* of argument which we must not reject, namely the simple notion of a divine deontological claim.

I, however, must identify an objection at a more fundamental level, namely by doubting the appropriateness of letting the most important specification of how persons should behave be one which separates them from brothers and sisters by saying that their calling under God is contradictory both to Christ's guidance and to what others should do.

But can it not be argued that we read in the New Testament a call to people to live within their social status? Slaves and wives are encouraged to stay where they have been placed (I Cor. 11). Do not the New Testament *Haustafeln* represent a kind of divine ratification of every individual's social station?[122] Certainly in some sense the *Haustafeln* reasoning enables us to relate to the giveness of social order. Yet these role definitions are not seen in the New Testament as selected vocations, distinguishable from others by their prescribing different moral obligations. They are rather dimensions of the life of everyone. Everyone may be in a position of subordination to someone else. Every father is first of all someone's son, and the free citizen is a ruler's subject. Even the slave may administer another slave. The wife may govern slaves and children. Furthermore the duty of the subordinate person according to the New Testament and that of the person in power are the same: both are called to be subordinate to one another.[123] The specific expression of that subordination will differ from one social context to another, but never in such a sense as to ratify the autonomy of a set of behavior patterns which are derived not from Jesus but from the fallen social order.

What I have already observed with regard to vocation applies especially clearly to the thought of Martin Luther about the state. When in his fundamental catechetical writings Luther dealt with government, his basis was not Genesis 9 (the death penalty) or Romans 13 (the sword of the ruler). He preferred to describe government as a part of the commandment to honor father and mother: i.e. government is an extension of the family, and as such an order of God's *good* creation. Yet that order bears the sword, which is an adjustment to the fallenness of the world. When the two orders, creation and fall, are juxtaposed thus uncritically, as the notion of "culture" does, it means claiming the authority of God as revealer to legitimate one of the most dramatic indices of the fallenness of humanity, i.e. of humankind's rebelliousness against him.

What we have thus far been observing as it is played out in Lutheran terms, under the heading of "vocation" or "station," is hardly structurally different from the function of the notion of "nature" in Catholic thought. There too it is assumed that a set of claims and demands is simply given, knowable, univocal. It is held to be known not through the particularity of the salvation story of Jews and Christians with their respective scriptures, but through reason, to which all humans have access. Because "nature" is accessible to all rational creatures, no one can be dispensed from its revelatory demands by not being in the church or not knowing the Gospel.

Relativism Revisited

As we accompanied Niebuhr along his promenade through the history of his theme, his a priori pluralism or relativism became

79

increasingly visible. It has now turned out that it was for him a formal prior commitment. It does not really arise out of the story itself. It was rather imposed on the story, as a methodological a priori derived from his mentor Troeltsch. Niebuhr's predilection for avoiding any one right answer serves to reinforce his positive claim that all the answers together somehow add up to the truth. The "conviction that Christ as living Lord is answering the question in the totality of history and life, in a fashion which transcends the wisdom of all his interpreters, yet employs their partial insights and their necessary conflicts" was stated at the outset (p. 2) as a "belief"; it is a presupposition of the book, and not its conclusion. Since it is the presupposition, the categories were set up from the outset to confirm it. "We shall need to exercise care lest we pre-judge the issue by so defining one term or the other or both that only one of the Christian answers to be described will appear legitimate" p. 11). To suggest that there is one answer would usurp the Lordship of Christ (pp. 232ff.). God's sovereignty dictates making faith relative. Yet the prior commitment to find more than one legitimate answer makes its own assumptions of a special kind about the truth question, which would have to be debated in their own right, and which would be shared by very few of the pre-modern people he describes.

Intellectual honesty will always make us admit that there may be some questions to which there is not one demonstrably right answer. According to some schools of thought it makes sense at that point to say that a special category of "paradox" is needed, so that a more adequate overall answer is constituted by an interlocking of several answers, which at first may appear contradictory. When, however, one suggests that five different answers are all valid, the pluralism has become irresponsible (quite apart from the observation, to which we were driven in this case, that as the presentation goes on, the five answers are not all equally right after all).

Pages 234–41 in *Christ and Culture* set out the case for relativism at greater length. There it is based in a call to modesty: our knowledge is inadequate, our faith is imperfect, the historical situation we claim to come to grips with is always changing, and the diverse values we seek to realize compete with one another. Yet all of those elements which call us to modesty and flexibility fail to make the case for the affirmation that numerous different answers to the same question are all equally true. Niebuhr makes avoiding a firm conclusion into a moral imperative, not merely a modest measurement of the limits of our knowledge. "Whatever our capacities to state relatively inclusive and intelligible answers to the problem of Christ and culture, they all meet their limit in a moral imperative that commands, 'thus far shalt thou go and no farther.'" p. 232). Where this "imperative" comes from, and who speaks it, is not made clear. What line it draws and why is not said. If there is not one right answer because the facts are obstreperous and refuse to be brought under one denominator, that is a conclusion arising from within the search, possibly produced by a fault of our categories, not a prior moral imperative. If there is not one right answer because our respect for various people who hold various positions keeps us from excommunicating them, that may be an imperative on the social and ecumenical level but does not resolve the truth question. The very end of the book makes it the essence of the definition of the church that we should simply believe that all the answers come together in some kind of higher synthesis or fusion or average. Why we should believe that, rather than holding that some valid answers are available and some heresies should be denounced (or that the whole realm is a meaningless mess), is not explained; it is an axiom of this urbane and ecumenical interpreter.

Although this tolerant equiprobabilism looks at first glance like a very refined ecumenical openness, we saw that it actually constitutes a firm formal bias against those views which hold that there is such a thing as *binding* revelation, valid knowledge, or a firm moral imperative. Although logically it should undercut all the other answers equally, in fact it is cited as if it counted especially against the "radical" option. Niebuhr supports his point by appealing to the transcendence or the uniqueness of God who stands above all our efforts to know him.

In the New Testament, on the other hand, and in most classical Christian theology, the concrete import of the appeal to the sovereign majesty of God is more or less the opposite. God's transcendence is namely the ground of the assurance that our knowledge of God's call, and to some extent of his nature, is reliable and binding because, even though partial, it comes from God when it encounters us in Christ. Niebuhr's use of the language of "absolute" is diversionary, to avoid rather than to affirm something definite. The "absolute" is what all the partial views add up to. But it is defined as beyond anything we can attain; therefore all our partial views are equiprobable. The "absolute" is thus appealed to in order to ratify relativism. The transcendence of God is a code term to reinforce our uncertainty about the normativity of the incarnation.

81

Now if this relativizing thrust were itself completely thorough in its unfolding, we could at least grant its possible sincerity, while doubting its faithfulness to the Christian tradition, or its methodological utility. But the claims for it become weaker when we discover that the pluralistic position is itself being advocated after all as the *right* position; that saying there is no one answer is itself the correct answer, so that "transforming," at the same time that it overcomes the shortcoming of all the other solutions, has no very precise profile. Its being inclusive and pluralistic, fitting to the Ivy League graduate school culture, makes it precisely the best view after all.[124]

So the notion of "being right" has been first of all set aside, but then quietly reintroduced, to be used in favor of the position that is morally the least decisive, because the most tolerant and inclusive, which nonetheless is advocated on the grounds that it is the best reflection of the conviction of God's transcendence. Niebuhr thinks he has a way to eat his cake and have it too. Divine transcendence forbids anyone else's truth claims and validates his own. The one thing such a God cannot do is to have bound himself to Jesus (or for that matter to Abraham or Moses). It is finally the modern moralist who claims the last word.

11. What Would Be the Alternative?

After having seen at some length how the analysis of C&C skews the problems it claims to survey, the reader will have some right to ask, "what then? Is there a right answer?"

One early decription of a book like this one, projected to include this study, a book project which then failed to materialize in the initially intended form (partly for that reason), had promised that my critique of Niebuhr should be followed up by a "a new typology of Christ and Culture."

The reader who has come this far with me will recognize why that is (as far as I can see) not an available or desirable alternative. If a question is wrongly put, we should rephrase the question, not the answer. If "have you stopped beating your wife?" is the wrong way to frame an issue, it will not be fixed by changing the tense to ask "*when* did you stop . . . ?" or changing the verb to ask instead "have you stopped embezzling?"

What was wrong with the question as H. R. Niebuhr set it up was the very notion that "Christ" as Niebuhr defined him (or perhaps rather "it," since the connections linking all the meanings Niebuhr gives to the term "Christ" to the man Jesus was not simple), and "Culture" as Niebuhr defines that, are so predisposed by his own particular angles on the history of the problem that there can be no right answer.

Some of the time (Glen Stassen claims on good grounds that this was not all the time) Niebuhr's very purpose was to avoid that there could be a right answer, in order thereby to make the case for a pluralism of principle, or for the indecision of the Ivy League intellectual above the fray, or for the agony of the existentialist torn apart within the fray, or for what early in his career he called "truly catholic."[125]

At other times, there is a right answer, and it is "transformation," the fifth cumulative synthesis-of-syntheses type. This preference is clear, built into the plan of the book. Yet the reader has not been provided any precise understandings of the criteria which distinguish valid from invalid modes of carrying out that project.

As we observed, the formal qualities of "culture," as Niebuhr used the term in argument, which would need to be challenged in order to make the concept responsible, were that it is "autonomous" and that it is "monolithic." Once however those qualities are named and called into question, then there remains no room for a slightly repaired typology where the term "culture" could still be univocal. The reader can legitimately ask "what should we do about all of these problems?" but the answer can not be placed on a grid of classical types. There is no reason that what we should do about war, and about farming, and about epic poetry, about elementary education and about pornography, about mothering and about heavy metal, would gain by our trying to treat each of those segments of "culture" in the same way.[126] What we need is rather a capacity for moral discernment, in the light of which Niebuhr's ability to call all of those things "culture" will no longer be permitted to get in the way of handling each issue in its own terms.

With regard to "Christ," at the other end of the relationship, we also noted the inherent inadequacies of Niebuhr's account. At the one end of the field of themes usually referred to as "incarnation," he downplayed the weight of the fact that Jesus was a particular kind of politically committed poor palestinian preacher of a coming Kingdom.[127] That Jesus was moved from center stage in favor of a transcendentalist purveyor of better insights about God, whose main concern

83

was to keep anyone's understanding of God from getting too concrete. We saw that Niebuhr's special definition of "humility" was the avoidance of concreteness in the name of transcendence.

At the other end of the scale of standard issues, by decrying "the unitarianism of the Son" as somehow worse than his own unitarianism of the Father, Niebuhr cut himself off from the issues which were the real historic stakes in the Nicene controversies (even though he appeared to be claiming to do so in the name of orthodoxy).

There can therefore be no simple fix to remodel the way Niebuhr shaped the probem. We can however attempt a few remedial steps which, when taken together, might add up to a better way to handle the whole agenda, by taking account expressly of the pitfalls he has helped us to identify:

a) how does the Bible deal differently with the "autonomy" challenge?

b) how does the Bible deal differently with the "monolithicity" challenge?

c) how does the Bible deal differently with monotheism's being radical?

I do not allude to "the Bible" here in any fundamentalist or obscurantist frame of mind, any more than Niebuhr was doing so when he wrote about the Jesus of the Gospels as differing from the Social Gospel. Our conversation should and does run up and down the centuries, a story for which the Bible is only the beginning. My reason for taking the Bible seriously is not the same as that of the protestant scholasticism to which some people in Niebuhr's setting were reacting defensively.[128] Yet it is the case that the biblical texts do in fact demonstrate fruitful ways of illuminating our moral agenda which at some points are more discerning, more helpful and more critical than Niebuhr's grid.[129]

As I start over, in the light of what we have learned from Niebuhr's misstatement of the question, to restate the Gospel, as it relates to our cultural obedience to Christ's Lordship, I shall by no means be seeking to refute Niebuhr every step of the way. As Glen Stassen has shown, most of the points which I make Niebuhr has made too. The difference has to do with the context in which they are made, the alternatives he rejects along the way, and the way he classifies other views.

The most inclusive synthetic description I know of the way the apostolic witnesses addressed the world around them with the proclamation of the Gospel is a list of five cases, five texts, from five different authors in five different settings, which I juxtaposed in my chapter "But We See Jesus."[130] In each of those five cases, the apostle faced the challenge of how to affirm Christ's Lordship in the face of a value structure, or a power structure, or a meaning system, which denied that Lordship." The five cases are utterly independent of one another in vocabulary, geography, and ethical stakes.[131]

A. John 1:1–14 uses the language of the Gnostics to reject the Gnostic strategy of putting Jesus in the box of a prior cosmological commitment. The writer does that with special reference to Jesus' humanity and his being rejected by "his own."

B. Hebrews 1:1–2:9 uses the language of a cosmology interested in priests and angels mediating between God and humankind, but places Jesus above rather than inside that ladder, accentuating again his humanity and his suffering.

The same accents are present, in a strict formal parallel, in

C. Colossians 1:1–28,

D. Revelation 4:1–5:4,[132] and

E. Philippians 2:5–13. The message is always the same.[133] In each text the first-century equivalent of Niebuhr's postulate of autonomy is rejected. To these five single passages I can here add two more cases with a different literary shape. The most coherent corpus of concepts whereby the New Testament deals with our theme is:

F. What the Pauline literature spoke about under the heading "principalities and powers." The thesis is now well established[134] that even though the textual basis for any synthesis is thin,[135] a solid and consistent world view underlies these texts. It is said about these "entities" at the same time that they are good creatures of God and that they are fallen, evil, oppressive. That fundamental ambivalence overrules at the outset the quality of Niebuhr's "culture" which we have had to label "monolithic." It identifies "autonomy" as their fallenness rather than as a positive value. Everything we call "culture" is both in some way created and creative and positive, and in other ways rebellious and oppressive. This is not a fifty/fifty mix, but a far more complex dialectical challenge, whereby we are called to exercise discernment. We should precisely *not* try to be consistent by affirming all, rejecting all, or paradoxing all, as the Niebuhr outline assumes would be consistent, but to be concretely discriminating, after rejecting any notion of an overall recipe.

85

Some aspects of human activity are thus less redeemable than others. In particular settings, Christians have rejected the theater; in others theater has served the gospel and the church. This is not inconsistency but concrete situational discernment. We need to ask not either/or questions but How? and When? questions. To some of them we shall soon turn. In the early Christian centuries the service of the state was rejected; in colonial Pennsylvania on the other hand, people with an ethical vision very close to that of the early Christians created a state. That was a contradiction only on the most formal level. The real difference was that the situation in Pennsylvania offered unprecedented chances. That made it possible that a man who loved foreigners (e.g. the original Americans)[136] could set up a government according to his own convictions, in which their dignity would be protected; a possibility which was unthinkable not only when the New Testament was written but any time since then. What was different about William Penn was not that he denied the early Christian vision about church and world, but that it was given to him to have a chance to implement that vision in a position where the Crown gave him some space.

G. It was again Paul, but this time the Paul of Acts, who faced the challenge of testifying in public address to a pagan audience about the impact of Christ. In Lystra (chapter 14), where a healing wonder had already caught the crowd's attention, he set his "News" about the God

> who made the heaven and the earth and the sea and all that is
> in them.

within his audience's world view of parallel cultures:

> he allowed all the nations to follow their own ways,

and of reliable cyclical nature:

> giving you rains from heaven and fruitful seasons, and filling
> you with food and your hearts with joy

Yet in so speaking Paul insisted that the proper response to this benevolent cosmos was not to sacrifice either to Barnabas or himself or to "these worthless things."

Not much later, in Athens (Chapter 17), challenged to respond to the curiosity of those who thought he was talking about two new deities, "Jesus and Anastasis" (resurrection), Paul again accepted conversing within the frame of their world view:

> From one ancestor he made all the nations to inhabit the whole

earth, and he allotted the times of their existence and the boundaries of the places where they would live.

Paul even conceded for purposes of discussion that there might be some authenticity to the Athenians' worshiping an "unknown God" (17:23) or

> that they would search for God and perhaps grope for him and find him.

Yet none of this creative readiness to meet his audience in their own terms diluted Paul's (original Jewish)[137] radical monotheism, his affirmation of God's creating all things and governing history, his rejection of graven images and sacrifice, and the final call to repentance in the name of Jesus whom God had raised from the dead.

So now we have on the table before us (A to G) seven specimens of the apostolic witness to Christ being addressed to the cosmology of the time. The seven cases are all parallel, except for the fact that the narratives of Acts are unfinished lively accounts, so that the reference to Jesus and to suffering is less explicit. Much of this witness is fully faithful to the already well-represented Jewish affirmation of creation and providence, rejection of idols and sacrifice. In these passages this monotheistic critique is affirmed in a culturally relevant way, in the language of the listeners or readers. It is in no way obscurantist or "sectarian." Yet to this is always added[138] the reference to Jesus, to death, to resurrection, **and** to the identification of the speaker or writer with what he reports, **and** to the call to the reader or hearer to respond in faith.[139]

What is quite absent in all of the NT is any trace of the Niebuhrian assumption that the pagan cosmology as a whole must be responded to somehow as a monolith, either affirming it all, rejecting it all, synthesizing with it all, or paradoxing it all. What Paul and the other NT authors do is **always** to transform, but the transformation always has firm material criteria. It takes account of (a) the Jewishness of Jesus (affirming creation and providence, rejecting graven images and sacrifice) of (b) the humanity of Jesus (especially his proclamation, his suffering, and his resurrection), and of (c) the involvement of the witness and the appeal to the addressee.

The call for discernment as to what constitutes authentic transformation invites us then to come up with criteria of at least two kinds. One kind will be procedural. How should believers proceed, in complex settings and in the face of major moral challenges, to make decisions about cultural values? What agencies, what institutions, should we use? To that I shall return.

The other half of the criteria question will be substantial. What is culturally good? What obligations and prohibitions follow from being a family? From being a master? a servant? a citizen? Are the teachings or the example of Jesus pertinent to such choices? We already noted that for Niebuhr, what matters about Jesus, the aspect which operates so as to provide the a priori "against culture" tilt, from which the shape of the rest of the argument flows, was not that Jesus taught love of enemy or unconditional promise-keeping or monogamy, but that his "radical monotheism" relativized everything human. The "everything human" which was relativized included concrete rules about enemy love and promise-keeping, not only their opposites.[140]

I already alluded to the "principalities and powers" cosmology of the Pauline writings as exemplifying a mode of moral interpretation which breaks the Niebuhrian grid.[141] Yet another functionally almost parallel testimony was powerfully represented by a lecture presented to the American Academy of Religion November 1992 by René Girard on "The Satan of the Gospels." Satan represents both order and disorder. Only paradoxical and dialectical discourse can do justice to the evil within human goods and the room for redemption within human sin.[142]

The "new song" which the saints and angels in the first vision of the apocalypse sang in praise of the slain lamb said that the lamb's sacrifice had purchased for God people who would constitute a royal and priestly people. This people would "serve God [i.e. function as priests]" and would "rule the world" [i.e. function as kings].[143] This is another place where the Niebuhrian world view breaks down. How does a community uniting in the celebration of the sovereignty of the slain lamb participate in his sovereignty and thereby in making the world go the right way? When the early creeds spoke of the risen Lord as "sitting at the right hand of the Father" this meant exercising a role as cosmic viceroy, with history in his hands, **even though** that rule was not transparent. The worship of the Johannine community was not social withdrawal but radical monotheism, participating in that Lordship as they stood in the midstream of world events, but refusing to confess any other Lord.

The way the simple reader, like Paul Ramsey's average college student in the 1950's, responded to C&C was to assume a "natural" or "rational" epistemology, according to which the moral content of "culture" is simply given, already "out there," defined by the way things are. Then we have to decide how to respond to it. We choose by which of the five logically available modes we shall be guided. The Gospel alternative we have gradually been watching unfold will rather deny that there is any such thing as an already given "nature" of things, "out there" or "as such," to which we could then choose to say simply "for" or "against," or with more nuances "above" or "tension" or "transform" (subject to an a priori premium on responding the same way to all of them).

Instead, each setting, each event, each relationship will open for us a set of options or challenges, where we shall need to decide how to love our enemies, how to feed the hungry, how to keep our promises, how to make the earth be fruitful, how to celebrate community, how to remember our heritage . . . The challenge "what will you do about this value we call culture?" far from helping us to be responsible, is something we are freed from, by the concreteness with which the Torah and the Kingdom message of Jesus describe our path.

One way to clarify why concrete discernment is indispensable is to survey the "culture" of our time. Our world is characterized by racism, by the punitive exercise of authority from the home to the state, by genocide, pornography, the glorification of violence in commercial entertainment . . . These are authentically "culture," but they are what an older reformation theology called fallen. In the face of these dimensions, Niebuhr's favoring the "transformation" vision correlates with a low estimate of the power of evil.

CHAPTER 2

The Social Self in the Pilgrim Church

D. M. Yeager

1. Christian Ethics and the Social Question

All pieties to the contrary notwithstanding, it is possible that "Christian social ethics" is an incoherent phrase, and because the pieties press upon us so forcefully at present, we have all the more reason to examine this question with care. It is certainly worthwhile to note that the distinctively American discipline of Christian social ethics had its origin in and was given its structure by the widely (though perhaps wrongly) maligned social gospel movement. The appearance late in the nineteenth century of an academic discipline devoted to the Christian analysis of social problems as a point of departure for the specification of appropriate programs of Christian action designed to achieve their resolution is a phenomenon which reflects the struggle of Christian thinkers to absorb and sort out the contribution of the great European architects of sociological thinking as much as it represents a Christian response to changing demographic and economic features of the social order at home. No one, of course, disputes the belief that Christian life unfolds under the command of neighbor love and that proper "neighboring" concerns itself with worldly well-being as well as spiritual salvation. It is not, however, difficult to imagine an argument that "Christian social ethics" is incoherent (1) because Christian ethics, structurally regarded, must be understood to be an ethics of personal conversion not structural reform and/or (2) because Christian ethics is an ethics without specific social content in the sense that it does not require any *particular* ordering of our economic, political, and social relationships—so long as those relationships are coherently and constructively ordered in some fashion.

Derivative Effects or Direct Address?

There is no need to search far among the classic texts of Christianity in order to find a representative argument that Christian ethics is concerned with virtue and character not with social reform because Christian faith is an affair of internal conversion addressed to the "vertical" relationship of the created person to the personal creator. Friedrich Schleiermacher provides a clear and convenient example:

> That a Church is nothing but a communion or association relating to religion or piety, is beyond all doubt for us Evangelical (Protestant) Christians, since we regard it as equivalent to degeneration in a Church when it begins to occupy itself with other matters as well . . . . However, not only we, but even those Churches which are not so clear about keeping apart Church and State, or ecclesiastical and scientific association, must assent to what we have laid down. For they cannot assign to the Church more than an indirect influence upon these other associations; and it is only the maintenance, regulation, and advancement of piety which they can regard as the essential business of the Church.[1]

Schleiermacher's sharp distinction finds few adherents among contemporary theologians, but one can still find careful and articulate arguments that the connection between faith and social action is indirect. Though Lisa Cahill's recent book *Love Your Enemies* is clearly offered as a contribution to Christian *social* ethics (the right and discriminating use of coercive force by civil powers and by Christians in civil positions) and though her purpose is to "[reestablish] the gospel as an integral base of Christian thought about violence,"[2] she acknowledges that her study is a study of "implications" rather than of imperative "social objectives." "The Sermon on the Mount does not suggest a 'social ethics' in any direct or usual sense. It depicts active, personal outflow of a total conversion by virtue of which ordinary religious and moral expectations are shaken to their roots and one is transfixed by Jesus' transparence to the reign of God" (p. 34). She appeals to Martin Hengel's *Victory over Violence: Jesus and the Revolutionists* as she develops her account of the requirements of the Christian life:

Jesus saw the primary source of evil in the world as the evil in the individual's heart, rather than Roman political domination, the priestly aristocracy, or large landowners. Thus the reign of God is not brought about in the first instance by socio-political transformation, but by the "transformed heart" which alone "is capable of new human community, of doing good."[3]

According to Cahill, the notion of the present reality of God's kingdom—with its attendant elevation of the virtues of forgiveness and compassion, together with its power to anchor and bind together a distinctive community—creates the pathway from the "hard sayings" and daunting example of Jesus to social action and to distinctively Christian political and ethical judgments. Cahill's unfolding of a substantive portrait of discipleship guided by the disclosure of the kingdom of God is instructive not only in the way it leans against more directly political readings of Scripture but also in its treatment of the way even a rigorously dispositional ethics can produce, and in the Christian framework may be expected to produce, a socially influential pattern of behavior. "From a standpoint any other than this conversion experience itself, it may be difficult for us to appreciate exactly how radical would be the impact on social life of a full personal commitment" (p. 233). Does she then hold that the maintenance and advancement of piety is the sole business of the religious community? No. She remarks, "To insist, as did Luther and many recent interpreters, that action flows necessarily and spontaneously from conversion seems right but inadequate once the incompleteness of the kingdom is acknowledged." Goodness is "fragile" and depends in some important sense on fortuitous social circumstances; consequently, the Christian community must never lapse into the illusion that goodness will take care of itself.

While the indirect or derivative influence of religious convictions on social behavior can be examined in this subject-centered way, it has historically been more usually traced through the works and obligations of charity. In their essay in *Evangelicals and Development: Towards a Theology of Social Change*, Vinay Samuel and Chris Sugden observe that from the first century to the seventeenth, "the motivation for the church's involvement with social change in relation to the poor was personal charity."[4] This view reflects and may well be derived from the argument made by Ernst Troeltsch in 1912 in his massive study of *The Social Teaching of the Christian Churches*. Troeltsch was, of course, one of the primary architects of the idea that Christian social responsibility could be and should be exercised in a way more direct than derivative. Considering the way in which the radical ethic of Jesus's teachings was both preserved and domesticated through centuries of practical activity, he noted that "social reform took the shape of philanthropy, which aided individuals and allowed conditions to remain as they were," a conservative habit that was not "overthrown" until the Calvinists saw that "spiritual values are conditioned by the material, external setting within which they are placed."[5] Though he was anxious in his own right to establish a structural justification of Christian political activism and of efforts to define a systematic Christian program of social reform, Troeltsch did acknowledge the extraordinary impact that early Christians exerted upon their social order, even in their deliberate indifference to programmatic action:

> Thus for many centuries the conservative attitude of Christianity towards political and social life was decided by this doctrine of Paul [that civil authorities must be obeyed because they rule by the order of God but that Christians are inwardly unaffected by civil arrangements]. It is a most remarkable thing that the entirely revolutionary and radical principle of unlimited individualism and universalism should adopt such a thoroughly conservative attitude to social questions. In spite of this, however, it actually exercised a revolutionary influence. For the conservative attitude was not founded on love and esteem for the existing institutions, but upon a mixture of contempt, submission, and relative recognition. That is why, in spite of all its submissiveness, Christianity did destroy the Roman State by alienating souls from its ideals, and it has a disintegrating effect upon all undiluted nationalism and upon every form of exclusively earthly authority [1:82].

While acknowledging the power of this secondary effect, Troeltsch judged it inadequate. Though he could trace the way in which "the immense spiritual energies of a revolutionary nature" embedded in the Christian worldview often "led to revolutionary changes in very concrete matters," he still wrote with disappointment that "through all this, however, Christianity always either tolerated the existing social order, while inwardly it undermined it, or by its comparative conservatism it supported and glorified it" (1:87). He thus, himself, chronicled with care the theological movements which sought and established "an inward connection and historical continuity between the general political, economic, and social situation and the values of personal religion" (1:88). What Troeltsch wanted (and what many

Christian theorists continue to want today) was a carefully grounded understanding of a thoroughly Christian "spirit which should penetrate, mould, and renew the common life" (1:126).

The question is not whether Christians will take thought for the neighbor or care about the social, political, and economic orders that form the background of their lives. The question is rather that of specifying theoretically the relationship between faith and social action and of specifying theoretically the relationship between the churches as social institutions and other social institutions. Troeltsch, of course, believed that only twice in Christian history had theology managed to weld the two together in a serious and convincing way: first in "the Theory of Ecclesiastical Unity of Civilization by the Thomist Ethic" which yielded the "Christendom" of the high middle ages and again in the theology of the Calvinists which produced at the practical level the pursuit of the "holy community." Both of these achievements were context-specific; thus, neither could be preserved as an adequate "solution" amid the social and intellectual structures of the twentieth century. Troeltsch then set us the task of defining a new understanding of the integral relationship of faith and social action, one that would fit the modern sociological situation. But before we rush to embrace the task Troeltsch set before us, we should first ask the question of whether this welding is desirable or even possible.

Domains of Concern

The first issue of concern is the development of a right understanding of the Christian view of human existence both with respect to the weight to be given to the individual's loneliness before God and with respect to weight and meaning of history. Even Troeltsch speaks of the "ontological individualism" fundamental to the Christian world view. Can Christianity accommodate the belief that structures and institutions have a primordial and shaping influence on individuals from which individuals cannot withdraw their minds and allegiances by simply saying "no" because they have no logical space for saying "no"? Can Christianity preserve the centrality accorded to personal relationship—most particularly the relationship of the individual agent to a fully personal God—while absorbing the contributions made to human self-understanding by contemporary social theorists and the modern sciences? This is closely related to the question of the proper

95

Christian construal of the religious significance of the social and historical order that is the context of life in time.

Secondly, at the nub of the problem we find the question of how the Christian community is to be conceived: What is the work of the church? Is the work of the church the conversion of individual souls, leaving to the converted Christians the work of altering the social order through their derivative activities? Or does the church have direct work to do in the world—is it, in fact, responsible to God for the principles of civil organization? Ought it to be a self-conscious political force? Ought it to operate among social institutions as a correlative social institution—a center of temporal power? Perhaps even more radically, we find a question as to whether the center of gravity of Christianity is to be construed individualistically or corporately. Is the Christian community a sort of holding company linking a collection of autonomous independent agencies which could go on about their business if the parent company dissolved? Is the Christian community best modeled as the mothering bosom to which we can return to be healed of the wounds received in battle with less hospitable powers; is it a final refuge, like the family, where "they have to take you in"? Or is the Christian community a company with an active purpose such that the members of the community receive their personal as well as their corporate identity through the execution of their specified role in accomplishing the distinctive work of this distinctive corporate agency?

2. Niebuhr and the Redemption of History

In "The Social Gospel and the Mind of Jesus," H. Richard Niebuhr poses the question simply: "Does the acceptance of the cosmic God and the eschatological Jesus reduce us to individualism in Christian ethics and to a passive attitude in social strife?"[6] Lennart Molin has not been alone in answering: For Niebuhr, apparently, yes. In *Hearts and Structures* Molin describes Niebuhr's ethics as "a personal system" which attends to the structural and social framework of our lives, but treats it as background. "What Niebuhr wants to change," Molin writes, "is the self rather than the world."[7]

Niebuhr is, to be sure, a theologian who combines, in an atypical way, a strong interest in sociology and in philosophical anthropology with a forcefully evangelical religious sensibility. Though he begins his career with great sympathy for the social gospel movement, he becomes increasingly critical of it with the passing years, gathering its principal spokesmen together as examples of the accommodationist type in *Christ and Culture*. Niebuhr's last and most searching treatment of the Christian moral life is a dispositional treatment of "the responsible self" which presents personal conversion from distrust to trust as the *sine qua non* of Christian living. His exceedingly powerful sense of God acting in history gives rise not to a confidence that Christians are called to accept from God the mandate to establish the kingdom, but rather to a sense of the degree to which all human endeavors fall short of God's will and are subject to God's sovereign judgment. For all his appreciation of the role the notion of the kingdom of God has played in American theology and for all his enthusiasm for that style of thinking which presents Christ as the "transformer of culture," his own writings are notably empty of any particular concrete suggestions, beyond the call for a contrite heart, as to how this flawed and aching world might be repaired. It is plain that Niebuhr traces all human wickedness to the unconverted or imperfectly converted structures of idolatry; the reversal or healing of wickedness must, then, begin with repentance and rebirth (usually construed as purely personal but also advanced as a process which a community might undergo as a community).

Convinced that inactivity is impossible for the converted, he trusts that Christians will have a significant social impact; indeed, the primary burden of the argument of *Radical Monotheism and Western Culture* is that radically monotheistic faith shows itself in and transforms every domain of activity. Yet, for all that, he resolutely refuses to dictate the outlines of right Christian response in economics, in education, in politics, in the arts, or in any other domain. There are at least three reasons for this: (1) In part it reflects his own faithfulness to his model of the answerer: the substance of "Christian social ethics" cannot be abstractly and definitively fixed but must be worked out by Christians interpreting and responding to their complex, varied, and changing particular situations. (2) In part it reflects the historicist vision he absorbed from Troeltsch. Since we never escape from the particularities of given place and perspective, we cannot judge our cultural structures against the possibility of perfection; neither does it make any sense for us to hope that we can put in place absolute structures representing the timeless preferences of God. The issue is not to make actual some new law or ideal paradigm (an aspiration owing more to Athens than to Israel); the issue is rather to elevate given actualities so that they become vehicles (or in Luther's word, conduits) for grace. The kingdom of God, as Niebuhr reminds us at the end of *Christ and Culture*, is "the world of grace,"[8] not a particular set of structural solutions to a particular historical situation. He is likewise skeptical of the notion of time-stamped evolutionary progress toward the kingdom of God (as if we in the twentieth century were closer to God or the kingdom than people who lived in the thirteenth); rather, he invites us, in *Christ and Culture*, to abandon the model of temporal, sequential substitutions in favor of the more spatial model of "lifting up" whatever institutions and practices and arrangements happen to be in place. However, (3) his refusal to, say, argue for economic reform as a religious duty also reflects his strictly religious conviction that we must perpetually resist the temptation to allow finite goods to usurp the place of transcendent ones. All cultural systems and institutions are context-relative human artifacts; none should be absolutized or idolized as "institutions of the Christ."[9]

In Niebuhr's view, the evangelical categories of faith, idolatry, and conversion are the categories through which all human experience—personal and communal, secular and religious—can be most reliably interpreted. Significantly, his favored paradigm, while labeled "Christ the Transformer of Culture," is ordinarily characterized in the text not as transformationist but as conversionist. The realization of the kingdom is essentially a matter of spiritual regeneration: false faith and antipathy must give way to authentic faith and reconciliation. Christianity does not bring a fixed law, a new order, a distinctive moral and social agenda; it is not a casting off but a reorientation. The fault is not to be sought in the values and practices of the community, but in the conception of the final good according to which the values and practices are ordered. Christians lift up the present law, order, agenda so that it serves not human ends but divine ends. The churches must not be construed as "safe houses" in a hostile "larger" culture, and the churches are not to be thought of as sacred repositories of moral values and spiritual goods that cannot be found elsewhere.

Yet this theologian who has read and acknowledged his debt to Paul, Augustine, Luther, Edwards, and Kierkegaard—and, not incidentally, Martin Buber—has also been shaped by the study of Troeltsch, Max Weber, and George Herbert Mead. From the beginning to the end of his career, he insists that the self is radically historical and irreducibly relational. His emphasis on the social character of the self is paired throughout his work with an insistence on the social character of sin and salvation. His early enthusiasm for the social gospel reflects his deep appreciation of the importance of the social gospel's shift of religious focus from the individual to the community, and he does not discard this corporate angle of vision when he begins to discard the moralism that he comes to attribute to liberal theology and "applied Christianity." The least that can be said is that this historicist understanding of the self gives to his evangelical commitments a new coloration. The secondary literature speaks skeptically of unresolved tensions (Kant and Weber, Barth and Troeltsch) and ponders whether the synthesis Niebuhr confidently sought to devise is, in fact, conceptually coherent or sustainable. That this question should be asked is inevitable; whether it is a pertinent question remains to be seen.

Niebuhr's notion of the social self is not the only conviction that serves to ballast his theology against the otherworldliness and individualism that so often mark the evangelical stance; of equal importance is his insistent affirmation that the sovereign God is indisputably Lord of history and is acting redemptively in all events—not just in rainbows and newborn babes but in the devastation of black lung disease, in concentration camps, in war. Hence, it is not we who are being saved out of the evils of history, but history itself that is being saved. Nothing is beyond the reach of redemption for God abandons nothing and no one. As "the dynamic driving force immanent in the events of time,"[10] God rules not in some distant heaven, not only in the individual heart, but in the social sphere—in all social spheres—as well. Yet Niebuhr does not develop a political theology out of this root conviction; indeed, he is critical of Christian social activism and of prophetic denunciations. Justus Doenecke rightly used his work in the mid-seventies as a platform for the critique of political theology.[11] To be sure, Niebuhr argues, in *Christ and Culture*, for the motif of social transformation, noting that "history is the story of God's mighty deeds and of man's responses to them" (p. 195).[12] Yet he himself sharply differentiates his proposed "transformation of mankind in all its cultural activity" (p. 215) from the more familiar Christian approaches to altering social realities—one of which Niebuhr characterizes as the Christ-against-culture attempt to create an alternative "holy community" and the other of which Niebuhr criticizes under the rubric of "Christ of culture" as a baptizing of various secular social agenda (for example, "the practices of prohibition" or "individualistic liberalism" or, in our own time, gender justice) by a process in which "Christ is identified with what men conceive to be their finest ideals, their noblest institutions, and their best philosophy" (p. 103).

Not surprisingly, various readers (not least among them his elder brother) have wondered what social transformation would mean and how it is to be accomplished if the tradition of kingdom theology is dismissed and if the prophetic stance is undermined. These concerns can best be pointed up through a brief examination of two recent critical attacks on Niebuhr's work, one which alleges that Niebuhr is naive in his failure to understand the structures of power, and the other which argues that Niebuhr's dismissive treatment of the Christ-against-culture type is unfair and ill considered since the creation of an alternative community is the only conceivable means by which Niebuhr's own ideal of cultural transformation might be achieved.

3. Two Sets of Questions

The first of these arguments is offered by Raymond Whitehead in a short article titled "Christ and Cultural Imperialism" which, significantly, appears in a collection titled *Justice as Mission: An Agenda for the Church*. Noting that "Niebuhr's typology [in *Christ and Culture*] neglects the question of power,"[13] Whitehead faults Niebuhr for failing to distinguish in his notion of culture between "cultural thought forms and structures of political and economic power" (p. 27). He further faults Niebuhr (though this is not stated so explicitly) for failing to appreciate the fact that the structures of "culture," whether they be symbolic structures or political/economic structures, are devices of social control and oppression. Thus, the duality of Christ and culture is an oversimplification, for "Christ" as a cultural symbol has functioned frequently as a device for cultural oppression. Contrarily, if we take "Christ" to signify precisely that which cannot lend itself to structures of oppression, we find that it must necessarily be *against* culture before it can propose transformation. Whitehead suggests that Niebuhr's rejection of the Christ against culture model is again an oversimplification which, failing to appreciate the dangers and obduracy of structures of power that oppress, fails to appreciate the fact that when Christians oppose "culture," they are usually rejecting not "the world" generally conceived but "a particular oppressive form of that culture" (p. 30) which in the name of Christ (on Whitehead's reading, he who opposes all impulses of domination) ought properly to be rejected, not "lifted up."

This argument has some affinities with the more extended argument made by Charles Scriven in *The Transformation of Culture*. Scriven sets the work of John Howard Yoder alongside that of Niebuhr in order to argue that "the true Niebuhrian way is the Anabaptist way."[14] By this he means that the transformation of the prevailing culture cannot be worked from within the prevailing culture since one cannot convert through capitulation. In order to work the transformation of the prevailing culture, the Christian community must develop a contrasting culture which it offers as an alternative. Scriven follows Yoder in the argument that Anabaptist separatism is not a rejection of culture and politics but is rather a profound act of political engagement:

> Anabaptist witness addressed social and political structures as well as individuals. It spoke judgment upon rulers and institutions while upholding an alternative form of social life as a way of changing the world. This was a form of political engagement. Anabaptists believed that the Bible requires such engagement, and I am saying they were right [170].

That they rejected "the close link between church and state that had to their day been a hallmark of Catholic and Protestant Christianity" (pp. 170–71) is not to be taken as a repudiation of culture or a retreat to an entirely spiritual understanding of the Christian life. Rather, it signals a fundamental criticism of a particular style of integrating Christian faith with political and economic affairs; the Anabaptists exercised themselves to construct Christian cultures or communities which displayed an alternative style of integration. His criticism, then, of Niebuhr is not that Niebuhr's impulse is mistaken but that Niebuhr fails to see that the project of the radicals is the only project by means of which the program of transformation can be achieved. Whereas Niebuhr interprets the Anabaptist separation from the prevailing cultural structures as an epistemologically naive attempt to escape from culture and as resolutely anti-political, Scriven and Yoder argue that it is, to the contrary, an affirmation of culture and an act of political engagement. It would seem, then, that Scriven's criticism could be laid to rest if Niebuhr would simply place the Anabaptists alongside F. D. Maurice among the transformationists and leave the category of Christ-against-culture to those, if any can be found, who are wholly other-worldly in their orientation.

Yet I think the differences between Niebuhr and Scriven are deeper than Scriven realizes, and their depth is betrayed by that passage quoted above in which Scriven asserts that the Bible does indeed require political engagement on the part of Christian communities. Scriven acknowledges Niebuhr's opposition to the belief that Christ brings a new law, but he regards Niebuhr's opposition as a curiosity—a point tangential to the central argument about the transformation of culture. In point of fact, it is pivotal in importance. Scriven reads the relationship of the Christian community to that of culture as fundamentally antagonistic; it is the mission of the church to identify false values and evil behaviors and to substitute true values and right behaviors in their place, creating an alternative social space in which the good may flourish. This program of substitution is, in Niebuhr's view, antithetical to conversion.[15] Conversion has as its model redemption by incarnation: by patiently entering into the world as it is and by bringing out its potential for the good, we heal it of its corruption. While some habits of action and patterns of organization may be incompatible with life in Christ and radically monotheistic faith, no habits of action or patterns of organization can, according to Niebuhr, be regarded as privileged of God. As he writes in "The Christian Evangel and Social Culture," "The good news which the Church of Christ must proclaim today has as little to do with the conservation or the victory of any existing human culture as it had in the days of Jesus or of Paul."[16] Even our highest achievements of justice must be recognized to be unjust in the eyes of God. Moreover, different constellations of historical circumstance require different patterns of social arrangements and practices, and Scriptural revelation is wrongly used if it is interpreted as a validation of or mandate for some particular economic or political system. From the point of view of Niebuhr, it would be arrogance and folly to imagine either that one could justly undertake to "Christianize the social order" or that one could institute a better approximation of the kingdom by extricating oneself from the institutions and values of the prevailing culture in order to begin again with godly practices and purified intentions. Christian social responsibility requires, according to Niebuhr, not the replacement of cultural values with different values, but rather the ordering of existing values (political, economic, intellectual, aesthetic, and moral) in relation to God through the personal conversion which makes possible rightly ordered loves.

The criticisms advanced by Whitehead and Scriven focus two important sets of questions for us: (1) Is Niebuhr, despite his assertions

102

concerning the social character of the self, sufficiently naive in his understanding of power to have failed to realize the implications of the notion of social solidarity for reflection on concerted Christian action directed toward the alteration of the structures within which we must work out our salvation? Put more pointedly, is Niebuhr's contribution to theological ethics limited or diminished by the absence of a plausible, realistic, and well-developed social theory? (p. 21) Is Niebuhr's Christian ethics finally "spiritual" and personal, rather than social, by reason of his rejection of all efforts to associate Christian culture with some preferred particular structures of political, social, and economic relationships? Does his resolute commitment to reconciliation rob his theology of moral force and prophetic vision? Isn't Christian faith compelled to pronounce judgment on unacceptable features of the prevailing culture, and isn't the proper stance of the Christian necessarily "against the world," particularly in heavily secularized cultures like our own?

In order to deal fairly with these questions, we must examine Niebuhr's treatment of the work of the church in the world because this represents an important, and largely unexamined, complement to his treatment of personal conversion. "The subject-counterpart of the kingdom," he writes in *The Purpose of the Church and Its Ministry*, "is never an individual in isolation but one in community."[17] The church is *not*, he is careful to say, the kingdom of God. It is a social institution and a human community infected by false faith, defensiveness, and distrust like any other—capable of apostasy and in need of perpetual "reformation." The church therefore must be understood to be a feature of the "world," not an alternative to the "world." At the same time, the church is unlike any other human institution and any other human community. As a unique community of memory and hope, worship and thought, it is, despite its relativity and limitations, "indispensable" in mediating human relations with the divine reality.[18] As a social reality in its own right, it has a distinctive mission, function, and office.

4. The Social Equivalent of the Evangelical Strategy

In order to understand both Niebuhr's evangelical conception of social Christianity and his views on the distinctive function of the church, it is helpful to examine some of his early efforts to sort out and appraise the strengths and liabilities of post–World War I theologies.

"The Social Gospel and the Liberal Theology" (1931) appeared in *The Keryx* of Eden Seminary and therefore has not been widely circulated. There he refuses the common impulse to assimilate the social gospel to "liberal" theology (of which he himself is quite critical), and he makes an argument that the "social gospel" can survive the decline of liberalism because it is not reducible to "social idealism" and because it has built into its premises what liberalism forgot: "the radical acceptance of the radical ethics of Jesus [in] their explicit and implicit references to man as a social being and to society as a sphere of sin and salvation . . . the experience of social condemnation and the promise of social deliverance and the duty of social repentance."[19] The crumbling of liberalism has the advantage of "releasing" the social gospel from the constraints of "innocuous optimism" so that "it may be as honest and as radical in its criticism of the social order of human sin as that order itself and the ethics of Jesus require" (p. 13). What the social gospel lacks, however, is solid theological grounding, and Niebuhr surprisingly proposes that the necessary theological foundations might best be found in the "eschatological conceptions" and "uncompromising doctrine of sin" advanced in Barthian theology. Though he admits that "the leaders of the new theology" themselves encounter "logical difficulties" when they undertake the task of explicitly "associating their ethics with their theology," he expresses the firm belief that the new theology can preserve "a social radicalism of pronounced type" and give it a secure foundation.

His 1933 essay "The Social Gospel and the Mind of Jesus," which he read before the American Theological Society but never published, represents the negative counterpart of the hopeful argument of 1931. Here he emphasizes the failings of both the social gospel theologians and "Barthianism." The social gospel misconstrues the "mind of Jesus": it presents Jesus as a humanist "whose morality is anthropocentric morality" and who teaches that God is compassionate and kind; it presents God as a moral ideal, often little more than "the ideal of a just human society"; it elevates human social struggles into religious quests but continues to define those struggles in temporal, material, and anthropocentric terms; and most importantly, the social gospel removes God from the arena of history, trusting to human capabilities to bring about the kingdom.[20] Ironically, the fault of Barthianism is formally no different; though it does a much better job of representing the mind of Jesus as the mind of "a God-centered, apocalyptic, revolutionary strategist" (p. 119), it likewise banishes God from history. It offers a static conception of God. "It has no faith in the God who is that which it is and who is the dynamic force moving toward glory. Its God is a mere transcendent point" (p. 126). In establishing the gospel criteria against which he tests the work of both Walter Rauschenbusch and Barth, he lays down, in three broad affirmations, the theological foundations for the conversionist type that he will commend eighteen years later in *Christ and Culture*. (1) God is a dynamic cosmic power, not a moral principle. This power is not careful of human desires and sensibilities; it destroys in order that it may bring forth. It bestows gifts and "makes for a glory," but does so as sovereign judge, not as a handmaiden to our independently worthy projects. (2) Because God is acting, we "cannot sit still" (p. 126), but what is required of us is resourceful exploitation of God-made revolutions and emergent opportunities. Christian social action is less the steadfast pursuit of a social justice agenda than a humble cooperative adjustment to new realities and an inspired transformation of problems into possibilities. The proper question is not What has God laid down that we must do? but What is God doing and what response is required? (3) Eschatology must be rethought in terms of present realities and in terms of the redemption of the community. The individualistic and otherworldly motifs so prominent in Christian soteriology are a consequence of the "amalgamation . . . of Jewish and Hellenic thought" (p. 125). Jesus himself was oriented toward the community ("he spoke less of the death of the personal individual than of the judgment on the social individual" [125]), and it is now possible to recover this "social gospel in the mind of Jesus" (p. 115) "because we, like the Jews, have become accustomed to think in terms of social rather than personal individuals, and because we, like the Jews again, take time seriously" (p. 125). We are better prepared than previous generations to accept temporal process as "the scene of divine judgment and salvation" (p. 126). While "the symbol of the resurrected body" expresses the importance of "faith in the conservation of personal values," resurrection is "secondary to the idea of the social or cosmic realization of hope" (p. 125). Yet this hope is genuinely eschatological; it is not the progressive teleological humanist hope of theological liberalism and most social gospel writers.

Differentiating Between Mission and Strategy

The 1936 essay "The Attack upon the Social Gospel" offers a third attempt to point a new direction through a differentiation and comparison of existing theological options. The tools Niebuhr develops here provide the theoretical resources for his later reflections on the work of the church. He distinguishes between, on the one hand, the issue of goals and objectives ("whether the individual or society is the proper object of Christianity's mission") and, on the other hand, the issue of strategy or "means" ("whether the Church is to employ direct or indirect means").[21]

His discussion of Christianity's proper object is notable for his refusal to dismiss the individualistic movement "as an error which might have been avoided" (p. 178). On the contrary, he suggests that the "individualist gospel" of the eighteenth and nineteenth centuries was peculiarly well fitted to the dominant requirements of the times. In an era in which individuals were willy-nilly cut free from stabilizing "political, ecclesiastical, and economic bonds," individually focused Christianity "splendidly . . . succeeded in supplying inner discipline in place of vanished external restraints" (p. 177). Moreover, persons do stand directly and individually before God, so concerns for the individual soul continue to be an appropriate component of the Christian gospel. Still, the twentieth century poses problems very different from those posed in the eighteenth. "The problem of society" is "the problem of the day" (p. 178); accordingly, the question of social salvation, so central in Hebrew history, has reasserted itself as the dominant concern and the proper primary object of the Christian mission.

Christians who agree about mission might, nonetheless, disagree about strategy, and Niebuhr undertakes to point the difference between direct and indirect means of achieving the desired objective. A *religiously* direct strategy is first of all one that the church can pursue within its own domain without recruiting mediating agents. It is secondly a strategy which takes account of "the priority of God—not as a human ideal, or the object of worship, but as the moving force in history—who alone brings in His kingdom and to whose ways the party of the Kingdom of God on earth must adjust itself" (p. 181). The political action and social agitation that mark applied Christianity are, by contrast, religiously indirect in two senses: (1) They involve an intermediary social institution with direct jurisdiction; thus, the church must persuade some other group (legislators, regulatory agencies, corporate executives) to pursue a particular agenda or program that they presumably would not pursue on their own. (2) They relegate

106

religion to a supportive rather than a primary role: faith is typically construed to do no more than provide the motivation for the pursuit of goods and values that are derived by rational reflection on social realities. So this muscularly "Christian" attempt to further the kingdom turns out ironically, Niebuhr thinks, to discount God's power in history and to deny the real effects of religious faith in reconstructing social arrangements. The religiously direct method to be adopted by the Christian community in the face of social ills and harms is vigorous attack on the "false faith" which produces, along with other consequences, social injustice and social misery.

Having thus distinguished the issues and defined the terms, Niebuhr proceeds to a comparative discussion of liberal theology or cultural protestantism, the social gospel or "applied Christianity," and "new theological movements" or "postliberal theology" (that is, the work of Karl Barth and other figures we have come to group together as neo-orthodox theologians). A simple table showing combinations of options may be helpful here:

Form of Theology	Object or Mission	Strategy
Evangelical Theology	Salvation of individuals	Direct
Liberal Theology	Salvation of individuals	Indirect
Social Gospel (Applied Christianity)	Social salvation	Indirect
Postliberal Theology	Social salvation	Direct

The first thing that he notes is that postliberal theologians look at the social gospel and denounce it as "a message of self-help, as an optimistic faith that men can enter the kingdom of God without profound revolution" (p. 176); in effect, they assimilate it to the rationalistic and individualistic liberal theology they have abandoned. On their side, the proponents of "applied Christianity" condemn the postliberal theological posture on the grounds that it "retreats from the battlefield of social life back to the line of individualistic and other-worldly Christianity" (p. 176) represented by the evangelicals. According to Niebuhr, neither side is correct in its interpretation of the other because they have not clearly identified the true point of controversy. The social gospel, noting the hostility of the new theology to *strategies* of explicit political and social action, misreads this as an

107

abandonment of the *objective* of social salvation; Niebuhr believes that post-liberal theology has not abandoned the notion that "society is the proper object of Christianity's mission" (p. 176). Conversely, post-liberal theology, noting the tendency of the social gospel to engage in and demand political and economic activity, has dismissed it as humanistic, melioristic, and superficial, thus failing to appreciate how much the two movements have in common in their understanding of the Christian mission. Post-liberal theology has ironically condemned as an enemy a movement it should be seeking to cleanse and reform.

What is needed, then, is a clear analysis of the strategies that are appropriate to the work of a church that is committed unequivocally to a social rather than an individualistic gospel. Niebuhr does not, to be sure, oppose political action, economic boycotts, the effort to influence legislators, the program of reforming education, or the determination to influence political parties to adopt particular platforms. He does, however, think that centralizing such activities is always somewhat misleading and can be religiously pernicious:

> Such measures are doubtless good in their place but as used by the church they represent the strategy of indirect action. They are not only efforts to get some other organization to do something about the intolerable situation but also presuppose the convictions that religion as such has no direct bearing on social life, that prophetic and Christian analysis of the situation with corresponding direct religious action are unimportant and that the analysis of society in terms of its political and economic arrangements is fundamental [179].

What, then, in Niebuhr's view, is the proper work of a church that understands itself to have a social mission in a world characterized by social injustice and extreme misery? The work of the church is to bring about justice and to diminish misery—but if its activity is to be truly Christian as well as truly effective in the transformation of society, it must choose religiously direct but socially indirect strategies: (1) It must analyze the problem in terms of false faith—that is, pervasive idolatry—rather than in terms of moral failure. (2) Since the problem is false faith, the church must issue the call to repentance. If social life no less than individual life can be an expression of false faith, so the social body, no less than the individual, must repent as a preliminary to the rebirth that transforms: "Men will be ready for no radically new life until they have really become aware of the falsity of the faith upon which their old life is based" (p. 180). Moral attacks and political activity are at best temporary in effect and limited in efficacy; Christian avengers can actually add tinder to the fires of false faith. It is the work of the church to bring the community to appreciate the need to fit itself to "the historic process" which is God's action in our spatial, temporal, and interpersonal environment; the direct work of the church is to preach "the adjustment of human ways to the way of God as revealed in Jesus Christ" (p. 181). He believes that because post-liberal theology has clearly laid hold of this truth, it represents a significant advance beyond both liberal theology and the applied Christianity of the social gospel movement. In its relationship to the earlier forms of evangelical protestantism, with which it shares the commitment to religiously direct strategies, post-liberal theology mounts no massive reaction against "Evangelical individualism"; thus, it is not difficult to understand why proponents of the social gospel have made the mistake of thinking that it represents a retreat to that posture. That it is not a retreat to individualism and passivity Niebuhr is quite confident; it is, rather, a search for something not yet clearly defined: "the social equivalent of the Evangelical strategy" (p. 181).

Religiously Direct Strategies for Social Redemption

The "evangelical strategy" is, of course, the call to individual conversion through repentance. It is not immediately clear what this might mean when we are talking about social institutions or structural social change, though two other essays from this same period enable us to trace the direction of Niebuhr's thought on the matter. One is the 1932 essay "Faith, Works, and Social Salvation"; the other is his justly famous *Christian Century* article, written in the same year, "The Grace of Doing Nothing."

"Faith, Works, and Social Salvation" objects to a muscularly political program of Christian social action because "advocates of the engineering point of view"[22] have betrayed the strategy of trust in favor of the strategy of "works." Their "faith" is wrongly placed, though they have rightly identified the social problems that require attention. They place their trust in human rationality, and this is a trust that is bound to be shattered, leaving them bitter and disillusioned. Rather, Christians should trust "the force of moral health, the divine 'grace' which operates in society as well as in the individual, to make its own way" (p. 429). This trust in "natural process" is a trust in "God's

109

agency" (p. 430). Our trustful activity should not be that of constructing new alternatives, but rather that of removing the obstacles which prevent God's agency from "making its own way." In terms of dealing with the failings of nationalism and capitalism, it means "non-cooperation" with these "great systems of self-interestedness." It means a patient waiting for and promoting of

> the development of a co-operative international commonwealth and of a co-operative economic order. For instead of faith in self-interest the faith of such a movement lies in the divine agency which manifests itself in co-operative life, in mutual aid, in the organic growing together of individuals and societies [430].

Only such tactics—loving tactics—are appropriate to the strategy of faith. To those who doubt the efficacy of such work, his only answer is that we must not picture "the growth of love as an automatic process." "There is no road to unity save through suffering, forgiveness, repentance, restitution" (p. 430).

"The Grace of Doing Nothing," together with the follow-up reply to Reinhold Niebuhr's intervention, explicitly repudiates "the inactivity of those who call evil good" as well as the inactivity of despair, resignation, and self-pity.[23] "Doing nothing" is not a general program of social passivity for Christians; it is, rather, the appropriate posture for Christians (individually and collectively) who find themselves in a very bad situation to which they have materially contributed and which they would only worsen by further action within the operant framework of interests and loyalties. In such a situation, Christian action must wait on the discovery of a way out of the "ceaseless cycle of assertion and counter-assertion."[24] That there is such a way is the content, he suggests, of authentic Christian hope, for faith in a real and sovereign God is the faith that love is not an impossible ideal but is, in reality, "an 'emergent,' a potentiality in our situation which remains unrealized so long as we try to impose our pattern, our wishes upon the divine creative process."[25] "Doing nothing" is graced activity to the extent that it is the consenting and contrite experience of the judgment of God, an experience that issues in repentance and forgiveness. "Doing nothing" is, as it were, only the first moment (he uses these metaphors: it eliminates weeds, tills the soil, clears the road), and this work of preparation comes to fulfillment in disinterested, constructive common action once the movement of God's creative and redeeming will has been discerned.

5. Assessing Niebuhr's Social Analysis

It is evident, then, that a remark like Molin's, "What Niebuhr wants to change is the self rather than the world," is misleading because it posits a disconnection between self and world that Niebuhr would not accept. Understanding the social world as he does, Niebuhr believes that the only way to bring about *durable* social and institutional change is to bring about spiritual change, a reorientation of faith. The effort to bring about spiritual change is, of course, slow, difficult, and unpredictable; a lot of innocent people may suffer injustice and oppression—may perhaps even die—while we wait for a change of heart on the part of the powerful. However, Niebuhr has a pointed and unambiguous answer to this complaint: Although the reform of practices, the reconstruction of institutions, the transfer of power into other hands may shift the pain to different shoulders and may even provide short-term relief, over the long term it leaves everything the same. In fact, it produces a deeper despair and a more intractable cynicism as people harvest the strange fruit of their supposed liberation. He is convinced that it is *not* more effective to be more direct.

Yet it is also clear that he does not have a strictly aggregative view of group life. That is, he is not among the party of those who hold that groups are simple sums of the individuals they contain, such that if you have changed the majority of the individual units you have changed the aggregate sum that is the group. He is quite clear in his insistence that a saved society is not the same thing as a society of saved individuals. Nevertheless, Niebuhr's conviction that there is a "social equivalent of the Evangelical strategy" establishes his belief that the "self" and the "world" are built on the same principles and can be addressed in the same ways. This contrasts sharply with Reinhold Niebuhr's equally strong conviction, displayed nowhere so effectively as in *Moral Man and Immoral Society*, that the life of groups is quite decisively different from the life of individuals—and is therefore ruled by contrasting moral requirements, expectations, and possibilities.

At first blush, it would seem that H. Richard Niebuhr has embarked on the dubious, quaint, and anthropomorphizing project of reading cultural institutions as complex "individualities" which can, as institutions, come to conceive of their false faiths, repent, and be born again. It is admittedly very difficult to think of institutions and bureaucracies on such a model. They are, to be sure, social organizations of a supra-personal sort which exert an immensely powerful impact on our

111

lives, but they seem to be vast impersonal networks of functions and practices, existing like the gigantic husk of a particular body of inter-related individuals, the shape of whose common project persists like a cretinous shell after the persons themselves have disappeared. This shell is all the more impermeable to change as a result of the passing of the lives that shaped it to a purpose and kept it flexible and capable of adjustment. It could be argued that, over time, there are only two possibilities, neither of which allows logical space for the personalist fictions of repentance and conversion: either (1) a new community comes to inhabit the husk with intentions similar enough to the originating body that the husk can be kept alive—thus capable of growth, change, even perhaps contraction—or (2) a dead husk, increasingly rigid and unresponsive to the needs of the community, constricts and obstructs the communal life. In this situation, violence, however destructive and regrettable, has a positive function; it is the mechanism for the destruction of the dead structures which can no longer be organically shaped to the situation but must be torn apart and scattered so that people may associate themselves together again according to their current needs and intentions. Yet the very language I have used here provides the clue to a better understanding of Niebuhr's intention. When he speaks of the *social* gospel and of addressing the Christian evangel to suprapersonal forces, he is speaking not of cultural forms but of the communities that create and maintain (and sometimes become victimized by) the various impersonal structural frameworks that are the most complicated and intangible of human artifacts. It is his belief that communities are creatures of faith—spiritual creatures held together by shared loyalties and capable of betrayal and regeneration. They are living, changeable, malleable beings, subject to moral suasion and, in some sense, morally responsible.

In this connection, his 1939 essay "The Christian Evangel and Social Culture" is instructive. He begins with the affirmation that it was the work of Jesus to try to bring the total life of the community under the influence of radical faith in God and that it is the work of the church today to continue that effort. In the second part of the essay, he draws a sharp distinction between "the gospel" and the cultural forms that are generated to embody and "conserve" it. The last part of this essay is one of Niebuhr's most direct acknowledgments of the degree to which he agrees with Whitehead's point that Christ has frequently been co-opted by "culture" and used as a device for oppressing the different and the vulnerable: "the evangelist necessarily becomes a church-father."[26] In this process, "other forces" also shape the "new habits and institutions" with the result that "such Christian culture is infinitely far from the Kingdom" (p. 48). The "Christ" that is used to oppress is precisely a cultural artifact and not the Christ of the gospel who relativizes all cultural artifacts and, indeed, all cultures—including, paradoxically, Christian culture. Augustine's failure was to become a defender of "Christian culture, that is, of the institutions and habits of the Christian society."[27] Religion itself can be used against God, and this Niebuhr notes, quoting Maurice, constitutes "the most terrific form of infidelity."[28]

Is Niebuhr, then, properly said to be naive about evil and power? Does he fail to grasp the oppressive and threatening weight with which culture obstructs the life of faith and the possibility of human flourishing? Would his theology and his contribution to theological ethics be sounder and more persuasive if he had developed a different and more realistic social theory? If it is naive to believe that God's creation remains fundamentally good and if it is unrealistic to believe that the substance of Christian faith is faith in the redemptive power of love *in history*, then Niebuhr is naive and unrealistic. He admits as much himself when he ends "The Grace of Doing Nothing" with the words, "But if there is no God, or if God is up in heaven and not in time itself, it is a very foolish inactivity."[29]

The more empirical question of the adequacy of his social theory is certainly an issue for further examination and debate for it has no easy answer. Once we draw the same distinction he draws between institutions and communities, it is harder to dismiss his treatment of social realities as nostalgic romanticism. He teaches us to ask whether the real theoretical naivete is to be found among those writers whose discussion of social life is so reductive that it discounts or altogether misses the spiritual dynamics—the loyalties, shared commitments, common reliances, defining memories, protective defenses, behavioral boundaries—of the common life of vibrant communities. We are left, though, with the very real question of what spiritual regeneration can and cannot do.

6. The Church Against the World?

Let us return now to the other dimension of the criticism that has been lodged by Whitehead and Scriven. Focusing on his argument in

Christ and Culture, both find him to be inadequately critical of regnant cultural forms; both believe him to be wrong in treating political engagement as a matter of (as he puts it at the beginning of "The Christian Evangel and Social Culture") indifference; and both fault him for failing to insist on the oppositional character of authentic Christian witness. That he contributed in 1935 to a book titled *The Church Against the World* and approvingly characterized that title as "the declaration of a position"[30] might tempt us to think either that their criticism is overdrawn or that Niebuhr himself is of two minds. But the material in this book must be interpreted with care. To begin with, in his introductory essay, Niebuhr reverses the terms; it is the church that is the object of opposition, and this is not new: "The world has always been against the church" (p. 1). Civilization makes its own aggressive claims upon the church out of its own needs, its own anthropocentric interests, and its own sense of the right and good. To the extent that the church adjusts itself to these claims, it betrays its religious mission and fails "as a reliable witness to the Christian faith" (9). Thus, the church must resist the seduction of worldliness within its own house, and in that sense only, it is, or should be, "against the world." The argument that is made here is congruent with his discussion in *Christ and Culture* of the failures of the accommodationist type. To the extent that the church ties itself to culture (even by well-grounded efforts at social reform), it becomes entangled in false faith and suffers corruption with the world (p. 123). He writes that the captive church must "emancipate" itself from the world, but he is careful to say that he means that it must emancipate itself from idolatry and lust, not civilization or nature (pp. 124–25). "How to be in the world and yet not of the world has always been the problem of the church. . . . Its main task always remains that of understanding, proclaiming and preparing for the divine revolution in human life" (p. 154).

By the time we advance to 1946, we find that Niebuhr has supplemented this early argument in some important ways, giving us for the first time a really clear outline of what he believes the church may permissibly do to be "in the world" without compromising its distinctive mission and office. In the essay "The Responsibility of the Church for Society," the motif of repentance and conversion remains, but it is now identified as only one of the three primary "functions" through the fulfillment of which the church satisfies its "social obligation."[31] Indifference (which might more properly have been termed disinterestedness) is no longer recommended as the appropriate pos-

114

ture of the church. The essay extends and advances the discussion of the entanglement of the organizational church in the ills of civil society, and it acknowledges again the material contribution the church has made to human misery through its inveterate tendency to collapse the distinction between relative temporal goods and transcendent realities. Thus, although "the responsibility of the Church for society" remains rooted in obedience to the command to love the neighbor and, even more basically, in faith in the promise that God is redeeming history, it also, in the present crisis, arises from

> the Christians' recognition that they have done not a little to make the secular societies what they are. In this respect the modern church is in a wholly different position from that which the New Testament church or even the church of Augustine's time occupied. The Christian community of our time, whether or not formally united, is one of the great organizations and movements in civilization; it is one of the oldest human societies; it has been the teacher of most of the nations now in existence [112–13].

The Roman Empire was not the creation of the Christian community, but present nations and cultures were "nursed and baptized by the Church" (p. 113).

In this sober essay, the consideration of the social responsibility of the church is played out against the background of the twin heresies of worldliness and isolation, with Niebuhr arguing that "the true measure of the Church's responsibility is not to be found, however, by attending to either extreme or by seeking for a compromise position between them but rather by attending to the two aspects of Christian responsibility *in the right way*" (p. 126, emphasis added). In trying to develop a means to speak of the responsibility of the church that will escape the perpetual conflict of the sacred and the profane, Niebuhr is adverting to and advancing a theme developed dialectically two years earlier in "Towards a New Otherworldliness." In that essay, he argues for a "two-world life," "conversion of this dual existence," "the double announcement that the Word has become flesh and the mortal put on immortality," and "the double injunction to seek the things that are above and to go into all the world."[32] His point there is that while "earth is not enough," a return to an "old" otherworldliness, indifferent to social realities and destructive of reverence for creation, would only represent another form of religiously destructive one-sidedness. Developing a striking metaphor, Niebuhr notes that in mystical Chris-

115

tianity and prophetic Christianity alike the wholeness of the Christian gospel is obscured and "the life of man, the migratory being, into whose structure the law of a seasonal movement is written, is thwarted and distraught by confinement to one world, whether it be the world of sight or the realm of spirit."[33] The challenge the Christian community must meet is not that of finding the right balance between God and neighbor, spirit and materiality; rather, the challenge is to generate a holy worldliness.

What, then, is "the right way" for the Christian community to attend to the two aspects of the gospel whether as the double announcement or as the double injunction, particularly if compromises of the sort worked out by his brother Reinhold are to be ruled out? In "The Responsibility of the Church for Society," Niebuhr resourcefully recasts the issue (so often presented in terms of church and world, spirit and flesh) in terms of responsibility *to* and responsibility *for*. The church is always responsible to God and only to God, but it is responsible for a variety of worldly tasks. He defines three specific "functions of the Christian community": the apostolic function, the pastoral function, and the pioneering function.[34]

The apostolic function represents a continuation of the argument we have already examined: namely, the argument that it is the primary business of the church to "announce the Gospel": "to proclaim to the great human societies, with all the persuasiveness and imagination at its disposal, with all the skill it has in becoming all things to all men, that the center and heart of things, the first and last Being, is utter goodness, complete love" (p. 127). Correlatively, it must preach the necessity for repentance; it must picture the life to which the social order must be born again. In this essay, Niebuhr seems less inclined to picture "society" as some sort of great willing being; however, he does explicitly note that the church must learn to think of society not merely as a "physical" but also as a "spiritual form of human existence" (p. 128). It is clear that he continues to think of the church's "mission to social groups" in terms of the structures of evangelization which have always characterized the work of the church "as apostolic messenger to individuals" (p. 126). He acknowledges that he and others experience difficulty in conceptualizing this activity, but he lays these difficulties to the fact that churchmen of his time have been caught in a transition period: "The Church has not yet in its apostolic character made the transition from an individualistic to a social period" (p. 127). Or again:

How the Church is to carry out this apostolic task in our time is one
of the most difficult problems it confronts. Its habits and customs, its
forms of speech and its methods of proclamation come from a time
when individuals rather than societies were in the center of attention
[128].

This is a difficult problem not simply because old habits die hard. It is
difficult because this new calling requires of us forms of imagination
that we have not yet developed and that Niebuhr himself remained
unable to specify. The tongues that speak and the ears that hear remain
individual tongues and ears.

The pastoral function: Throughout church history, he notes, the
pastoral interest of the church in individuals has "forced" it "to take
an interest in political and economic measures or institutions" (p. 129).
He notes that the political activities of "the early leaders of the social
gospel movement" were the natural and necessary extension of their
pastoral concerns with the suffering of their individual parishioners:

The Church cannot be responsible to God for men without becoming
responsible for their societies. As the interdependence of men increases in industrial and technological civilization the responsibility
for dealing with the great networks of interrelationship increases
[129].

This concern for social structures because of their impact on individuals he characterizes as an *indirect* pastoral concern with social structures: "if the individual sheep is to be protected the flock must be
guarded" (p. 129). Alongside this is a *direct* pastoral concern with social
life which arises because "the Church responds to the God who not
only creates men but also their societies. This pastoral mission of the
Church to the nations includes all those measures of large-scale relief
and liberation which the times call for" (p. 129). It seems, then, that
Niebuhr here means to gather back into the work of the church the
activities characteristic of "applied Christianity." This is, in all likelihood, a conscientious concession to his growing consciousness of the
church as a negative social force which has a responsibility to God to
right the wrongs to which it has actively and materially contributed.
Now insisting that the church become responsible for society, he makes
space within the Christian mission for those "indirect" economic,
social, and political strategies that ten years earlier he had treated as
distracting and perhaps corrupting. Nonetheless, he leaves this function undeveloped and returns immediately to the direct ameliorative

ministry in which the reach of "compassion and concern" must be enlarged to include not just suffering individuals but suffering peoples. Thus, the church's indirect pastoral interest "in political and economic measures and institutions" (p. 129) remains subtly subordinated to its direct mission in the established and long-standing pastoral work of charity: "to feed the hungry and clothe the naked" (p. 130).

The pioneering function: Finally, he argues that the church, as "that part of the human community which responds first to God-in-Christ and Christ-in-God" (p. 130), may function for the whole of society in something like the way Christ functions: it can provide the model of right response which will move the larger community of which it is also a part. He is not, he argues, reverting to the model of the sect which is related to God precisely in its opposition to the larger culture; rather, the church serves as a model precisely because it is representative of the larger culture, not distinct from it. As a representative of culture, "it repents for the sin of the whole society and leads in the social act of repentance" (p. 131). The church is the sub-culture which first discerns what is required of the whole community; it is the first sector of the community "to obey Him when it becomes aware of a new aspect of His will" (p. 131). It can lead society precisely because it is representative of rather than inimical to society. Interestingly, Niebuhr closes the essay with the observation that this pioneering function, rather than the apostolic function earlier emphasized, is "the highest form of social responsibility in the Church" (p. 132).

The Purpose of the Church and Its Ministry (1956) does not take up this very interesting delineation of a triple function (probably because this text is very heavily an internal critique of church practices and theological education), but it does further clarify Niebuhr's conception of the distinctive niche occupied by the church in the temporal social ecosystem. Niebuhr identifies "world" as "the community of those who are occupied with temporal things." To be occupied with temporal things is not, in itself either good or bad. Neither does it serve to set the world somehow against the church. If the context of this attention to the temporal is a feeling of being rejected by God and of in turn rejecting God, then the preoccupation is idolatrous; however, if this community "is occupied with [temporal things] as gifts of God—whether or not the consciousness of grace becomes explicit—it [world] is partner of the Church, doing what the Church, concerned with the nontemporal, cannot do; knowing what Church as such cannot know."[35] The church should not be and cannot be an institution

118

for civil governance; that is not its office. However, the church and the institutions for civil governance can be (though this is a rare achievement) "partners" or "companions" in the kingdom, each pursuing faithfully its own function. The church is "the subjective pole of the objective rule of God" (p. 19), and while all human communities can be and should be "directed toward the divine reality," the relation of the church to that reality is unique: "there is made available to it, or revealed to it, a characteristic and meaning in the Object—the divine reality—unknown from other perspectives" (p. 20). The office of the church is simply to be a faithful witness to what has been entrusted to it alone: the knowledge of the "reconciling nature and activity" of God. If the church fails in this task, there is no other community and no other institution that can keep alive this witness.

The full dimensions of Niebuhr's unusual understanding of "church" become evident when we examine the closing summary he offers in the 1948 essay, "The Gift of the Catholic Vision." What he calls "*Protestant Catholic* vision" is an inclusive vision which relativizes the competing claims of all Christian churches and denominations. The word "church" thus takes on a new meaning that Niebuhr undertakes to make clear:

> For now we see that the human response to divine action is not so much religion as Church. It is not the Christian religion with which we are concerned, as our predecessors were concerned with it, but the *ecclesia* which worships, to be sure, which has religious ideas and religious rites, but which is something more inclusive and more strange than a religious association. What is this body of Christ, this *Civitas Dei*, this new people? It stands in succession to and is akin to that other strange community of Israel which is not simply a religious society nor yet a political or a racial community. The Church always tends to retreat into religion and to become the religious institution of a civilization but cannot remain content with that role. Its members forever transcend the boundaries of what men call religion; they form sects, societies within society yet apart from society; they enter restlessly into the political and economic life of the civilizations in which they dwell; they seek a Zion which cannot be located in any part of earth and yet are not content to find their beatitude one by one in a heavenly Paradise. It is a pilgrim community which makes strangely enduring settlements. It is an abnormal community which does not fit into this world and yet forever seeks to make itself at home in a world that is a Fatherland.[36]

119

7. Affirming the Good

With this notion of the pilgrim community trying to be at home in a land that could be its home but is not yet its home, with this notion of the pioneer community which seeks its own integrity not against the larger community but somehow in representation of and in behalf of it, we are ready to return to the notion of the "lifting up" of cultural forms which plays such a significant role in the "conversionist" chapter of *Christ and Culture*. Niebuhr's theological commitment to holding together creation and redemption "in one movement" underwrites his critique of those strands of Christianity which, though they properly accent the sovereignty of God, make too much of sin, becoming mesmerized by evil:

> What made Maurice the most consistent of conversionists . . . was the fact that he held fast to the principle that Christ was king, and that men were therefore required to take account of him only and not of their sin; for to concentrate on sin as though it were actually the ruling principle of existence was to be enmeshed in still further self-contradiction.[37]

Our task is not so much to resist evil and struggle against adversaries as to remove the weights and obstacles which so burden the good that it can scarcely any longer be known for what it is; in consequence, Niebuhr believes that the social task of the Christian community comprises (1) the evangelical work of tracing misery to its true source in the personal sin of self-will and the social sin of "anthropocracy"[38] in order to disclose the only alternative to this condition of self-contradiction; (2) the relativizing work of setting existing intentions and structures against the background of a larger pattern and teaching people to see them in terms of a more inclusive community; and (3) the creative work of glad cooperation with the new reality that God is bringing to be in the midst of old and passing forms. The stance of opposition betrays faith by feeding cynical hopelessness and by fostering separation (thus denying unity and foreclosing reconciliation) and negation (thus diminishing creativity and increasing defensiveness).

For this reason, the methods employed by Christians individually or corporately must never under any circumstances be divisive methods. Conflictual models are unscriptural and unacceptable. It is because of this stress on the motif of unity and reconciliation (as opposed to conflict and struggle) that Niebuhr insists that the way to the kingdom is exclusively the way of repentance. In a very revealing passage in

Christ and Culture, he applauds the contribution of Maurice, who, he writes,

> rejected every dualistic tendency to turn from positive to negative action, from co-operation to attack on nonco-operation, from the practice of unity in Christ to conflict with dividers of the church, from forgiveness of sinners to their exclusion from the church. Every effort of this sort involves a recognition of the power of evil—as though it exists otherwise than as a spirit of self-seeking, self-willing, and self-glorification; as though it can be located somewhere outside ourselves. Hence it evokes Satan to cast out Satan. . . . This is not compromising with evil, but accepting evil as our good; for between good and evil there can be no compromise, however much good and evil may be mixed in persons and actions [224–25].

The turn to critical denunciation and attack, the work of identifying wickedness and focusing attention upon it, is here represented to be a wholly wrong-headed strategy that belongs to the party of Satan and mistakes evil for the good. What marks Christian action is not the object of its wrath, but the contrition with which it applies itself to the positive tasks of cooperating, forgiving, overcoming conflict through the discovery of common causes, and drawing the structures of our common life, whatever they may be, toward their final end in God.

Though whatever is is good, not everything that is is right, and Niebuhr is not inviting us to romanticize or underestimate the faith and humiliation, the sacrifice and devotion, that are required of Christians who embrace incarnation as a mode of redemption. The covenant has been broken, our lives are ruled by the mythology of death, our religion is idolatrous, our "communities" are largely lies. There is much that needs to be reconstructed, and the changes will be painful and costly. Niebuhr's point is simply that we must begin the process of change by casting out the beam in our own eyes. If sacrifice is required, we must require it first of ourselves. If structural change is recommended, it must be advanced in a spirit of repentance for our own failings; structural change is not to be recommended as a correction and chastisement of the failings of others. The religious community cannot reliably criticize racism elsewhere until it has genuinely welcomed representatives of all races into its own worship. A church that believes sexism is wrong must witness to that belief by opening its own ministry to women. Moralism that condemns the sins of others with no awareness of its own sin is one of the most intractable, self-deceived, and dangerous forms of self-assertion.

Important as that insight is, Niebuhr's deeper point is that Christians must believe, with heart and soul and sinew, that good is more powerful than evil. To incarnate the good in our common life is to become the vehicle of the redemptive power of the implacable goodness of God. Thus, a Christian community, acting as a Christian community, wastes its time in denouncing failure and error; its work is to lift into view, to rehabilitate, to transvalue the obscured good wherever it can be found, confident that this activity will serve as a beacon for rectifying the confusion, self-contradiction, and guilt that afflict the lives of people not only within the Christian community but outside it as well.

In principle this is a plausible model, and the suggestion that the Christian community might do this as a representative of the larger culture, as part of its work of "lifting up" that larger culture, is an intriguing and attractive suggestion. The difficulty lies in specifying where we would find this pioneering church-as-repentant-community. Certainly Sunday morning worship services do not constitute it, and even socially active congregations lively with works of charity in their neighborhoods would not constitute such a pilgrim settlement. Churches today do, of course, comprise vast complex networks of social organizations (hospitals and nursing homes; colleges and seminaries; the church bureaucracies with their various governing boards, support staffs, and research groups; relief agencies; missionary organizations; publishing houses, print publications, radio and television stations; lobbying groups), and it is by no means clear that these institutions are presently paradigms of social justice or loving practice. It is pertinent to notice that Scriven mounts his critique of Niebuhr from the context of the Seventh Day Adventist Church, a church that undertakes more self-consciously than most to witness to its beliefs in its communal and organizational life. We might well wonder whether there is any great substantive difference between the Christian community witness that Scriven recommends and Niebuhr's understanding of the pioneering church—however significantly they may differ concerning the legitimacy of the oppositional stance.

When we consider the sheer scale of institutional structures in urban industrial America and when we reflect on the systemic character of most of the problems that capture our attention, we might well wonder whether there is practical and logical space to imagine a religious community as a social pioneer modifying its practices in order to model for the larger community a more generous, just, and flourishing way of life. Could Georgetown University survive as a major American university if the women who teach languages were paid the same salaries as the men who teach economics? Would students enroll here if they had to clean and repair the residence halls themselves, eat low on the food chain, and abandon blasphemous language and conspicuous consumption? Would faculty continue to teach here if there were no parking lots and everyone had to come to work by bicycle or public transportation? If wage thresholds were established at Georgetown University and Georgetown Hospital according to the standard of the family living wage rather than the federal minimum wage, would these institutions remain competitively viable? I don't know the answers to these questions, but it would be interesting to begin to have this sort of conversation.

Still, as Niebuhr reminds us so forcefully both in *Christ and Culture* and in so many of the earlier essays, whenever Christians try to capture the gospel long enough and materially enough to embody it in relative cultural forms, many other forces come into play. For that reason, despite his very provocative remarks about the potentially transformative power of the pioneering church, he continues to remind us that "the great point of the Gospel is that the new beginning, the new birth, the new life, is not an event that depends on a change in temporal history" (p. 201). The apostolic function of the church remains, after all, its most important function. The Christian calling is not to create the kingdom on earth but to live on earth in the kingdom.

8. Assessing Niebuhr's Conception of the Eschatological Community

So we come back at the end to Niebuhr's own question: "Does the acceptance of the cosmic God and the eschatological Jesus reduce us to individualism in Christian ethics and to a passive attitude in social strife?" Certainly from the point of view of Troeltsch—and probably from that of Molin, Whitehead, and Scriven as well—Niebuhr's contribution represents a disappointing retreat from "the social question." Yet from Niebuhr's point of view, Troeltsch's analysis of the sociological situation would seem excessively dualistic, positing the church and the world as two powers that must be yoked together. The categories and contrasts we typically use to think about these problems are too simple to accommodate the finely balanced symmetries and curiously subversive fusions that mark Niebuhr's argument.

123

We have seen that the "indifference" that Niebuhr recommends is not an irresponsible apathy but a quality of detachment rooted in a sense of the relativity and ambiguity of all social artifacts. The church cannot save us and we cannot save ourselves; we must look to the Lord for salvation, and salvation is not dependent on any particular constellation of earthly conditions. The converted Christian may work passionately in the service of civil justice, and the authentic church may model justice in its own affairs—these are the very means by which faith "permeates" cultural life. But these are consequences and not conditions of deliverance. To culture the Christian brings "the spirit of a disinterestedness that does not ask what cultural or gospel law requires directly, or what profit for the self may be gained; but rather what the service of the neighbor [and God] in the given conditions demands, and what these given conditions really are" (p. 186).

His failure to address imperialism, oppression, violence, and injustice with prophetic, righteous anger is not an oversight; neither is it a consequence of preoccupation with individual souls or (as his brother thought) spiritual purity. It is a consequence, as he unfailingly insists, of his theocentric faith—of living in the faith that goodness is powerful, that creation is good, that incarnation is a means of redemption, that sin is self-will, that eternity is now, and that God is the Lord of history. For from this faith rises the conviction that, converted by love, we can only convert by loving. If the witness ever falters and adopts the strategies appropriate to the unconverted, she contributes to the very obstructions that it is her office to remove.

The church is not against the world; it is responsible for the world to God. This means two things: (1) The faithful community cannot abstract itself from civilization and the relativities of history any more than the eternal order of existence can be abstracted from the temporal. (2) To the extent that the redemption of history requires right response to what God is doing, it is the responsibility of the church to say again and again to a forgetful world that "every moment and period is an eschatological present, for in every moment men are dealing with God" (p. 229). The church is therefore the servant of the world—to the extent that the world belongs to God. That is to say, in humble theocentric faithfulness and repentance, the Christian community must not only draw attention to the universal condition of self-contradiction but must also name to the world its goodness and awaken its dormant hope.

There are, of course, worthy questions that can be posed in

connection with this argument, just as there are further questions to be resolved in connection with his social theory. Chief among the concerns raised by his celebration of the redeeming power of love would be (1) concerns about the defensibility of the critical realism that underlies his persisting distinction between the truth and power that are embodied in cultural forms and the relative and replaceable forms themselves and (2) concerns about the sustainability, even the plausibility, of his anchoring conviction that unity and harmony represent, as it were, the base-line case in light of which division and conflict are known to be abnormal and diseased conditions. The first of these is an exceedingly large question, perhaps the most difficult bequeathed us by the historicist revolution, and it cannot be answered with respect to Niebuhr's work alone. The second is scarcely more manageable for it likewise touches on bedrock convictions concerning "the way things are." Still, concerning the second, it is at least important to say this much: Niebuhr's universalism (if that is an accurate term for it) is quite remote from the myth of sweet reason's fixed and timeless findings concerning "nature, man, and God." Niebuhr's historicism is deep, genuine, and consistent. Commenting on Maurice, he writes, "The full realization of the kingdom of Christ did not, then, mean the substitution of a new universal society for all the separate organizations of men, but rather the participation of all these in the universal kingdom of which Christ is the head."[39] Inasmuch as the legacy of sin is understood to be the self-assertion that fractures wholes into parts, denies relations, and disrupts community by setting interest against interest, redemption must be imaged as the reestablishing of that whole, that web of interconnections, that community of shared concerns. As early as 1929 he wrote, in *The Social Sources of Denominationalism*:

> The way to the organic, active peace of brotherhood leads through the hearts of peacemakers who will knit together, with patience and self-sacrifice, the shorn and tangled fibers of human aspirations, faiths, and hopes, who will transcend the fears and dangers of an adventure of trust. The road to unity is the road to repentance. . . . The road to unity is the road of sacrifice which asks of churches as of individuals that they lose their lives in order that they may find the fulfilment of their better selves.[40]

Though unrelentingly personal, his argument offers no shelter for conventional individualism. Though bracing in its penetrating critique of the intentions and strategies that inform much Christian activism, his evangelical focus on faith does not return the religious life to the cocoon of private piety. Like Troeltsch he expects of Christianity "a spirit which should penetrate, mould, and renew the common life," but unlike Troeltsch he does not measure this by the Church's ability to "initiate . . . social reform."[41] Eternity is "the dimension of divine working" in the medium of time.[42] According to Niebuhr, our deepest religious responsibility is to love creation and hallow it—in order that it may be changed.

CHAPTER 3

Concrete Christological Norms for Transformation

Glen H. Stassen

1. Authentic Transformation and the Triune Sovereignty of God

Many think we should be embarrassed by the fact of our historicity. They seek, perhaps unconsciously, to avoid the particular beliefs and perceptions that come from our history, just as many try to get rid of their hometown accents and learn to speak like television announcers. They seek some universal viewpoint that might enable them to escape their historical particularity. That, I would argue, is a mistake. If we can know only what enters our history, it is folly to deny what is in our history and seek an ahistorical viewpoint. It is folly because it leads us to deny what we can and do know. It leads us to pretend to know what we do not know. As John Yoder's essay reminds us, it is folly to pretend that we have universal knowledge from the Creator and only historically particular knowledge from Christ, and therefore to privilege creation over Christ. Whatever we know of creation we see from our own historical viewpoint. I know more now about the Creator's care for the creation—the whole ecological system—than I did two decades ago, because of our place in history now, when we see the damage and the depletion more clearly. My new, historically shaped knowledge is true knowledge. I also know more of the meaning of Jesus' teaching on peacemaking now, because of our historical experiences of war and peacemaking, and that, too, is real knowledge.

Because Niebuhr wrestled with these questions so early, so consistently, and so perceptively, he represents us. He was there ahead of us, a scout on the ridge to see the valleys we are only now traversing. He saw the problems posed by historical relativism and scouted them out more fully than any theologian or ethicist of his generation or ours. He was a postmodernist long before the term became fashionable. His wrestle represents our wrestle; his problems are our problems. This is all the more true because his writings have been so influential for a whole generation of Christian ethicists. Not only because he was here before we arrived, but also because he trained the guides who are now pointing the way for us, the problems that he discovered in his efforts to see clearly are our problems. *Many have read, or misread, the signs that he left along the path to mean that we should avoid Christ-centered concreteness. We should claim that Jesus taught no new law, which means no new ethic, which means we should not seek concrete guidance from the prophetic ethic Jesus taught for our authentic transformation.*

I want to argue for the importance of historically situated, historically particular, concrete ethical norms disclosed in the particular history of Jesus Christ, continuous with the tradition of the Hebrew prophets and especially the prophet Isaiah. I want to argue that Christian discipleship and Christian ethics need those concrete norms. Our rejection of provincial narrow-mindedness, racial and nationalistic prejudice, authoritarian dogmatism, and apathetic disengagement—as well as our inclusion of the outcasts, our attention to the voices of the others and the strangers, and our peacemaking affirmation of the valid interests of our adversaries—are not based on our ability to achieve a detached, abstract, ahistorical viewpoint disengaged from our communities. They are based on historically particular revelation in a Jew in Galilee, who taught repentance, conversion, faithfulness, love, justice, prayer, mutual servanthood, delivering justice and transforming initiatives of peacemaking. Our response to injustice is also based on a method of validation, correction, and continuous repentance (*metanoia*), which Niebuhr developed in ways that are faithful to a sovereign God, not merely the possession of our particular knowing. It is a mistake for Christians to try to escape historical situatedness by avoiding historical concreteness, or by avoiding the historical, incarnate Jesus.

I will make that argument in the pages that follow via a historical narrative. I will ask us to consider the actual testimony of the life of H. Richard Niebuhr. I will ask us to begin with his beginnings, to understand his life's path, to notice obstacles that blocked him from proceeding as he intended, and to notice ways he developed for proceeding around those obstacles. The testimony of the life of H. Richard Niebuhr, seen in this way, points us in a direction not very different from the direction toward which John Howard Yoder points.

And once we see that testimony, we may also see a way to integrate what Diane Yeager's essay yearns for: the conversion of faith, the dynamic presence of God, and the social presence of the pilgrim church. That way may not become visible, however (if it does become visible), until our book's conclusion.

So I begin with Niebuhr's trinitarian understanding of the sovereignty of God, the importance of God's concrete historical self-disclosure in Christ, and historical realism, in order to correct interpretations of Niebuhr that evade those themes. I do so via a narrative history, a testimony from Niebuhr's lifelong experience of scouting the way.

A Faith That Conforms

As early as his first book (*The Social Sources of Denominationalism*, published in 1929), H. Richard Niebuhr was already calling for a Christianity that would not conform to the world but transform it. He agonized over the racism, regionalism, nationalism, and classism that had separated churches into denominations: the difference between African Methodist Episcopal churches and United Methodists is racial; the southern versus northern splits of many denominations still reflect the regional loyalties out of which they arose; the German and Swedish Baptists (now North American and General Conference Baptists), Norwegian Lutherans, and Greek Orthodox were formed by nationalism; the early Anabaptists and Quakers, the Salvation Army and Pentecostals were a movement of peasants and the working class, while Presbyterians and Episcopalians were typically of a more comfortable class. The shape of the churches is not separation by theology but separation by surrender to divisive social forces. "The church which began its career with the promise of peace and brotherhood for a distracted world has accepted the divisions of the society it had hoped to transform and has championed the conflicts it had thought to transcend." The New Testament vision of all as one in Christ has been lost and the church has conformed to the "cynical distinctions of the old humanity." The original vision of "the time when the kingdom of this world would be transformed into a kingdom of our Lord" has faded. Instead racial, class, national, and regional divisions are "the church's confession of defeat and the symbol of its surrender" (SSD, 264–65).

In other early essays, Niebuhr wrote calls to repentance for racism, nationalism, self-centeredness, sexual permissiveness, greed and economic materialism. These loyalties demonstrated the power of social forces to compel churches into accommodation, and the powerlessness of churches to resist. Not the gospel of Jesus Christ, but the divisive power of culture was shaping our actions. Niebuhr's conclusion was an appeal for "an integrating ethics" powerful enough to resist and transform the divisive forces whose shaping power he had demonstrated. I propose we join Niebuhr in this search.

He saw no strong and helpful ethical norms in the prevailing ethic of the compromising churches, nor in the early Karl Barth and crisis theology as he understood it then (SSD, 275–76). All Niebuhr could appeal to in the 1920s was a liberal-idealist reading of what he called the ideals in the gospel: love, brotherhood, the fatherhood of God, the beloved community, the fellowship of reconciliation, peace and peace-making (SSD, 278ff.). These ideals gave *The Social Sources of Denominationalism* prophetic clarity and critical sharpness. But he had demonstrated in the same book that mere ideals were powerless in the face of strong social forces. Ideals could appeal to idealistic persons, but could not produce a strong, transformationist church. The logical result was ethical despair.[1]

Then came the Great Depression of 1929, and Adolf Hitler's takeover of Germany in 1933. The case for ethical despair was all the more persuasive. Caring deeply about the millions who suffered from the Depression, and being himself a bilingual German-American who anticipated the pain of the impending war that Hitler's seizure of power portended, Niebuhr experienced a profound collapse of hope.

A Faith That Transforms: The Experience of the Sovereignty of God

In 1934 Niebuhr reported his own "tower experience"—a Reformation in his own faith.[2] He experienced the death of hope in ethical idealism and the resurrection of a new faith in the sovereign God who judges our ideals.

"The axe has been laid at the root of the tree of modern life."[3] Faith in progress and the triumph of human ideals was being felled by reality.

> We can no longer ask what we must do in order that we may achieve the ideal of a warless world. We must inquire far more desperately and seriously what must be done in order that we may be saved from the storm of war that is even now gathering upon the horizon. . . . The blood, the pain, the misery of our brothers cries up to heaven against us. What must we do to atone for this brutal common life of ours?

In the midst of this crisis, he discovered the foundation for faith and central theme of his theology and ethics: "The fundamental certainty given to me then . . . was that of God's sovereignty."[4] It was a decisive "break with . . . liberal or empirical theology" that "defined God primarily in value-terms," and a trust in the sovereignty of God as the center of faith. "It does not mean to believe in a kindly spirit somewhere who may help us in our more or less pious endeavors, but it does mean that we have seen the enemy and the judge of our sin as our redeemer."

Niebuhr's advocacy of the sovereignty of God included three essential themes: (1) *the reality of God's rule in and over all, including the bitter and the tragic*; (2) *the independence of the living God from subjective values and human institutions, which God judges*; and (3) *the redemptive manifestation of God in Christ, within our real history.*

All three of these themes are essential for Niebuhr's understanding of the relation between Christ and culture. Niebuhr's insight in 1934, pointing to the experience of the sovereignty of God, gives us powerful grounding for authentic transformation, grounding that is realistically validated in historical experience. To help us hear his strong intent, I want to show how deeply these three themes are rooted in the development of his own faith and ethics, beginning with his essay on the death of idealist hope and the resurrection of faith in the sovereign God.

The Universal Rule of God

> The events of our time insist that we shall not be able to find the basis of the faith by which we can live and must live save in the "I am that I am" on which we are utterly dependent for our being and our meaning. These events wring from us again the faith which no will to believe can establish, the faith in that last reality which is our creator and our slayer.[5]

Niebuhr wanted to recover his own roots in the Evangelical and Reformed tradition and his own affinity with the God-centered prophetic tradition of Paul, Augustine, Luther, Calvin, and Jonathan Edwards.[6] The only way to be freed from destructive idolatries such as nationalism, racism, and greed, is to discover a true loyalty to the living God as the source and judge of all life.[7] It was just this sovereign God, the real ruler in and over all, whom Niebuhr discovered in his "tower experience" in the midst of the crises of 1929–1933.

The Independence of the Living God from Subjective Values

"The gods we worshipped have shown themselves to be idols, dependent upon us for their existence." We can no longer place our faith in ideals or institutions such as "democracy, science, technology, industry, church and education."[8] Niebuhr made a passionate and prophetic attack on liberal idealism—an idolatry that had engulfed church and world alike, substituting subjective human desires and optimistic human ideals for God: "A God without wrath brought men without sin into a kingdom without judgment through the ministrations of a Christ without a cross."[9] The center of theology became not God, but human psychology, human ideals, human faith.[10] Instead, he commended those movements of religious realism that "are united by a common interest in maintaining the independent reality of the religious object. . . . They represent a movement distinctly different from nineteenth-century liberal theology which found its center of gravity in the idea of the ethical value of religion."[11] Niebuhr did not mean that God is unrelated to human values. God judges human values, transforms them, and establishes a grace-relationship in which God is the valuer more than the valued. The life of faith is founded on God's initiative; God is not founded on the life of faith. God is the living God, dynamic and personal; not a static God who could be possessed by, contained in, or identified with any doctrine, church, ideology, or institution.

The Manifestation of God Within Our History

Niebuhr saw that the sovereignty of God must include a third element: that God is revealed within our history; we can know God's character and the shape of God's actions. If theology is to be based on the sovereign God rather than on subjective values, it must be based on the self-disclosure of the sovereign God and not our wishes. God must be known in our experience, in Christ. Otherwise theology has only subjective values to work with, and meaningful affirmation of the independence of God from our subjective values is undercut.[12] Thus the sovereignty of God includes God's grace in revealing in Christ the character of the sovereign to whom we are responsible.

In his 1934 essay declaring the axe has been laid to the root of the tree, Niebuhr wrote: "But more than that, the answer to our question what must be done in order that we may be saved . . . directs us to Jesus Christ." He pointed to Jesus Christ not as a teacher of moral values and an example of religious ideals, nor as the proclaimer of the church's faith and human self-understanding, but as the disclosure of the "I am that I am" within realistic history. Jesus Christ is "that segment of history in which sin and tragedy and the God who brings sin to its tragic and redeeming consequences come to fullest appearance." The Jesus Christ Niebuhr pointed to is no wish nor dream but "a very bitter reality" in whom "we have seen the enemy and the judge of our sin as our redeemer." The sovereign God is disclosed in human history—in fullest clarity in Jesus Christ.

The Kingdom of God in America: Testing Faith in the Laboratory of History

Niebuhr's despair over the powerlessness of ideals to deliver the churches from social conformism led him to a study of those periods of U. S. history when churches exhibited the power to resist social forces and transform society. Here, as his ethics was being formed, long before he wrote *Christ and Culture*, his central concern was for a transformative ethic. The results of his research became his second book, *The Kingdom of God in America*. He was trying to discover, he said, the

> hard, unyielding core which kept religion from becoming a mere function of culture; which enabled it to recover its initiative, to protest as well as to acquiesce, to construct new orders of life as well as to sanctify established orders; which accounted for its reformist activities, explained its relations to the democratic, antislavery and socialist movements, and its creativity in producing ever new religious groups (KGA, x-xi).

He found that such a transformative, prophetic faith had erupted in the early, democratic Puritan period (by contrast with the late, self-righteous Puritanism that gave the movement a bad name), in the

Great Awakening and the antislavery and reform movements it spawned, and in the Social Gospel movement. Niebuhr's life-changing discovery was that in each prophetic period, faith with authentic transformative power was marked by three essential characteristics:

1. The early Puritan-Calvinist belief in *the sovereignty of God over all of life* gave courage and commitment to the struggle for transformation. It was the antidote to compartmentalizing life into a private realm under Christ's lordship and a societal realm of accommodation to some other lord. Faith in God's rule over all of life was strong not only in the early, Puritan movement, but also in those other periods when Christian faith transformed American society (KGA, 39f., 120ff., 130–39). The prophetic faith that had transforming power emphasized "the living reality of God's present rule, not only in human spirits but also in the world of nature and of human history" (KGA, 51).

2. The sovereign God remains *the living, dynamic, eternal Judge and Redeemer*. No doctrine, no matter how orthodox, no institution, whether political or ecclesiastical, no human good will, no matter how pure and moral, can claim to possess God's goodness. If the norm of Christian ethics is the living *God*, then the will of God must be found in biblical study under the guidance of the Holy Spirit, in God's own self-disclosure in Israel, in Jesus Christ, and in the presence of the Holy Spirit. Furthermore, if the norm of Christian ethics is the *living* God, the Christian life is never arrival but always *metanoia*, always permanent revolution.[13] Therefore, all human powers and causes are restrained from claiming sovereignty for themselves.

   "The rule of limitation of all human power" is one of the principles of constructive Calvinism. It produced the checks and balances in the U.S. Constitution, which Niebuhr contrasted with the unrealistic optimism of the French Constitution (KGA, xiv-xv, 22f., 66–79, 129f.). Prophetic faith applies the principle of checks and balances to church authorities as well as economic and other powers (KGA, 83, 96–100, 104–105).

3. Furthermore, it is crucial for transformative faith that *God's will is known with structure and content*. Otherwise there is no shape, no revolutionary strategy, no constitutional structure, and faith is vague and diffuse. The period of transformation when the

revelation of God's will in Christ was most clearly emphasized and the proclamation was most Christ-centered was the time of the Great Awakening.

We may add: those churches which have grown, and continue to grow, most profusely in American soil are the churches that have been most influenced by the Great Awakening and are most Christ-centered. Their Christ-centeredness is their strength. Their God is not so abstract as to be unknowable; they have a personal loyalty to God as revealed in a personal Jesus Christ. Their weakness is manifested when their "Christ" becomes a mere symbol without concrete biblical and theocentric content, without an incarnate Jesus who teaches and embodies concrete criteria for being transformed rather than conformed. At such a point the name "Christ" is in danger of becoming a gnostic cover for hidden, idolatrous ideologies and interests. Their personal loyalty to Christ needs clarity about the concrete discipleship content of the disclosure of God's character in Christ; otherwise the vacuum is likely to be filled by hidden ideologies.

Niebuhr writes that the key to revolutionary transformation is the transfer of the will's trust and loyalty from distrust to trust in God. That key comes in the form of God's action in Jesus Christ. "The divine sovereignty, according to the Awakeners, is fundamental . . . in a second way. God has acted and is acting in history; in Jesus Christ God has brought in the great change which has opened to us the kingdom of liberty and love" (KGA, 102–3). The required revolution occurs when we come to love the source of all being as our true good and to love our neighbors as creatures of that being. "That is precisely the possibility that has been opened in Jesus Christ" (KGA, 115).

The early Puritans "did not begin with an idea of God made up out of the most amiable human characteristics . . . ; they began rather with that last being which crowns with destruction the life which proceeds from it. This being they had come to trust and to worship because of its self-revelation in Jesus Christ" (KGA, 51).

Moreover, they believed both church and state are equally "subject to a common constitution, the will of God declared in Scripture and nature" (KGA, 39).

> The principle of Christian constitutionalism is directly corollary to the principle of God's sovereignty. Since God is the source of all power and value, his nature and will rather than human nature and human desires or ideals need to be consulted in all human actions.

135

Furthermore, if God is really the beginning, his character and intention need to be learned from himself and not prescribed to him from elsewhere . . . (KGA, 59; see also 60–62 and 120).

He wrote of the "great dilemma" in the prophetic tradition:

How could such a principle be used for the construction of a new order of life? . . . What ethical construction was possible to a formalism which proclaimed, "Obey God, love God and do what you please"? What definite counsel could be given? . . . It was easy to use the idea of the kingdom as a critical principle for the overthrow of usurpers of God's absolute authority, but very difficult to employ it for the purpose of establishing a new system of political order (KGA, 27, 30–32).

He was critical of Luther at this point, and praised Calvin for more realistic advocacy of checks and balances and specific constitutional norms (KGA, 38–39). Some constitutional pattern, some norms, are needed. This need points to the importance of the third theme, "the constitutional pattern," the normative content of revelation in the incarnate Christ. Without this theme, God's dynamic rule lacks ethical character, and its nonreducibility is only a negative, critical principle lacking concrete ethical content. The book's final words are: " . . . there was no way toward the coming kingdom save the way taken by a sovereign God through the reign of Jesus Christ" (KGA, 198).

Had Niebuhr written the book three decades later, he surely would have included the Civil Rights movement as a dramatic demonstration of transformative faith. We can test his results by looking at that transformative period as well. In Martin Luther King and the Black church tradition, one cannot help but be struck by the strength of faith in God's providential care and dynamic rule.[14] African American churches have solid reason to exercise a critical perspective on the claim of any social group to be just. They also have strong emphasis on humility about all claims to purity and righteousness. Certainly this tradition is thoroughly Christocentric. Redemptive love as revealed in Christ was central for Martin Luther King, Jr., as is clear in his book *Strength to Love* and throughout his writings. His decisive breakthrough came when the power of love as described "in the Sermon on the Mount and the Gandhian method of nonviolent resistance" were fused together into a concrete strategy. He saw that fusion in the struggle in Birmingham. It gave him a concrete strategy for change.[15] Only when he saw the connection between the nonviolent, redemptive love of the Sermon on the Mount and Gandhi's strategy of nonviolent direct action did King experience the fusion of light and energy that enabled him to see so clearly and lead so prophetically. He wrote:

> I became deeply fascinated by his campaigns of nonviolent resistance. . . . Prior to reading Gandhi, I had about concluded that the ethics of Jesus were only effective in individual relationships. . . . When racial groups and nations were in conflict a more realistic approach seemed necessary. But after reading Gandhi, I saw how utterly mistaken I was. For Gandhi love was a potent instrument for social and collective transformation. It was in this Gandhian emphasis on love and nonviolence that I discovered the method for social reform that I had been seeking for so many months. . . . I came to feel that this was the only morally and practically sound method open to oppressed people in their struggle for freedom.[16]

The Ethics of Response

Niebuhr's "tower experience," his study of transformative faith in *The Kingdom of God in America*, and his threefold understanding of the sovereignty of God, form the basis of his ethics of responsible selfhood as he presented it in his annual Christian ethics lectures at Yale.[17] Many students have heard him urge that the Christian life is response, in our social context, to the action of the sovereign God as Creator, Ruler, and Redeemer. "Responsibility affirms: 'God is acting in all actions upon you. So respond to all actions upon you as to respond to God's action.'" Such an ethic takes its shape from the character of God's action. Without specificity in the disclosure of the character of God's action, the ethic lacks specificity.

Christ and Culture

When we turn to *Christ and Culture* with this threefold understanding of the sovereignty of God in mind, we can solve what many have thought was a mystery: Is Niebuhr merely describing five different types of Christ-and-culture relationship, or is he actively advocating one of them? Now we can see that he is clearly advocating the transformationist relation to culture that he sought in *The Social Sources of Denominationalism* and that he advocated in *The Kingdom of God in America*. He describes five ways of relating Christ and culture: Christ against culture (radicals), Christ of culture (accommodationists), Christ above culture (synthesists); Christ and culture in paradox (dualists), and Christ transforming culture (transformationists). He evaluates all five types according to how well they express the three dimensions of the sovereignty of God.

The Reality of God's Rule in and over All

Radicals fail to relate adequately "the content of [Jesus'] commandment, . . . his law or reign, to that power which governs nature and presides over the destinies of men in their secular societies" (C&C, 81). The accommodationists fail to relate their "immanent, rational, spiritual, and moral principle" to God. They cannot escape the question whether "the Almighty Creator of heaven and earth is . . . pitiless and blind force . . . or the Father of Jesus Christ." (pp. 114–15). "There is an appealing greatness in the synthesist's resolute proclamation that the God who is to rule now rules and has ruled, that His rule is established in the nature of things. . . . He expresses in this way a principle that no other Christian group seems to assert so well but which all need to share: namely, the principle that the Creator and the Savior are one" (p. 143). Dualists do not see this so clearly; they see "law, state, and other institutions as restraining forces, dykes against sin, preventers of anarchy, rather than as positive agencies through which men in social union render positive service to neighbors advancing toward true life." They tend "to relate temporality or finiteness to sin in such a degree as to move creation and fall into very close proximity, and in that connection . . . do less than justice to the creative work of God" (p. 188). Transformationists succeed in emphasizing the creative activity of Christ-in-God, the "beneficence of the Ruler of nature." They emphasize Christ's participation in creation, and Christ's incarnation along with death and resurrection. They avoid the dualist error of almost identifying creation and fall; the fallen creation is corrupted, but is still good creation (pp. 192–94).

The Independence of the Living God
from Human Ideals and Institutions

Radicals underestimate our sinfulness, and so become legalistic. They underestimate the church's sinfulness, and so over-identify the Christian community with God's will (pp. 79–80). Likewise, accommodationists underestimate their own sin. Therefore, they, too, "incline to the side of law in dealing with the polarity of law and grace." They forget that "if we say we have no sin we deceive ourselves" (p. 113). The synthesists tend toward "the absolutizing of what is relative, the reduction of the infinite to a finite form, and the materialization

138

of the dynamic." They tend toward cultural conservatism, defense of the culture with which they have struck a synthesis, and identification of the grace of Christ with the institution of the church. "They do not in fact face up to the radical evil present in all human work" (pp. 146–48). "Perhaps a synthesis is possible in which the relative character of all creaturely formulations of the Creator's law will be fully recognized." When they do recognize this, synthesists are on the way to becoming transformationists with their "continuous and infinite conversion" (pp. 145–46). The advantage of the dualists is their accurate reflection of "the strength and prevalence of sin in all human existence." More than others "they take into account the dynamic character of God, man, grace, and sin" (p. 185.). The transformationists are clear about "the nature of the world's perversion." They consistently contrast "the response of Jesus Christ to the Father with that of the world of men to its Creator" (p. 198).

The Manifestation of God's Redemptive Character in Our Present History Through Christ

Niebuhr is impressed by the clarity of the radicals' profession of New Testament norms, and by the sincerity of their practice of those norms. Because of their clear and consistent witness, they have significantly more transformative impact for their numbers than do other groups (pp. 46–48, 66–67). Among the accommodationists, however, "one seeks in vain . . . for a recognition of the hard demand which the Sermon on the Mount makes on the Christian" (p. 90). Niebuhr devotes three full pages to scoring accommodationists for their "consistent tendency to distort the figure of the New Testament Jesus. . . . He has been abandoned in favor of an idol called by his name." Even so, they cannot "proceed in their reasoning without reliance on the purely given historical fact, and without references to an action of self-disclosure" of God in "Jesus Christ in history" (pp. 109–112). While accommodationists simplify "the nature of the Lord in a manner not justified by the New Testament record," synthesists do not. "The commandments of Christ to sell everything for the sake of following him, to give up judging our fellows, to turn the other cheek to the violent, to humble ourselves and become the servants of all, to abandon family and to forget tomorrow, cannot, the synthesist sees, be made to rhyme . . . with civilized society by allegorizing them," compromising them, or diluting them (pp. 120–21). "The dualist joins the radical Christian in maintaining the authority of the law of Christ over all . . .

and in stating it in its plain literal sense" (p. 157). But dualists have so little hope of regeneration in Christ that "spiritual transformation cannot be expected this side of death. . . . It is at this point that the transformationist *motif*, otherwise very similar to the dualist, emerges in distinction from it" (p. 189). Transformationists live more in the divine now than the other types, more in "the divine possibility of a present renewal" (pp. 195, 201). The prototypical transformationist, F. D. Maurice, "begins with the fact that the Christ who comes into the world comes into his own, and that it is Christ himself who exercises his kingship" over us, not some other lord "separate from the incarnate Word." Maurice insisted that "the center is Christ. In him all things were created to live in union with God and each other; he reveals the true nature of life and the law of the created society as well as the sin and rebellion of its members; he redeems men in and for community with one another in God." "The conversion of humankind from self-centeredness to Christ-centeredness was for Maurice the universal and present possibility" (pp. 221f. and 225).

Niebuhr prefers transformationist hope over dualist pessimism: we can live under the lordship of Christ. He identifies strongly with Martin Luther's and Jonathan Edwards' emphasis on regeneration as cleansing the springs of action, as freeing the Christian to love, and as conversion from distrust to trust in God. Conversion transforms not only our basic trust but also our loyalty and faithfulness to the cause taught and embodied by Jesus Christ.[18] But Niebuhr criticizes the pessimism of dualists about living a new, Christian life. The dualists' pessimism undercuts the authority of the ethics of the New Testament Christ and leads either to conservatism or to lawlessness. He climaxes *Christ and Culture* by emphasizing the transformationist theme of the lordship of Christ and the grace-based possibility of living a renewed life under Christ. This echoes the theme that he found crucial in transformationist faith, especially in the revivals of the Great Awakening: the experience that regeneration, the new life in Christ, is taking place now. He puts the two themes together, conversion to trust and conversion to loyalty to God's cause disclosed in Christ, in the normative principle by which he measures all five types: "the primacy of grace and the necessity of works of obedience" (C&C, 119).

Thus, Niebuhr has announced his criteria for evaluation of the types. His criteria are the three dimensions of the sovereignty of God he has consistently advocated. He is arguing for transformationism as the more adequate relationship, and sees the other types as failing on

140

one or more of the dimensions of the sovereignty of God. Niebuhr has given us a threefold, theocentric basis for our task of redefining the relation between Christ and culture.

I want to suggest that Niebuhr's threefold criterion is at least implicitly trinitarian. The reality of God's rule in and over all is the reality we speak of as God the Creator. The living, dynamic character of God, present in our experience but not reducible to human ideals, is what we point to as God the Holy Spirit. The manifestation of God's redemptive character in Christ is what we witness to as God the Son, God the Redeemer.[19]

Much of Yoder's criticism of Niebuhr is based on the doctrine of the Trinity. In his summary statement, he says Niebuhr used "the doctrine of the Trinity as his rhetorically most powerful way of arguing that the teachings and example of Christ need to be 'corrected' or brought into balance by appeal to nature and to history."[20] I would argue, however, that another understanding of the Trinity than the one Yoder criticizes is central to Niebuhr's writings, and that it is much more than merely a rhetorical device; it is Niebuhr's fundamental faith in the sovereignty of God. It guides his evaluations of different ways of relating Christ and culture. And this understanding has much to teach us for our constructive definition of authentic transformation. Niebuhr has demonstrated historically that the three trinitarian norms are crucial for an authentically transformative faith, a faith that does not merely accommodate to secular forces like a chameleon, but changes their direction toward God's will like a prophet. Our effort to define authentic transformation should take Niebuhr's argument very seriously.

In reaching this conclusion, I agree with Yoder's argument for the importance of a trinitarian understanding of the unity of God as disclosed in Christ. Yoder argues that the doctrine of the Trinity emphasizes that the character of the one God, the Creator and Ruler, is disclosed in Christ. That is exactly what I am arguing is essential to Niebuhr's program, as he developed it from *The Kingdom of God in America* through *Christ and Culture*.

Yoder also argues that it is dangerous to claim to know some other will of God disclosed in creation or in history that contrasts with the will of God disclosed in Christ. It is dangerous because it threatens God's unity and depreciates Christ's lordship. It creates another, autonomous ethic, separate from Christ. The ever-rationalizing human spirit is all too quick to see in nature or history a justification for racism,

141

greed, militarism, jingoistic nationalism, special privilege, or other forms of unjust domination. We must correct our understanding of God as Creator and Ruler of history by our understanding of God revealed in Christ. God is one. God cannot have a different character as Creator or Ruler than God has in Christ. This is the point of the doctrine of the Trinity.

I believe Niebuhr agrees. He praises synthesists for upholding better than dualists "the principle that the Creator and the Savior are one" (C&C, 143). He criticizes dualists for tending "to separate the two principles; and to posit two gods, or a division in the Godhead" (C&C, 159). The strength of the transformationists, over against the dualists, is that they make clear that Christ is Lord of all of life. He praises F. D. Maurice for beginning "with the fact that the Christ who comes into the world comes into his own, and that it is Christ himself who exercises his kingship" over us, not some other lord "separate from the incarnate Word." Maurice insisted that in Christ "all things were created to live in union with God and each other; he reveals the true nature of life and the law of the created society" (pp. 221f. and 225).

Yet there is a point to Yoder's criticism. There was another side to Niebuhr, a side that became dominant in the 1950s when Niebuhr rebelled against what he called Karl Barth's Christomonism. This other side made his ethics more abstract and relativist, as Yoder says. Hints of it are beginning to show in *Christ and Culture*, especially in the latter parts of the book.

Yet the point I would make is that Niebuhr did advocate a three-fold or trinitarian understanding of the sovereignty of God that has promise for answering Yoder's criticism. *This understanding has demonstrated, in the laboratory of history, that it bears fruit: it produces an authentically transformationist relation to culture.* It can provide guidance for our task of developing an understanding of prophetic faith that is authentically transformationist.

2. Concrete, Theocentric Norms Within the Limits of Historical Realism

Yoder criticizes *Christ and Culture* for lacking specific ethical norms: We need "to see by what criteria adequate and less adequate 'transformations' would be discerned. Yet Niebuhr identifies no such cases or criteria. The 'transformation' chapter proceeds on a higher level of abstraction than the others."[21] "This vacuity about moral substance is especially odd because of the choice of the terms 'transform' and 'convert' to label it. Those words for change would ordinarily . . . call for someone to define with some substantial clarity one's criteria or lines of direction for change."[22]

Yoder's criticism is perceptive. Although *Christ and Culture* clearly argues for the authority of "the Jesus Christ of the New Testament" (p. 12–13), and although Niebuhr clearly affirms the importance of the lordship of Christ and of the norms disclosed in Christ for the latter two types, dualist and transformationist, he indicates almost no New Testament norms advocated by those types. The farther the book goes, the less specific it gets about the ethics of the New Testament Jesus. Although the norm in his presentation of transformationism is drawn from Jesus Christ, it remains very general: theocentrism and giving love to the world (pp. 198–200). Nowhere does the chapter on transformationism indicate Christ's ethics or practices. The result is that readers may be convinced to call themselves transformationists without committing themselves to any specific ethics. Yet as Niebuhr has shown repeatedly, an ethic that has the power to transform rather than be conformed needs clear norms revealed in Christ. A vague stance for conversion without standing for anything specific is unlikely to have strong transforming impact. More likely it will degenerate into cheap grace and accommodationism, a mere symbol without concrete biblical and theocentric content, or a cover for hidden, idolatrous assumptions. In order to be authentically transformationist in our relation to culture, we need ethical norms, a prophetic plumbline, with which to measure the rightness or wrongness of different parts of culture.

Niebuhr says as much. He praises the dualists' strong emphasis on grace and trust, but criticizes their weakness in advocacy of clear norms. "Something is to be said" for the indictment "that dualism tends to lead Christians into antinomianism and into cultural conservatism." (C&C, 187). Lacking concrete norms for transformation, dualists tempt Christians to rationalize and to rely on the status-quo norms of the culture. "The church chose more wisely than Marcion did when it associated with the epistles of Paul the Gospel of Matthew and the Letter of James," with their specific teachings about Christian discipleship.

He criticizes Bultmann for deleting the content from the specific virtues that Jesus teaches and embodies. "This existentialist Jesus is more Kantian than Markan or Pauline or Johannine. Bultmann can find no real content in the gospel idea of obedience." Furthermore, the idea of God that he "ascribed to Jesus is as empty and formal as the idea of obedience." The result is

> a caricature of the New Testament Christ. For the Jesus who is radically obedient knows that the will of God is the will of the Creator and Governor of all nature and of all history; that there is structure and content in His will; that He is the author of the ten command-ments; that He demands mercy and not sacrifice; that He requires not only obedience to Himself but love and faith in Him, and love of the neighbor whom He creates and loves (C&C, 24f.).

In *Faith on Earth*, Niebuhr again criticizes Bultmann for reducing faith to a momentary response to the absolute claim of a transcendent God, without any content. He points out that even Bultmann has to pay attention to "the historical actuality of Jesus Christ, as presented in the New Testament" (*Faith*, 10–11). Why, then, was Niebuhr not more specific about the teachings of the incarnate, historical, Jesus Christ?

Yoder sees the root of the problem in Niebuhr's definition of Christ in chapter 1 of *Christ and Culture*. There Niebuhr presents a Jesus who "points away" both from the world and from himself to his Father who alone is worthy of loyalty. Jesus does not judge selected aspects of culture as more sinful than others. Rather, "in his single-minded direction toward God, Christ leads men away from the temporality and pluralism of culture."[23] This makes Jesus a rejecter of culture and irrelevant to culture. Niebuhr "has so set up the question as to make it clear from the outset that Jesus must be *by definition* inadequate."[24]

Yoder does admit that this is only half of Niebuhr's definition of Jesus Christ. Niebuhr also says we see in Jesus a movement of God toward humankind and human culture. This movement of God incar-nate in Christ toward humankind is a mediation of "the Father's will toward humankind, . . . the perfection of divine *agape*, . . . command-ing obedience not to his own will but to God's. . ." (C&C, 28). Thus Niebuhr's Christ is not only an otherworldly rejecter of culture, but a mediator of God's will toward culture. Yoder contends, however, that this is empty: "it provides his hearers no commands to obey nor examples to follow."[25]

One could defend Niebuhr in several ways. In my summary of Niebuhr's trinitarian evaluation of the five types, I indicated Niebuhr's use of the Sermon on the Mount and the commandments of Jesus as criteria for evaluation of two of the types. Niebuhr insisted that our various understandings of Christ need to be checked by the objective picture of "the Jesus Christ of the New Testament; and that this is a person with definite teachings, a definite character, and a definite fate" (C&C, 12–13). This Jesus teaches that "there is structure and content" in God's will (C&C, 24f.). Nevertheless one can hardly dispute that Niebuhr's description of the teachings of Jesus affirmed by each type gets less specific as he proceeds, and that his recommended type, transformationism, lacks concrete ethical criteria or content. The result is that it is too easy to claim to be a transformationist without standing for anything in particular.

Curiously, in spite of Niebuhr's criticisms of Bultmann, his own ethics lacked concreteness, especially in the 1950s. Lonnie Kliever says the absence of specificity "is considered a serious weakness in Niebuhr's ethics by some of his closest followers as well as his sternest critics." For some reason, Niebuhr seems to have a "reluctance to give more specific content to his ethics."[26] Joseph L. Allen and John C. Bennett both puzzle about the lack in Niebuhr's thought of "concrete moral principles," about the absence of "an intermediate link between radical monotheism and concrete action," and about "his reluctance to carry his reflection . . . over into such areas as the family, politics, the economy."[27]

Niebuhr is not alone in this. He exemplifies a problem most of us have. The problem is that we are influenced by the relativism of our century. Experiencing the intermingling of many different cultures, we realize people have different beliefs because they come from different historical, social, and religious backgrounds.

Furthermore, many of us still believe that the only real truth is universally objective: reasonable people everywhere should agree. Yet in our time of cross-cultural encounter we are aware that ethical values are not universally objective. Different people from different historical contexts have different ethical values. So we conclude that ethical values are not *objectively* true. They are subjective, like your preference for lime sherbet and mine for toasted almond fudge ice cream.

Many ethicists, spooked by historical relativism, shy away from rules or concrete guidelines.[28] Ironically, their awareness that we cannot help but be shaped by our historical context leads them to flee from being historically concrete. They become general, vague, in their ethics, lest they show their own historical relativism.

This is the problem of postmodernism—which Niebuhr saw early because of his study of Ernst Troeltsch, the philosopher of relativism.

The Enlightenment of the eighteenth century shaped the modern age. It was aware that different people have different perceptions and beliefs according to their particular historical situations and their particular faiths. So Enlightenment thinkers tried to escape by relying on reason, which they thought was universal, not relative to particular history. They would base morality and religion on universal reason in order to be objective. Three problems arose from this attempt at universality and objectivity, however. First, relying on universal reason meant abandoning or slighting whatever was not derived from universal logic—that is, particular religious beliefs, particular ethnic loyalties, particular community memberships, historically concrete and specific ethics. This produced a very thin set of abstract moral principles, lacking in the richness and depth of what makes community and faith real. It pushed many who affirmed particular loyalties into a reactionary, authoritarian insistence on the absoluteness of those loyalties and a hostile rejection of others who differed. This sort of fundamentalist reaction seems to have erupted in all cultures which have felt the impact of modernist Enlightenment reason. Second, we became aware that the allegedly universal principles of the Enlightenment were themselves a product of their own history. Because there is no escape from history, the Enlightenment, too, was historically relative. Third, belief that our principles are universally logical, and not dependent on our own particular history, blinds us to the particular loyalties, group memberships, hidden faith, class, race, gender, and nationalistic biases that shape our ethics. We end up powerfully influenced by loyalties, interests, passions, and faith that we do not acknowledge, examine, or correct. For example, Gerd Theissen shows that in the first decades of this century, 80 percent of German pastors and most theologians opposed the democratic Weimar Republic. They mostly favored the conservative German Nationalistic Peoples' Party. Accordingly they systematically neutralized Jesus' social criticisms. They handed down to us an individualistic and otherworldly picture of Jesus that does violence to the evidence and to the scholarly methods they claimed to be following. Their biblical interpretation claimed objectivity, but its very lack of concreteness showed it was historically relative. This is particularly true of Bultmann, whom Niebuhr also criticizes.[29]

Awareness of the dilemma of historical relativity and the failure of allegedly nonrelative reason is the basis of postmodernism. Postmodernism criticizes modernism and the Enlightenment for assuming that objective reason rises above the changing tides of historical particularity, and that whatever is not universal and unchanging is merely subjective. There are different kinds of postmodernism, but all see reason and truth as based on the diverse flows of the movement of history. We do not stand on unmoving granite; we travel on a pilgrimage, following a living God who moves us in real time.

Trying to avoid the problem by avoiding historically concrete norms is a logical error. It not only fails to escape historical assumptions, but obscures them, hiding them from critical view. Furthermore, it undercuts authentic transformation, which requires historically concrete norms. Unless we stand for something, we shall hardly move the world.

Niebuhr may be able to help us find a remedy. He wrestled with the problems of relativism more extensively than any other theologian. With his clear focus on the sovereignty of God, combined with the historicity of our faith, he had to ask: How is God's character disclosed within our history? How do we know valid, theocentric, ethical norms within our concrete historical context? How do we answer these questions in the face of the historical relativism of our time?

To answer these questions, Niebuhr developed a richly suggestive method of historical realism. It meets the challenge of historical relativism and the need for both Christlike inclusiveness and critical evaluation of the diverse faiths in our global culture.

Overcoming Kantian Agnosticism About Theocentric Norms

From the very start of Niebuhr's scholarly career, he identified the influence of the Enlightenment philosopher Immanuel Kant as a source of serious error. In his doctoral dissertation, Niebuhr argued that Ernst Troeltsch's intention to provide a strong foundation for Christian ethics was thwarted by the lingering influence of Kant.

According to Kant, God cannot be known by human knowledge. Human knowledge is limited to natural experiences. God is infinite, absolute, and supernatural, beyond our experiential categories.[30] If Kant is right, then we must *infer* our understanding of God indirectly from some human feeling or value that we *can* know. Kant inferred God from our moral values. Others, after Kant, based knowledge of God on immediate feeling (Schleiermacher), existential self-understanding (Bultmann), or some other allegedly universal human awareness. Niebuhr attacked this indirect approach for becoming "a 'faithology' or a 'religionology'" which turned attention away from God to religious feelings and made the religious consciousness the object of confidence," instead of the sovereign God.[31]

He pointed out that Troeltsch had two contradictory understandings of how we know God. One was Kantian agnosticism, but the other resembled the experiential philosophy of William James and Henri Bergson. It affirmed experiential knowledge of God, and was consistent with Troeltsch's central theme of the historical concreteness of all that we know. He criticized the Kantian side and advocated the more experiential and historical understanding.[32]

Rejecting Kantian Universal, Detached Rationality

The second Kantian assumption that Niebuhr attacked is universal, detached rationality. Kant argued that we should validate the truth of moral norms by their rational universality. That is, true moral norms are based on assumptions that are necessary for anyone who thinks rationally. And their content, their principles, must apply to everyone. This is the ethics of a rationality detached from historical differences. But if we accept universality as the criterion of truth, the resulting ethics must be extremely abstract and thin. It must reject the differences of different cultures, different societies, different communities, different religions, different situations. Only what is universal is true. This devalues all that is historically specific, all that is rich and concrete in religious faith, all that is the peculiar love (and joy) of human community. It reduces truth to a very thin lowest common denominator, if such can be found. It drains the concreteness from the ethics of Christ and reduces his teachings to a historically detached universal principle or two. Gone will be everything particularly Jewish or Palestinian. Gone, too, will be everything concrete in what the ethics of Christ means for our time and our particular challenges.

Niebuhr saw this clearly from the start. He agreed with Troeltsch that all our knowing is conditioned by our location in history. Therefore, our religious knowledge "cannot mean eternity, universal validity and absoluteness."[33] Still Troeltsch seemed to accept Kant's assumption that whatever was grounded in transcendent reality would be perceived by all humankind. In spite of his awareness of our historical situatedness, he still clung to a desire for universality.

Here, too, Niebuhr showed there were two fundamentally different methods of knowing in Troeltsch's thought. The Bergsonian or Jamesian way of knowing was empirical, realist, and historical.[34] This

method could establish authoritative norms within the limits of historical particularity without falling into subjectivism. The other, the way
of Kantian universal rationality, rejected historically situated knowledge as merely subjective.[35]

We can see the force of this criticism by looking at the conclusion
to Troeltsch's highly influential two-volume work, *The Social Teaching
of the Christian Churches*.[36] Troeltsch asks whether we can discover an
objective element in Christianity that will be normative for contemporary Christians. Its objectivity, he assumes, should be demonstrated by
its being universally normative in the teaching of all churches of all
times:

> Can we not learn something from a large work of this kind to help
> us to overcome our miserable ecclesiastical situation, which is daily
> becoming worse? . . . Does [this study] not also teach something
> lasting and eternal about the Christian social Ethos, which might
> serve as a guiding star for the present and for the future, something
> which could aid us not merely to understand but also to transform
> the situation?

The answer was "yes," but the content was meager, and the voice
was weak and quavering. At the end of a one thousand page book,
Troeltsch's proposed norms amounted to a page and a half pointing to
five ideals: individual personality, divine love, mutuality, active helpfulness, and the idea of the future kingdom of God. Ironically, these
"universal norms" now appear peculiar to nineteenth-century liberalism. Furthermore, they are thin and abstract. They lack the richness
and concreteness of Troeltsch's historical study.

Why this thinness? Troeltsch was still looking for "the permanent
ethical values which are contained within the varied history of the
Christian social doctrines."[37] He was still expecting true Christian
norms to be universally maintained by the various churches throughout
the centuries of church history. What was not universal, Troeltsch
treated as merely subjective.[38] When the honest historian searched for
universally accepted norms, he had to admit the results were very thin.

Furthermore, his Kantian side caused Troeltsch to believe Christian
truth must be based on a universal truth implicit in all religions, times,
and places. But his historical studies contradicted that claim, and
Troeltsch struggled with skepticism all his life.

In *The Meaning of Revelation*, Niebuhr rejects Kantian universalism. He insists that "we are not trying to describe a common human
certainty gained in a common human experience; yet on the other hand

we are not seeking to set forth a private and mystic assurance which is not subject to the criticism of our community" (MR, 141). He argues that from our historically particular location, we do see real truth, and develops a method of validating truth and correcting error that does not depend on universality. We can affirm concrete, historically situated norms that are not merely subjective.

Affirming Historical Realism

Niebuhr urges us to face squarely the twentieth-century "realization that the point of view which a man occupies in regarding religious as well as any sort of reality is of profound importance. . . . No universal knowledge of things in themselves is possible. . . . No observer can get out of history into a realm beyond time-space" (MR, 6–7, 16). "We can speak only about that which is also in our time and which is seen through the medium of our history. We are in history as the fish is in water and what we mean . . . can be indicated only as we point through the medium in which we live" (MR, 48). Furthermore, the time that is in us is "not abstract but particular and concrete, . . . the time of a definite society with distinct language, economic and political relations, religious faith and social organization" (MR, 13).

From a Hebraic, rather than Kantian, perspective, this awareness need not be disconcerting. In the biblical narrative, the people of Israel were well aware that what they saw differed from what the surrounding cultures saw. The prophets of Israel saw what others in Israel, who would not soften their hearts and change their practices, did not see. Jesus often said people did not see what is happening; they were blinded by faithlessness or hard-hearted practices. What we see is relative to our historical situation and our loyalties.

Accepting our historical limitations is disconcerting only if we also accept Kant's (and Plato's) assumption that true knowledge must be based on what everyone rational agrees with. Because Niebuhr rejects Kant's assumptions, he can accept our historical limitations without accepting subjectivism. He adopts the critical limits he learned from Troeltsch's historical side, but not the Kantian side, in order to overcome agnosticism and subjectivism. "It is not apparent . . . that those who understand how all their experience is historically mediated must believe that nothing is mediated through history." For example, even though "great eighteenth-century phrases such as 'the natural rights of men,' 'the system of natural liberty,' . . . and 'the iron law of wages'" are relative to their historical background and to "specific interests of certain social groups," they "doubtless refer to objective relations; doubtless too they were and largely remain useful instruments for the analysis of actual relations. . . ." The truth in human rights "grows out of a communication with reality. . . . What we see from the democratic point of view is really there, even though all men do not see it" (MR, vii, 10–11, 18–19).

Niebuhr experimented with various terms for his position which I will call *historical realism*. Historical realism proceeds "with confidence in the independent reality of what is seen, though recognizing that its assertions about that reality" have their meaning from a historically relative standpoint (MR, 10–11 and 22). It accepts our historical limitations realistically: what we see is strongly influenced by our historical context—our experiences, interests, loyalties, practices, communities, and faith. We can no more build ourselves up to God's level than could the builders of the Tower of Babel, standing on their crumbling hand-made bricks put together with tar that was bound to melt under the hot sun of the Plain of Shinar. They were looking in the wrong direction for God, who was not up above history, but had come down to their level—to be heard within the strife of the different language groups, and the power-seeking of the Babylonian Empire.[39] Within our history, on our level, with our strife and our differences, we hear God's truth. We can hear it nowhere else.

Historical realism points us to what we can and do know. We can know events, persons, social and cultural forces and organizations; beliefs and values held by particular communities or persons; actions and experiences that have occurred within history. We can know drama and narrative: patterns of action and interaction that give unity to our life. These are the stuff of our knowledge and our ethics.

Narrative in Community: Social Existentialism

Niebuhr developed a *social* existentialism that affirms specific, concrete knowledge of a self in action within history. This is crucial for the point I am arguing: Niebuhr's logic calls for concrete disclosure of God's character in Israel's history and in Jesus Christ as normative for Christian ethics. He criticized *individualistic* existentialism, which shies away from concrete knowledge of a self. Individualistic existentialism says the self is *hidden behind* its relationships. The self cannot be the object of knowledge. Thus individualistic existentialism reduces

151

revelation to an encounter between the unknowable self of God and the inner self of the believer, an encounter devoid of structure, content, and history.[40] It resembles Kant's agnosticism: no knowledge-content comes from our encounter with God. Furthermore, it produces a dualism that compartmentalizes Christ and the believer in an inner realm of private selfhood, shut off from guidance for responsible selfhood in an outer realm of society, law, and nature.[41] It shuts religion into a private realm, and makes society secular.

When Niebuhr speaks of God as the self we meet in history, his model for selfhood is not the private and unknowable self, but the social and responsible self, the self in faithful relation, who makes binding covenants. God's particular way of relating within real history is not merely a historical accident disconnected from the real, unknowable God. The real God is in covenant relationship, not in abstraction from relation. A responsible self is a self who acts, within the drama of historical interaction, and who is known in those actions. "Selves are known in act or not at all" (MR, 145–46; see also pp. 65–73 and 129–30). "The self that I acknowledge in my act of trusting is a being that acts with a peculiar kind of freedom and under a peculiar necessity. It has the freedom . . . to bind itself by promises . . ." (*Faith*, 48). This means that the relative historical particularities of God's actions and covenants, their existential and physical embodiments and their repeated patterns, are a part of the disclosure. Revelation is historically concrete, has rich descriptive content, and is subject to historical verification or correction.

Such acts of disclosure are not merely mystical inward encounters. Revelation provides the kinds of truths that are given when the character of a person is disclosed: truths about ways of acting and about intentions expressed in the actions. "It is like a decisive moment in the common life of friends. In the face of some emergency a person may act so as to reveal a quality undisclosed before. Through that revelatory moment a friend is enabled to understand past actions which had been obscure and to prophesy the future behavior of the revealer" (MR, 129).

In Niebuhr's social existentialism, the self that is revealed is not unlimited and unconditioned. The self and its faithfulness of character are revealed, involved, and committed in its own act of disclosure. In Jesus Christ we do not see a God who is detached and removed; in Christ "we see the righteousness of God, his power and wisdom" (MR, 93). In our unfaith we had thought of God as the impersonal "fate which lowers over us . . . in our communities;" now this fate "reveals itself to be a person in community with us" (MR, 153). When the Christian faith speaks of Jesus Christ, it is not enough to speak of human loyalty toward a hidden Infinity. "Unless there enters into our existence the demonstration, as it were, of the loyalty of the Lord of Heaven and earth to this One who was so loyal to God and so loyal to his fellow humans we can't believe in God."[42] In the cross of Christ "the great divine, dominating purpose" is demonstrated for us (MR, 123–25). To this demonstration of the faithful commitment of God, we owe the origin, the calling forth, of our faith.[43] The involvement and commitment of this person in community with us is a strong biblical theme; it is called promise and covenant:

> To have faith is to believe *in*, to count upon or rely upon another, particularly on another person as one who has made promises or has bound himself in covenant relations to the person who has faith in him. It is this meaning of faith which Luther especially emphasized, and in doing so seems to have been in harmony with the Hebrew scriptures. . . .[44]

Niebuhr emphasizes that the self and actions of the other are not merely isolated moments without recognizable pattern. "They are particular demonstrations of an enduring movement or particular parts of a continuous discourse" (RS, 77). We remember other acts of disclosure, and we are therefore able to interpret patterns, meanings, and intentions that are both hidden behind and expressed in events that occur in our relation with the other (RS, 62–63 and 136). Twelve times in *The Meaning of Revelation* Niebuhr uses the term *drama* to point to the knowable pattern of God's action that enables us to interpret our lives in a unified way—or to our false interpretion of life as a drama in which we, rather than God, are the protagonists.[45] In that false interpretation, we exclude others and isolate ourselves arbitrarily. By contrast, the drama of God's creation, judgment, and redemption increasingly includes other persons and other dimensions of life in a reconciled unity.

Our understanding of God is not limited to what we observe by ourselves. Our neighbors give us more information and help us interpret the pattern of God's actions. For the Thou whom we seek to know is a Thou whose actions of disclosure occur "in constant response-relations to other Thou's and It's" (RS, 77). The community of persons that has given us our language, and that continues to converse with us, clarifies and enriches our understanding of the Thou (RS, 77–78; see C&C, 245–49).

In an unpublished manuscript, "Reinhold Niebuhr's Understanding of History," H. Richard criticized his brother's use of "myth" for not making clear that creation, fall, incarnation, and resurrection are not mere stories but historical events which recur.[46] "Sofar as I understand his use of this term [myth] it means that an effort must be made to state in story form what is in fact not a once-and-for-all event but a pattern in repeated events or an aspect of human existence." H. Richard says rather that "the coming of Jesus Christ into the flesh is [the] profoundly significant, once-and-for-all historical event which makes the distinction between B.C. and A.D. exceedingly important and does not quite permit the treatment of all human history as equally subject to the reign of sin and equally characterized by the defeat of suffering love." He affirms the resurrection of Jesus as an historical event by which God gives us our faith. He urges his brother to adopt a prophetic interpretation, which "faithfully describes history as *dramatic encounter* between God and man in which the initiative always lies with God," and in which God is disclosed and known, *Deus Revelatus*. This contrasts with Reinhold's apocalyptic rather than prophetic interpretation of history, in which "God is dealt with as hidden and veiled, *Deus Absconditus*."

In "The Story of Our Life" (MR, chapter 2), Niebuhr suggests a narrative method that has since blossomed into narrative theology and narrative ethics.[47]

> The Christian community has usually—and particularly in times of its greatest vigor—used an historical method. . . . The preaching of the early Christian church was not an argument for the existence of God nor an admonition to follow the dictates of some common human conscience, unhistorical and super-social in character. It was primarily a simple recital of the great events connected with the historical appearance of Jesus Christ and a confession of what had happened to the community of disciples. . . . Christian evangelism . . . began directly with Jesus and told in more or less narrative fashion . . . "of all that Jesus began both to do and to teach" (MR, 43 and 45).

Narrative is history from the perspective of persons in community, existential selves with their own faith, participants in the history they are telling about. "When Christians speak of revelation they point to history . . . as it is remembered by participating selves."[48]

Niebuhr developed his narrative method in order to answer the question, "How can revelation mean both history and God?" (MR, 59; see also p. 54). He emphasizes that what is disclosed in revelation as drama or narrative is not merely some doctrines or some ethical rules, but first of all the presence of God, in faithful relationship. Revelation is personal and God-centered. But second, truths about God, the content of God's will, the shape of ethical faithfulness, are also disclosed (MR, 156–58). In the revelation of the person of God in Jesus Christ an indication is given of the way in which . . . "the dualism between revelations of a person and of his will [must be] overcome" (MR, 164–65). Emphasizing that it is God and not simply some doctrines or moral rules that we receive in revelation, Niebuhr writes: "Jesus Christ gives us, *first of all*, no new ethics but reveals the lawgiver whose implacable will for the completion and redemption of his creation does not allow even his most well beloved son to exempt himself from the suffering necessary to that end" (MR, p. 166; emphasis added). Notice that Niebuhr does not say that Jesus "gives us no new ethics," but that a new ethics is not the *first* thing Jesus gives us. Most important is that Jesus reveals God; revelation is first of all personal. But part of revelation is also the disclosure of God's will, God's covenant, with specifiable content. Emphasizing that in revelation we also receive a disclosure of the content of God's will, Niebuhr writes: "It cannot be enough to say that in revelation we meet the divine self, for if this meeting is pure immediacy which does not provide us with truths about God it would remain incommunicable and unable to provide the reasoning heart with principles of understanding." (MR, 175–76; see also *Faith*, p. 11). Niebuhr points to new truths about God revealed in Christ that revolutionize the moral assumptions we had held: God is revealed as

the oneness of a will directed towards unity of all things in our world; . . . the one to whom Jesus prays as the Lord of Heaven and Earth; . . . [the provider of] the descending rain and the shining sun, careless of the distinctions which we make between the good and evil. . . . The power of God is made manifest in the weakness of Jesus, in the meek and dying life which through death is raised to power . . . and . . . exercises sovereignty more through crosses than through thrones. . . . The essential goodness of the Father of our Lord Jesus Christ is the simple everyday goodness of love. . . . Here is goodness that empties itself, and makes itself of no reputation, a goodness that is all outgoing, reserving nothing for itself, yet having all things" (MR, 183, 186f., 189f.).

God treasures the neighbors we did not prize; God desires a justice different than the justice we sought. God requires and grants forgiveness of sins, repentance, faith, trust in God's mercy, the hope of the world to come (MR, p. 190).

In a beautiful, climactic passage, Niebuhr says the revelation of God in Christ gives us both a new trust in God as faithful and a new ethical standard to follow. It is like the historic event when Egyptologists, who until then could not decipher ancient Egyptian hieroglyphics, discovered the Rosetta stone. On that one stone the same text was written in three parallel versions: easily read Greek script, ordinary Egyptian script, and previously undecipherable hieroglyphics. Suddenly, they were able to translate and make sense of a world they could only puzzle at before.

> When we speak of revelation we mean that moment when we are given a new faith, to cleave to and to betray, and a new standard, to follow and deny. . . . From this point forward we must listen for the remembered voice in all the sounds that assail our ears, and look for the remembered activity in all the actions of the world upon us. The God who reveals himself in Jesus Christ is now trusted and known as the contemporary God, revealing himself in every event; but we do not understand how we could trace God's working in these happenings if he did not make himself known to us through the memory of Jesus Christ; nor do we know how we should be able to interpret all the words we read as words of God save by the aid of this Rosetta stone (MR, 154).

Validating Norms Within the Limits of Historical Realism

But how can our understanding of this new ethical content revealed in the Rosetta stone of Christ be validated and corrected, if we do not use Kant's method of universal rationality? Are we left with fideism—affirming whatever we take to be Christian norms without ways to subject our understanding to criticism and correction? Does historical realism mean mere subjectivism? Does it mean the ethic of apartheid or gas ovens or protracted nuclear warfare is just as valid as the ethics of Moses, or Jesus, or Dietrich Bonhoeffer, or Dorothy Day, or Martin Luther King, Jr.? Is there a way to validate or correct an ethic within our historical limits? To answer these questions, Niebuhr worked out a method of validation within the limits of historical realism, a method that has not been sufficiently noticed. Some have assumed his narrative concept of the inner history of the Christian community insulates faith from correction by external history, the way Kant insulated practical reason from theoretical reason. That is a serious error. Niebuhr's critical method is Troeltschian, not Kantian (MR, x, 11, 31, 65, 163–64).[49] To correct this fideistic or subjectivistic understanding, one wonders if we might be better off to speak of historical-realist theology and ethics, rather than narrative theology and ethics, or to use the biblical terms *testimony* and *witness*. These terms appear frequently in the Bible; story and narrative do not. Or, to follow Frank Tupper's insightful category, perhaps we should speak of *dramatic history*, which combines imagination with a "strict regard for the plain truth." [50]

Validating from Outside the Community

Christian ethical norms can be tested from perspectives outside the community of faith in four ways:

1. External Histories of Our Community

The perspective of "faith in the God of Jesus Christ" tells us that we still practice idolatry, distorting the truth in order to exalt our own community. Therefore, we are called to continuous repentance and ongoing correction. When a critical perspective—say a sociological study of the church, or a Marxist interpretation of the church's interests—confronts us with judgments of the injustice of our actions or the racism, sexism, or classism of our institutions, we need to listen. We find it "necessary to accept the external views of ourselves . . . and to make these external histories events of spiritual significance, . . . occasions for active repentance" (MR, 84–85).

2. Reiteration of Our Experience in Other Communities

The living God who is revealed within our history is the Creator of far more than we know, beyond our subjective values. Therefore,

> just because the Christian community remembers the revelatory moment in its own history, it is required to regard all events, even though it can see most of them only from an external point of view, as workings of God . . . and so to trace with piety and disinterestedness . . . the ways of God in the lives of men. Thus prophets, for whom the revelation of God was connected with his mighty acts in the deliverance of Israel from bondage, found the marks of that God's working in the histories of all the nations" (MR, 86–87).

This continuous process of correcting our understanding resembles the

157

verification process in any scientific undertaking. It tests hypotheses for their ability to make sense of ever wider groups of phenomena. Michael Walzer, whose method in many ways resembles Niebuhr's, calls this the method of reiteration:

> We know that . . . we have genuine national unity and a real nationalist movement [in Israel]; why should we assume that these do not exist among the Arabs? We must try to see the world from the perspective of the other. It is important to stress, however, that this is the very opposite of another [Kantian] commonplace, which enjoins us to step back from every particular perspective, to detach ourselves, to take a God's eye view of the world. The first mode, stepping into rather than stepping back from, is the more modest enterprise.[51]

Reiteration invites us to walk in the shoes of another community. When we see others reiterating our experience in the Exodus, for example, it confirms or corrects the truths we see from within our community.[52] Reiteration is not the same as Kantian universal rationality. Our own history is particular, concrete, rich in detail and drama, not reducible to a universal principle. We should accord the same right to others' histories, refraining from reducing them to a universal principle or to exactly the same experience we have had. Reiteration has universal intent, but expects and respects local differences.

3. Our Own Critical History of Our Community

In the central Christian drama, disciples misunderstand Jesus' teachings, betray and deny Jesus, and need confrontation and correction. We cannot exempt our community from the sin and finitude that characterize all other human communities. We must write an external history of our own community to show how it is one in its humanity with "a Judaism to which it often, in false pride, feels superior"; and with mystery faiths, feudalism, and capitalism; and "to know itself as the chief of sinners and the most mortal of societies" (MR, 88f.).

4. Critical History of Events and Practices that Shape Us

Christian faith is about events and experiences that happen within history and that are open to historical testing. It is embodied in books, monuments, documents, the Bible, and the practices of Christian groups and the institutional church, and these can be investigated critically and assessed from nonchristian perspectives (MR, 89–90). Jesus is thoroughly human and mortal—a teacher from Nazareth who gets hungry, tired, and angry, and becomes a victim of the Roman Empire's method of torture, terrorism, and death for those who threaten it. Christian faith does not claim that Jesus is not human or not accessible to historical study. It claims that in this thoroughly human teacher from a particular village in real history God acted to disclose God's own person and God's will. Jesus is not exempted from historical verification. Furthermore, the Christian community is shaped by its participation in society's practices, including the material conditions of work and domination, war and family structures. Therefore it needs to learn from social analysis of the society's practices and structures that shape its character.[53]

Validating from Within the Community

Faith is not merely subjective: a large community of Christian witnesses checks what we claim to see. Nor is the community always right: Niebuhr describes an interpretive process of progressive validation that resembles psychotherapy for the community. He calls it "continuous *metanoia*" (repentance), "*semper reformandum*," and increasingly extensive and intensive inclusion.

1. Inclusiveness of a God-Centered, Not Self-Centered Drama

The primary source of error is our practice of interpreting whatever we care about as "a dramatic action in which the self is the protagonist." We interpret what others do, and what God does, as aimed at what we want. "The group also thinks of itself as in the center. So all nations tend to regard themselves as chosen peoples." The result is isolation from others, and exclusion of others from the heart of the drama within which we interpret our lives. Our images for understanding "leave great areas of life unexplained" and "lead to confusion and disaster" (MR, 99–102). We understand ourselves with images that exalt our class, race, or nation above others, and that enable us to ignore the injustices we have committed. "We drop out of our consciousness or suppress those memories which do not fit in with the picture of the self we cherish" (MR, 110–14). Their effects endure in class prejudices and race divisions.

If instead our image for understanding is the revelation of the one Lord of all, who both condemns us and forgives us, then "the revelatory event resurrects this buried past. It demands and permits that we bring into the light of attention our betrayals and denials, our follies and sins." Every personal and social history becomes a confession of what we had been ashamed to remember. It becomes a reaching out toward those we have marginalized because of our anxiety, shame, or guilt toward them.

If Jesus is understood as the representative of all humankind and God is understood as the Sovereign of all creation, then "the whole of history becomes our history. Now there is nothing that is alien to us." Niebuhr measures the adequacy of our normative paradigms by their tendency to reconcile communities with one another. Nowhere does he criticize so strongly as where he sees a defensive narrowness that alienates people from one another or from the living God. Central here for Niebuhr is the reconciling action of God in Christ. In the space of six pages, he points out ten times how we are led through Jesus Christ to appropriate the history of others as our own and to include them in our drama of life (MR, 115–21). In Christ's grace, suffering, forgiveness, loving and judging, we are led to accept our own sin and the sin of others, and to affirm others' suffering, loving, and faith as well as we do our own.

2. Responsibility with Transforming Power

Another source of error is our habit of evading responsibility. Niebuhr criticizes "external, non-participating" interpretations of the drama of life, which leave out participative responsibility. He attacks positivism, especially, for ignoring our responsibility and interpreting life as controlled by impersonal forces (MR, 103–8).

We have already seen his search in *The Social Sources of Denominationalism* and *The Kingdom of God in America* for the faith that motivated churches to transform culture rather than conform to it. He advocates "the need of testing the abstract ideas of theology and ethics in the laboratory of history." What he searches for in that laboratory is a transforming, prophetic faith. Every one of his books expresses his hope for a church that is transformationist rather than conformist; and always that means being responsible to God rather than passively allowing external forces to shape its life.

3. Focus on the Sovereign God, Not Another Center of Value

A third source of error is focusing not on God as revealed in our experience, but on lesser centers of value—moral principles or human needs or feelings. Then we define God as the guarantor of those human values. Niebuhr insists that by revelation we do not mean a hypothesis that has only instrumental value. "We mean rather that something has happened which compels our faith and which requires us to seek rationality and unity in the whole of our history. Revelation is like the kingdom of God; If we seek it first all other things are added to us but if we seek it for the sake of these other things we really deny it" (MR, 139).

4. Accurate Description of Revelational Experience

Our false images alienate us from others: they "are unsupported by what other members of [the] community experience;" hence they lead "at last into the frustration of utter solitude" (MR, 99). What is truly seen from the faith perspective can be verified by the community, "that is of all those who occupy the same standpoint and look in the same direction toward the same reality to which we look as individuals" (MR, 141). Biblical study, church history, theology, ethics, and other disciplines all contribute to the communal verification of the revelatory event and its meaning for past, present, and future existence, as does the worship experience of ordinary Christians. They validate, invalidate, or correct our perceptions (MR, 20f. and 141f.). After indicating the great variety of views of what it means to believe in Jesus Christ, Niebuhr concludes:

> Yet this variety in Christianity cannot obscure the fundamental unity which is supplied by the fact that the Jesus Christ to whom men are related in such different ways is a definite character and person whose teachings, actions, and sufferings are of one piece. The fact remains that the Christ who exercises authority over Christians . . . is the Jesus Christ of the New Testament; and that this is a person with definite teachings, a definite character, and a definite fate. . . . The Jesus Christ of the New Testament is in our actual history, in history as we remember and live it. . . . He can never be confused with a Socrates, a Plato or an Aristotle, a Gautama, a Confucius, or a Mohammed, or even with an Amos or Isaiah. . . . There always remain the original portraits with which all later pictures may be compared and by which all caricatures may be corrected (C&C, 12–13).

I conclude that as long as Niebuhr remained consistent with his rejection of Kantian universal rationality and Kantian agnosticism, he developed a strong basis for theocentric ethical norms that can be historically concrete and full of the rich character of historical events, historical drama and narrative, specific teachings, covenants, and community experiences. He had a basis for concrete, theocentric norms that can give backbone to the authentic transformation he sought. And he developed a method of validation that works within the limits of our historical knowledge—no small accomplishment in our postmodern age of historical relativism.

Seven Concrete, Historically Realistic Processes of Deliverance

So far we have analyzed Niebuhr's discovery of the sovereignty of God and its transformative power, his evaluations of the five types in *Christ and Culture,* and his development of a method of historical realism. These pivotal themes in Niebuhr's ethics have all pointed us in a clear direction for our search for the ethics of authentic transformation. In each case we saw a threefold understanding of the sovereignty of God, the third item being the disclosure of God's character in the historically incarnate Jesus Christ, in the context of the prophetic faith of Israel. The concreteness of Niebuhr's ethics depends largely on the Rosetta stone, God's disclosure in Christ.

Niebuhr began *Christ and Culture* with the section, "Toward a Definition of Christ," in which he sought "a moral description" of Christ. He said our interpretations of "the Jesus Christ of the New Testament" will differ as we look from our different standpoints, but "there always remain the original portraits with which all later pictures may be compared and by which all caricatures may be corrected" (C&C, 12–13; 24–25). How then would we proceed "toward a definition of Christ" for our understanding of the relation between Christ and culture?

We would try to point concretely to "the Jesus Christ [who] is a definite character and person whose teachings, actions, and sufferings are of one piece; . . . the Jesus Christ of the New Testament . . ." (C&C, 12–13). In Niebuhr's words, we would begin with "the original portraits," the Jesus of the gospels. We would not *reduce* the teachings, actions, and sufferings of the Jesus Christ of the gospels either to a set of doctrines about Jesus, or to a set of Enlightenment-style moral principles, or to the conclusions of a revised quest for the historical Jesus *behind* the gospels. Niebuhr's emphasis on "inner history," and on the dynamic presence of God confronting us in the testimonies of our contemporary Christian community to the living Jesus Christ, are right in not reducing Jesus to "external history."

At the same time, however, we would be reminded by Niebuhr not to isolate our inner history from the corrections of external history.

Niebuhr has taught us how our culture and society distort our perception of the Jesus Christ of the New Testament. Our post-Enlightenment, consumerist, economic-power-driven, individualistic, privatistic, secularist, domination-system culture causes our perception of the incarnate Jesus to be distorted in ways we are not even aware of. It causes us to thin out Jesus in order to accommodate him to a culture that is oblivious to Jesus' and our Hebraic roots, oblivious to covenant commitments, oblivious to God's caring for faith and faithfulness rather than to secular prestige, and to God's caring for compassionate, delivering justice rather than for the special privilege of our own kind. Therefore we do need to learn the richness of Jesus' own Hebraic context. We need to root Jesus in his concretely incarnate struggles and conflicts in first-century Palestine. We need to appreciate Jesus' loyalty to the prophetic tradition of Israel, and his transformative corrections of the culture of his time, with its sense of God's distance and silence. We need to learn historically realist discipleship rather than individualist and universalist ahistorical principles; Hebraic covenant community rather than individualistic/privatistic greed; covenant justice rather than secular special privilege. We can learn from those scholars who quest for Jesus' historical context to understand him in the richness of his Jewish and first-century context. We need to correct our own culture's distortions by recapturing some of Jesus' historical concreteness. Thus we would pay attention to what Niebuhr has taught us about historicity, and about the eight ways of validating historical disclosure. We would root our interpretation of Jesus in the historical context of Jesus' time, and in the historical documents that we have (the New Testament) and their historical context (the Hebrew Scriptures and Roman and Jewish history). Our interpretation of Jesus' ethics would be historically located and concrete, and open to historical criticism. Beyond that, we would study different understandings of the meaning of the ethics of Christ in subsequent periods of history to determine which understandings led to transformative and faithful Christian discipleship, and which led to unfaithful conformation to unjust structures. History is the laboratory in which our faith and ethics are tested.

Since Niebuhr wrote, several scholars have given new attention to the historically concrete ethics of Jesus. They have sought to pay attention to the New Testament witness, to its historical and sociological context in the faith of Israel and the early church, and in Palestine and the Roman Empire. In that respect, their methods fit nicely with the historical realism and methods of validation for which Niebuhr argued. We may learn (carefully and critically) from their work and sketch—all too briefly—some of the historically concrete normative practices that they emphasize. We may see these as an extension of the logic of Niebuhr's historical realism, developed in dialogue with recent scholarship. In so doing, we surely conclude that at least the seven following bedrock normative practices are clearly emphasized by the concretely incarnate Jesus. These seven are not exhaustive, but they are fundamental tests of the extent to which we are being faithful to God's revelation in Christ, or are practicing evasion and accommodation.

1. **Not judging, but forgiving, healing, and breaking down the barriers that marginalize or exclude:** In both word and deed, Jesus witnessed to the God of mercy, and invited a remarkable array of outcasts and sinners to participate in community.[54] The legalism that excludes was laid to rest; the mercy that includes stood at the heart of Jesus' new way. In the culture of Jesus' time, people's sickness, blindness, and lameness were blamed on their own sin, and so the sick, blind, and lame were marginalized and excluded. Jesus' healings were acts of compassion, and also of inclusion, peacemaking, and challenge to exclusionary legalism. For example, Jesus said to the paralyzed man who was lowered through the roof, "Son, your sins are forgiven. . . . I tell you, get up, take your mat and go home." The teachers of the law who were observing thought this blasphemy (Mark 2:1ff.; see also Luke 5:12–15; 7:36ff.; 8:40ff. 13:1–17; Matt. 6:12–15 and 7:1–5; John 9:1ff.). Jesus' execution on the cross of slaves and rebels revealed the legalism, unjust domination, and violence practiced by the authorities, and demonstrated Jesus' forgiveness even for the crucifying powers.[55]

2. **Delivering justice:** not hoarding money greedily, but giving alms, forgiving debts, breaking bread together in the common meal, feeding the hungry, announcing good news for the poor, sharing goods, investing money in God's reign and God's delivering justice. These were not mere wishes or ideals, but actual practices in the Galilean villages where Jesus taught, and in the early church. In the time of Jesus, and of the writers of the Gospels, there was great need for economic justice.[56] The Essenes, the insurrection movements, and the followers of Jesus all made thoroughgoing criticisms of unjust wealth and possessions.[57] Furthermore, practices of restoring economic justice were essential marks of the coming reign of God or kingdom of God

in Isaiah 40–66, and Jesus saw God's rule already beginning in these practices.[58] "Do not store up for yourselves treasures on earth, where moth and rust destroy, and where thieves break in and steal. . . . But seek first his kingdom and his righteousness, and all these things will be given to you as well" (Matt. 6:19 and 32–33; See also Matt. 6:1–4 and 12; 18:23–25; 19:16–22; Mark 4:19; 6:30–44; Luke 4:18; 6:30 and 34; 12:13–24; 14:21–23; 16:1–31; 19:1–10).

3. **Evangelism, preaching the gospel and calling for repentance and discipleship**: not timidly seeking honor in society and respect in one's family, but preaching the good news of God's deliverance and calling for conversion and commitment, for repentance and faith expressed in action, for following Jesus. Jesus stands in the traditions of the Old Testament and apocalyptic faith, understood not as end of the world but as dramatic establishment of God's reign. "He proclaims the rule of God which is already beginning in secret. . . . Primitive Christianity took over this conviction: it believed that with Jesus this new world had already begun, even if it is not yet visible. . . . Now is the time for conversion and ethical testing."[59] Now is the time of joy, repentance, and faithful action, the time to share the gospel and call for response. How we respond to Jesus' words now is how the Son of Man will respond to us in the future. Jesus also proclaims judgment on those who reject his words and are of little faith and little obedience; who neglect the weightier matters of the law—justice, mercy and faithfulness; who show by their life that they are not ready for the reign of God; who serve some other God than the Lord. "If anyone would come after me, he must deny himself and take up his cross daily and follow me. For whoever wants to save his life will lose it, but whoever loses his life for me will save it. . . . If anyone is ashamed of me and my words, the Son of Man will be ashamed of him when he comes in his glory and in the glory of his Father and of the holy angels" (Luke 9:23–26; see also 19:9; Matt. 4:19; Mark 1:14–15; 6:6b-13; 8:34–38).

4. **Nonviolent transforming initiatives**: not returning evil for evil but taking initiatives of peacemaking. In Jesus' day, frequent insurrection movements erupted in the countryside and in Jerusalem. Finally the Jewish revolt against Rome resulted in disastrous defeat, Rome's destruction of Jerusalem and the Temple in 70 C.E., and the scattering of Jews as a people without a country.[60] Jesus taught and practiced an alternative strategy that was historically realistic. He directly contradicted the practices of the nationalistic insurrectionists of his time,

affirming and eating with Gentiles and tax collectors, pronouncing woes not on foreigners but on Israel, emphasizing God's inclusive compassion and mercy rather than vengeance—praising a Samaritan, a tax collector, a Roman centurion, and many kinds of sinners, lepers, lame, outcasts, children, women, poor people and Gentiles, who were outside the pale according to crusaders for nationalistic purity. He taught a practice of nonviolent transforming initiatives like that carried out successfully by Jews to reverse oppressive policies of the imperial government in 26 C.E. and 39 C.E., just before and after Jesus' ministry. It was not an impossible ideal, but a concrete practice.[61] It was not mere renunciation, but surprising nonviolent direct action, confronting injustice and hostility, willing to suffer, asserting the dignity of both sides in a conflict.[62] Like his healing of the lame and blind, it was a healing of the angry and hateful, a shalom-making of the body of society and of the spirit. In Hebrew, shalom means both peace and health; it points to wholistic healing. As Jesus' healing brought outcasts into community, so his peacemaking brought enemies into community. "Do not be violently resisting by evil means, but . . . if someone compels you for one mile, go with him two . . ." (Matt. 5:38ff. [author's translation]; see also 5:9; 21ff.; 43–48; Luke 19:42).

5. **Love of enemy**: not vague words and sentiments of love, but "the deed of love . . . : table fellowship, emergency aid, release of debt, healing." Jesus names the neighbor "concretely: tax collector, prostitute, victim of robbery, woman threatened with divorce. . . . He thinks in terms of concreteness."[63] "The new feature is love." Not an emotional bond, but love of enemy and "solidarity with the weak. . . . In this love" God is revealed.[64] By contrast with the resistance movements, "the Jesus movement . . . gradually opened its ranks to foreigners." They found doors opened to them in the Hellenistic cities "because they could offer prospects of a resolution of the tensions between Jews and Gentiles. . . . The Jesus movement was the peace party among the renewal movements within Judaism."[65] "So in everything, do to others what you would have them do to you, for this sums up the Law and the Prophets" (Matt. 7:12). "'Love the Lord your God with all your heart and with all your soul and with all your mind.' . . . 'Love your neighbor as yourself.' All the Law and the Prophets hang on these two commandments" (Matt. 22:37–40).

6. **Mutual servanthood**: not patriarchal domination but community with mutual and egalitarian servanthood.[66] Jesus criticized "the domination system." He initiated an egalitarian community by prac-

166

ticing economic equality, modelling mutuality among men and women, welcoming children, sharing table fellowship with outcasts, breaking down ethnic and racial divisions, and freeing disciples from patriarchal family structures.[67] He initiated an egalitarian community by practicing economic equality, in which debts were forgiven, lending was practiced without expecting return, goods were shared, and the values of prestige were turned upside down. He modelled mutuality among men and women, welcomed children, and freed disciples from patriarchal family structures. "Whoever wants to become great among you must be your servant, and whoever wants to be first must be slave of all. For even the Son of Man did not come to be served, but to serve, and to give his life as a ransom for many" (Mark. 10:43–45; see also Mark 3:31–35; Matt. 15:21ff.; 23:8ff.; Luke 14:7–14; 18:15–17; 22:24–30).[68]

7. **Prayer**: not for show, but for God's will to be done and deliverance to come. Prayer includes facing the evil that is in ourselves. It asks to be allowed to participate in a drama of grace and deliverance in which it is God, not us, who is the chief protagonist.[69] Prayer is not only speaking; it is listening—listening to God's Spirit praying in us.[70] Prayer is for *participation in delivering grace*. The characteristic community prayer is for God to deliver us. The three "thy" lines in the Lord's Prayer pray for God's delivering rule to happen on earth as in heaven:

> Thy name be hallowed;
> Thy rule come;
> Thy will be done.

And the four "us" lines pray for God to deliver us from four concrete threats—hunger, debt, temptation, and evil:

> Give us our daily bread;
> Forgive us our debts;
> Lead us not into temptation;
> Deliver us from evil.

Prayer is asking God's delivering grace to happen; *and* it is participation in that grace and deliverance.

Ethical Norms as Historically Realistic Processes of Deliverance

These seven norms are not legalistic rules, or future ideals, or

167

individual virtues. They are historically realistic processes of deliverance, based on the grace of God's dynamic rule. They fit the criteria Niebuhr has developed intriguingly well.

They are theocentric and grace-based. They are not recipes for perfection or self-righteousness; nor are they the virtues of individuals. They are processes of deliverance, shared in community, that participate in God's gracious, dynamic rule. They are eschatological signs of God's delivering action, already beginning in present action and connected to future promise. Forgiveness and healing, community with mutual servanthood: these are gifts of God's delivering grace as described by the prophets of Israel. Restoring economic justice is an essential mark of the reign (or kingdom) of God, fulfilling the descriptions of that reign in Isaiah 40–66. The good news we proclaim is God's gracious, forgiving presence and deliverance, already beginning to happen, and shaping the future. The repentance and discipleship we teach are participating in and conforming to the shape of God's mercy. Transforming initiatives and love toward enemies are what God does for us in Christ, in which God calls us to participate. Prayer is basking in God's presence and grace, and seeking God's gracious deliverance.

As Niebuhr has written, Jesus' teachings in the Sermon on the Mount are based on the conviction "that God now rules" and that the character of God is mercy. "This divine mercifulness is not for Jesus something added to God's justice; it is the very heart of the goodness with which God is good." What God is, is mercy; and mercy is what God requires of us.[71] Jesus' ethic is based on the grace of God's rule; it calls us to participate in that grace by practicing it.

These delivering processes are historically realistic actions, not impossible ideals. Each includes a social criticism of the vicious cycles engaged in by hierarchies, power structures, and people and communities. In other words, these processes of deliverance do not constitute merely a private ethic of individualistic virtues in a dualism between private and public spheres. They mark the characteristics of God's rule in and over all.

Each of the seven norms is a **dynamic process of deliverance, not a fixed, rigid, static requirement, nor the possession of an institution or a doctrine.** Each has a critical edge that supports independence from ideological captivity by a human system. Each is a process of deliverance from one or another vicious cycle: judging and legalism; hoarding, greed, and poverty; living an empty life whose meaning is darkness and alienation from God; violence and returning evil for evil; antagonistic exclusion; patriarchal domination, status-seeking and living for prestige and hierarchical honor rather than aiding the powerless; praying hypocritically to impress others.

The norms are dynamic processes of deliverance, not legalistic rules that must be repeated by rote, rigidly and unimaginatively in all contexts. They have functional flexibility; they take place in *analogous* ways in different societies. Church feeding programs, government aid for the poor, and advocacy of human rights for persons of all races, nationalities, genders, and classes in our society are the first-century analogues of sharing bread, giving alms, and seeking community-restoring, delivering justice. Evangelism takes different forms in different historical contexts, as does peacemaking. They need to be practiced concretely in a way that fits the needs of people in each society. Their continuity is their faithfulness to God's delivering action. And God, as Niebuhr says, is not the possession of our static doctrines, but the living God who surprises us and calls us to continuing repentance.

The seven norms are **historically concrete and historically realistic practices**:

A. They are incarnational. God's delivering action is not merely a timeless principle, but becomes concrete in these delivering processes, within our history. They are historically situated, concrete, visible actions that God enables people to engage in; to "hear these words and do them" (Matt. 7:24–29. Cf. James 1:20–25).[72]

B. They are not gnostic escape from history but prophetic enactment of the historic tradition of Israel.

C. They are sociologically actual in Jesus' time and the time of the early church.

D. They are not merely wished-for ideals, but are practices embodied in the life of actual communities then and now.

E. They are communally situated practices, not merely individualistic virtues. As Troeltsch indicated, disembodied ideas and official church teachings have little historical impact; first they need to be embodied in church practices, procedures, policies, and structures.

F. They are not isolated one-time acts, but are regularly repeated acts in a way of life. As Larry Rasmussen says, "Practices must be the connective tissue in a whole way of life that *in toto* steadily shapes the participants."[73]

G. They engage the church in creating innovative alternatives to standard operating procedure in the secular society, and thus generate an experiential base for selective support and criticism of specific societal structures and practices.

The seven norms also **meet Niebuhr's tests of validation** remarkably well. They are grounded in the historically particular and concretely situated Jesus of Galilee, in continuity with the prophets of Israel. They are taught by specific writings that refer to historically definite events and locations, accessible to historical testing. They include others in the drama, make peace with enemies, and correct alienating and unjust practices we would prefer not to confess.

The seven practices work within the limits of historical realism. They are based on the central event in our internal history, which calls us to identify with others' histories. Its reconciling characteristic is not its ability to achieve universal agreement beyond historical limitations, but its loyalty to the prophetic faith of this particular Israel and this particular Jesus, which call us to be a "light to the Gentiles" (Luke 2:32; cf. Rom. 1:16, Rom. 11, Isaiah 2:2ff, 49:6, 51:4, 60:3.)

Something like these normative processes is what Niebuhr's emphases on the sovereignty of God and historical realism point to, if they are not blocked by other considerations. In fact, they closely resemble what Niebuhr suggested were the new truths about God revealed in Jesus that revolutionize our morality (see above, p. 154).

Varieties of Ways to Relate These Delivering Processes to Culture

These norms need to take specific shape in different social contexts. What they mean in medieval France differs from what they mean in twentieth-century Kazakhstan. To achieve concrete embodiment and clear communication it may be wise to make at least temporary coalitions between these norms associated with Christ and selected norms in the culture. It may be wise to be "a Greek to the Greeks and a Jew to the Jews." Thus Ernst Troeltsch, Niebuhr's mentor, pointed to three epochs when Christian faith had strong transformative impact: the Augustinian, the Thomist, and the free-church Calvinist period.[74] He concluded that they made such impact partly because each made a synthesis with a set of norms in the culture of their day: St. Augustine with neoplatonic and Constantinian norms; St. Thomas with Aristotle and medieval-feudal norms; free-church Calvinism with democratic, human rights, internationalist and peacemaking norms. The synthesis gave them concreteness and widespread persuasive power. Niebuhr resisted "synthesis," and preferred instead to speak of "dialectical affirmation." Nevertheless, each of Niebuhr's periods of transformative faith did advance a fairly specific diagnosis of problems in their time and did advocate norms that resonated in their culture. The early free-church Puritans diagnosed the problems of hypocrisy, monarchy and religious persecution, and advocated faithful living, democracy, religious liberty, and human rights. The revivalists of the Second Great Awakening diagnosed the problems of unregenerate hearts, loose living, and slavery, and advocated conversion, discipline, abstinence, and the abolition of slavery (KGA, 121, 149, and 155–59). The social gospelers diagnosed the problems of individualism, greed, and corporate power, and advocated social justice, democratic socialism, and radical democracy. The civil rights movement, as well, was clear in its diagnoses of the society's injustices, and clear in its linkage with the tradition of human rights and nonviolent direct action. Therefore we might add one more characteristic of transformative faith to those Niebuhr pointed out: transformative faith selects appropriate ethical understandings in the culture and makes temporary or dialectical coalition with them, thus increasing the concreteness and persuasiveness of its advocacy. John Howard Yoder writes eloquently of our freedom to make these "tactical alliances." We are freed by the incarnation, by God's entry into the particular, concrete history of Jesus, "in his ordinariness as villager, as rabbi, as king on a donkey, and as liberator on a cross" to enter into tactical alliances with particular historical movements in our time.[75]

Other ways of understanding the relation between Christ and culture may want more definite syntheses with cultural norms and not merely temporary coalitions, or may see the danger of losing independence and criticize such coalitions. Some may argue that the seven norms are not practical in our culture and want to dilute or change some of them, while others may see them as absolute laws that should not be changed according to the social context. Some may want to limit the norms to a private realm and bar them from civil society, or limit them to the church or the inner life or a future time. Others will argue they are God's will and God is Sovereign Lord in and over all of life.

171

Some may favor a few of the norms and ignore or argue against some of the others. Some may want to redefine the norms or add a few more. These different interpretations will signal different ways of relating Christ and culture.

These different interpretations should become matters for explicit discussion. I propose that we not dilute the ethics of Christ from the start, before we have brought the question of how to relate them to our culture up on to the table for open dialogue and debate. Instead, we would do better to start with a theocentric, dynamic, and historically concrete Christ. Then let us discuss and debate the practicality and relevance of the ethics of Christ openly. Let us not decide the issue in advance by defining the ethics of Christ abstractly and ahistorically. Jesus' teachings and actions are so striking and memorable because they are not abstract essences but concrete and historically real. Let us begin our discussion with Christ and not a pale reflection.

What I have called delivering processes (or elsewhere, transforming initiatives), John Howard Yoder has called practices, especially in his recent book, *Body Politics: Five Practices of the Christian Community Before the Watching World.*[76] Yoder identifies five practices of the early Christian churches, three of which overlap closely with the delivering processes above, and the other two of which (consensus process under the guidance of the Holy Spirit and dialogical process of conflict resolution) deserve to be included. He also calls them *redemptive* (or dialogical, pastoral, social, and rabbinic) *processes.* Their characteristics are:

A. They are grace-based: "When humans do it, God is doing it. . . . God would at the same time be acting 'in, with, and under' that human activity (Luther). . . . Each is a way God acts. Each of the practices is described as involving both divine and human action, and as mandatory" (pp. 1, 48, 55, 71).

B. They are ordinary human behavior, not esoteric or mysterious; a social scientist could watch them happening (pp. 44 and 71).

C. They are community action of the kind that sociology studies.

   One can extrapolate from each of them into a secular or a pluralistic frame of reference. . . . All five of the practices . . . can be spoken of in social process terms. They can be translated into non-religious terms. The multiplicity of gifts is a model for the empowerment of the humble and the end of hierarchy in social process. Dialogue under the holy Spirit is the ground floor of the notion of democracy.

172

Admonition to bind or loose at the point of offense is the foundation for conflict resolution and consciousness-raising. Baptism enacts interethnic social acceptance, and breaking bread celebrates economic solidarity (pp. 44 and 71–72).

D. They "are described in the New testament as derived from the work of Jesus Christ. . . . Yet this closeness to Jesus does not do without the Holy Spirit . . . or the Father" (p. 44).

E. They all

have a social meaning at the outset. None begins with a statement about inward experience or with conceptual information or illumination from which the social meaning needs to be derived indirectly. Each activity is at the outset—by its nature, not only by implication— social, practical, and public. . . . They are not only political in that they describe the church as a body with a concrete social shape; they are also political in the wider sense that they can be commended to any society as a healthy way to organize (p. 46).

F. They are not rigid and legalistic, but are procedural approaches that "foster flexibility and readiness to approach any new challenge. That frees them from bondage to any one cultural setting; it frees them for evangelical integration into any new missionary context. They are all good news, all marks of the new world's having begun" (p. 46).

It is striking how Yoder has come via his route, criticizing Niebuhr, and I have come via my route, learning from Niebuhr (and Yoder), and we have arrived at a very similar understanding of criteria for an ethics of authentic transformation.

3. What Blocked Niebuhr's Concreteness?

From several different directions and at several different levels, we have seen that Niebuhr's central affirmation of the sovereignty of God depends on the disclosure of God's redemptive action within our real historical experience, in Christ. Likewise, his commitment to an ethic with transforming power requires concrete norms that are theocentric, dynamic, and not reducible to an ideal or an institution, but experienced within our history, in Christ. Concrete historical revelation in Christ is central for the sovereignty of God, for authentic transformation, for the ethics of response, and for Niebuhr's answer to historical relativism.

God as the One Universal Beyond the Many
Historical Particularities

Yet in the decade of the 1950s, something blocked this essential step in Niebuhr's intended trajectory. During that period, he seldom spoke of God's self-disclosure in Christ. He adopted a more abstract and distant language, speaking of God as the One beyond the many, the Universal who is infinitely distant from all particulars, the Source of all Being.

What blocked his concreteness?

The first answer is his decade-long reaction against Karl Barth's exclusive Christocentrism. In an address at Union Theological Seminary in 1960, Niebuhr said that for the last decade he had intentionally leaned in the opposite direction from Barth. He compared theology to riding a bicycle: one needs to keep correcting imbalances by leaning the opposite way. Barth had leaned theology in a too exclusively Christ-centered direction, and so he had leaned in the opposite direction as a counterbalance.[77]

The second force blocking Niebuhr from greater concreteness and historical particularity was his definition of idolatry. He assumed that idolatry is treating the relative as universal or the finite as absolute.[78] Sometimes he spoke of God as The Universal or the One, in contrast to the relative or the many. Defining idolatry in a way that distanced God from everything relative or finite caused him to shy away from affirmations of what is historically particular. It caused him to avoid concreteness in his ethical norms and his description of the content of revelation. This understanding of idolatry resembles Kant's definition of truth as what is universal and not particular, and Kant's rejection of particular disclosure of God. In spite of Niebuhr's clear intention to reject Kant's method, this Kantian residue was always incipient in his thought, and it came into dominance when he reacted against Barth's particularism.

In the 1950s, Niebuhr clearly emphasized the beyondness of the Universal One in a way that conflicted with the historical particularity that he had so clearly advocated. Previously he had spoken of God in concrete, biblical, and historical terms as the living God who acts in history in particular ways, judging our disorder and reconciling us to one another and to God. He had criticized Tillich's definition of God as Being-itself for being too abstract; he wanted more concrete terminology: God as self-in-faithful-action revealed in the history of Israel and in Jesus Christ.[79] He had insisted that God has met us in Christ "not as the one beyond the many, but as the one who acts in and through all things," whose unity is a single will directed toward reconciliation (MR, 183–85).

Yet a tendency toward abstraction was already beginning to show itself in *Christ and Culture*:

> As Son of God he points away from the many values of our social life to the one who alone is good; . . . he points away from all that is conditioned to the Unconditioned. He does not direct attention away from this world to another; but from all worlds, present and future, material and spiritual, to the One who creates all worlds, who is the Other of all worlds (C&C, 28).

This is the passage Yoder criticizes for defining Christ as irrelevant to the world. Niebuhr does immediately say, however: "Yet this is only half the meaning of Christ, considered morally." The other half is the movement of God toward us in Christ.

A few years later, in *Radical Monotheism and Western Culture*, he speaks of God more starkly in terms which he had previously called abstract and pre-Christian. God is the One beyond the many, the principle of being and the principle of value, and the Universal, in a way that rejects the relative and the particular. Niebuhr writes: "When the principle of being is God—i.e., the object of trust and loyalty—then he alone is holy and ultimate sacredness must be denied to any special being. No special places, times, persons, or communities are more representative of the One than any others are" (RMWC, 52; see also pp. 24 and 37, and PCM, 36). If all places and persons are equally non-representative of God, where then is any disclosure of God's character within history? Where is the content of historically specific faith, the structure to our knowledge of God's will? Are we moving back under the sovereignty of Kant and Kantian agnosticism? God seems to become the abstract universal transcendent, so far removed from discriminating relation to concrete history that no "relative value system" can be evaluated as "above the others." (RMWC, 112). We expect Niebuhr to say none is absolute save God, but here he says nothing is even relatively more valuable than anything else.

When God becomes abstract, something more concrete becomes the hero of the drama. That something is faith, and particularly the radical faith called monotheism. Niebuhr says faith as some kind of trust in and loyalty to a cause is an inescapable and universal human necessity (RMWC, 18–23). He defines God in terms of this general sort of faith (RMWC, 24). The central battle now is between monotheism and other forms of human faith. And the incarnation now means "the historical incarnation of . . . *faith* in Jesus Christ" (C&C, 255; italics added). The incarnation is "the coming of radically monotheistic faith into our history, meaning by it the concrete expression in a total human life of radical trust in the One and of universal loyalty to the realm of being" (RMWC, 40 and 42). He almost seems to be falling under his own strictures against the perversion of evangelical ethics—transferring God's attributes to faith. "This seems to happen when faith is separated from its divine object and when the subjective condition of confidence is made the object of trust. Then we say to ourselves that we are saved by faith rather than that God alone saves us."[80] In 1949 he wrote that speaking of faith as gift of God "can easily be perverted into the fido-centric heresy which substitutes faith in faith for faith in God. . . ."[81]

Niebuhr's shift in the 1950s to this abstract perspective may explain what has seemed like a mystery in *Christ and Culture*. In the substantive chapters Niebuhr clearly argues for transformationism, based on the three dimensions of the sovereignty of God. But the concluding chapter denies any preference for any one way of relating Christ and culture. Niebuhr wrote the substantive chapters in 1948 as a series of lectures delivered in January, 1949. Later, when he submitted them as a book manuscript, his publisher asked him to add a concluding chapter. In the intervening time (the book was published in 1951), his reaction against Barth took over, and his sovereign God became almost equally distant from all types of Christian ethics. This is what Yoder criticizes as equiprobalist relativism.

Concrete Norms for Peace and War

We can see the effect of this shift by comparing Niebuhr's writings on peace and war before and after 1950. We can, in other words, test its effect on his ethics in the laboratory of history.

In the 1930s he wrote essays critical of nationalism and warned of Hitler's danger. In 1932 as his turn to the sovereignty of God was just beginning, he and his brother Reinhold engaged in a debate about how Christians in the United States should respond to Japanese military attacks on China.[82] Reinhold misinterpreted him as arguing that the

United States ought to do nothing. H. Richard had simply *assumed* we were in a situation where "we seem condemned to doing nothing," and wrote about the intriguing ethical question, "How shall we do nothing?"[83] His answer, characteristically, focused on how to interpret what was going on. He saw God both judging and redeeming, through economic forces, race relations, and revolutionary changes. His judgment/redemption paradigm supported a concrete ethic. It led him to confess U.S. economic, nationalist, and hypocritical interests. It gave hope for active preparation for change, when change would become possible. He criticized nationalism and capitalism, advocated international ecumenical conferences, and called for self-analysis, repentance, and forgiveness. He argued that we should choose either realistic coercion as Reinhold does, or consistent Christian pacifism, but rejected idealistic arguments for pacifism as the most effective means to utilitarian ends.

In 1942 and 1943 he wrote a series of articles interpreting World War II as judgment and as crucifixion.[84] Basing his analysis on the action of the sovereign God as Creator, Judge, and Redeemer gave him a theological/ethical way of interpreting the experience of war. He alluded to specific actions and teachings of Jesus Christ, the incarnate teacher, the crucified victim, and the resurrected Lord and giver of hope. He called for mercy after the war, and for more attention to political action, justice, and social structures. He also called for specific, concrete practices: acknowledging our wrongness and participation in "that whole series of past acts and present desires . . . which in the order of creation led to the consequence of war"; repenting for American nationalism, greed, self-righteousness and isolationism; refraining from judging and condemning each other; pressuring states to limit the destructiveness of war; praying for all people including our enemies; empathizing with the powerless and the innocents on whom the suffering of war falls as much or more than on the evildoers; administering relief to all the sufferers of war; pushing for clear declarations that the aims in war focus on the protection of the weak; making the actions of war fit the declared aims; not withdrawing while our weaker neighbors remain imperiled; waging war in a way that enables a just endurable if not a just and durable peace to result; and hoping for reconciliation rather than vindictiveness after the war is over.

After the war he wrote two additional articles arguing that the church in the United States cannot announce the mercy of God without pointing out how this nation transgresses the limits assigned to us when it defrauds the Negro and refuses to condemn itself for the indiscriminate manner in which it made war in its use of obliteration bombing, or deals with defeated nations in the spirit of retribution rather than of redemption.[85]

When we turn to the decade of the 1950s, however, we notice a puzzling lack of essays on nationalism and peace and war. This is the decade of the Cold War, the Korean War, the McCarthy anticommunism crusade, the growth of the United Nations, and many decisions by the United States about new responsibilities in Asia, Europe, Africa, and Latin America. It is a period of struggle for arms control and a nuclear test ban. Yet none of these problems appear in Niebuhr's writings. His silence contrasts curiously with his prophetic calls in the previous decades to resistance against Hitler, to repentance for obliteration bombing and racial injustice, to equal justice for Germany and Japan, to compassion for war's victims, to reconciliation with all.

The fifth chapter of *Radical Monotheism* does discuss "Radical Faith in Political Community"— something like civil religion—in very general terms. But it lacks discussion of specific issues, norms or advocacy.

Niebuhr's ethics, as seen from the many different angles we have examined, requires knowable structure and content in God's self-disclosure in Christ. That is what his reaction against Barth, or the Kantian residue still in his thought, caused him to shy away from in the '50s. In 1935 he had written: "So long, of course, as the church has no faith in a divine revolution and no strategy of its own for participation in that revolution it will need to commit itself to some other revolutionary faith and strategy or remain conservative."[86] The image of the divine revolution and the strategy and tactics for participation in it seem to be missing from *Radical Monotheism* and weakened in other writings of the 1950s. An adequate ethic for authentic transformationism needs that image and that strategy.

The increased abstractness of Niebuhr's ethics in the 1950s also may have exacerbated the problems Diane Yeager has identified. In the previous decades Niebuhr had done more social analysis and more critical analysis of power structures. When his thought became more abstract, it also became less historically and socially critical in the senses Yeager discusses. Similarly, Elizabeth Bounds writes: "Especially in his later writings, the particular historical community became more and more abstract until it seemed to disappear behind 'a universal society and a universal generalized other, nature and nature's God.'"[87] Niebuhr's critical assessment of economic interests and structures, and of racial injustice, also became more silent and less critical.

The Rock and the Rosetta Stone

Another problem became more painful for Niebuhr in the 1950s. He had written of the sovereign God as "the Rock against which we beat in vain," the all-determining power who causes all that we experience to happen. The Protestant faith that he commended speaks of God's rulership as absolute and as temporally immediate (KGA, 25–26). God is the all-determiner; God is to nature as a hand is to a glove.[88] This radical affirmation of God as the all-doer and all-determiner was partially balanced by his affirmation of God as revealed in Christ the Rosetta stone: some kinds of evil and tragic power that we encounter surely are not the will of the God whose character we see in Christ.[89] Yet Niebuhr did not spell out very fully what that character is. He said that "the power of God is made manifest in the weakness of Jesus, in the meek and dying life which through death is raised to power. . . . We cannot come to the end of the road of our rethinking the ideas of power and omnipotence. . . . His power is made manifest through weakness and he exercises sovereignty more through crosses than through thrones" (MR, 187). We recognize here a tension that he cannot finish rethinking. He frequently mentions suffering as needing more adequate interpretation (for example, MR, 120–22, 124, 125, 128, and 130).

During the 1950s, when he radically de-emphasized Christ as the Rosetta stone, God became the all-determining power encountered universally in all power, and the One Beyond. The result was a painful struggle with the problem of evil. God as all-determiner was hard to trust in the face of tragic evil that Niebuhr experienced both personally and historically, and that we experience. Only if the character of the kinds of actions that God intends is known to us can we say of some bitter cruelties and tragedies: "Those are not the kinds of actions God intends. God intends reconciliation not alienation, love not hate, peace not destruction, justice not injustice, healing not affliction." In the conclusion to *Christ and Culture* Niebuhr identifies God with "the power we call fate and chance." He asserts that in Christ we are convinced that this same power is loyal and trustworthy. But he offers no indication of how this conviction modifies our concept of God's power (C&C, 254–56). To do so, he would need to say more about the character of God as revealed in Christ.

Testing in the laboratory of history leads to the conclusion that Niebuhr's reaction against Barth and his holding back from emphasizing concrete norms revealed in Christ weakened his ethics and troubled his theology. This conclusion has wide implications because very many Christian ethicists have been influenced by Niebuhr, and by Niebuhr's reaction in the 1950s. Others of us are influenced by the presence of many different religions and faith perspectives. If historical diversity leads us to flee historical particularity and seek a universal perspective, it is likely to lead to the kind of abstractness, and the loss of prophetic edge, that happened to Niebuhr temporarily in the 1950s, and that was always lurking at the door.

The Incarnate Jesus as the Way to Correct Exclusivism

We can ask whether there is a way around the obstacles that blocked Niebuhr's intended trajectory. We can ask how to follow Niebuhr's historical realism to its conclusion, affirming concrete norms for an authentically transforming ethic, without succumbing to Barthian exclusivism or our own idolatry.

What had Niebuhr found so needing correction in Barth? In 1931 he had praised Barth's realism. He praised Barth for opposing Kant's agnosticism and for advocating a realism that affirms God is known and experienced in Christ. Barthian theology's "realistic interest and its critical method remain . . . the source of its religious strength." But he criticized Barth's exclusivism, his decision to exclude all other historical experience and limit knowledge of God only to revelation in Christ. The result is "a Kantian agnosticism in which God remains forever unknown," except in a Christ-centered revelation. Therefore the revelation in Christ cannot be confirmed by other experience.[90] Theology, impervious to correction by other experience, "tends to become a dogmatism."

In a meditation in 1953 at Union Theological Seminary, he lamented that the Lord's Prayer "has become the prayer of an exclusive group, so that the prayer which was the prayer of a Jew has become the prayer of Christians, and Jews, who find themselves in this community, feel themselves excluded when this prayer is prayed." Again, the problem is exclusivism. Niebuhr's solution is to confess that we lack the full sincerity to be able to pray this prayer; only because Jesus represents us and prays it for us can we pray it. We pray it as part of the people whom Jesus represents and prays with—not only Christians praying to a Christian God, but all humankind, on whose behalf Jesus prays, asking for daily bread and deliverance from evil for all of us.[91]

In 1962, Niebuhr repeated the criticism in words that remind one of his criticism of the "Christ Against Culture" type in *Christ and Culture*. In fact, his criticisms of that type may have Barth partly in mind, which would help explain the inaccuracies Yoder rightly points out. Tolstoy and the Mennonites did not claim they were doing without culture. But listen to Niebuhr on Barth:

> In our time the effort to achieve a completely Christo-centric and solely Christo-morphic form of thinking and acting has been . . . Karl Barth's theology. . . . Barth . . . attempts to dismiss all analogies, all metaphors, all symbols from Christian speech and conduct except Jesus Christ. But, of course, he cannot interpret the meaning of Jesus Christ without the aid of other metaphors and symbols . . . (RS, 158; see also RMWC, 59–60).

The result, Niebuhr says, is exaltation of the Christian religion over against other religions and even Judaism. This is the kind of exclusivism and divisiveness that Niebuhr's method of validation, and Jesus' inclusive love, must reject (PCM 31, 44–46).

There is an ironic twist in Niebuhr's metaphor of theology as a bicycle that gets off balance, and his decision to lean in the opposite direction to correct Barth's lean. When a bicycle gets off balance, the rider actually turns *toward* the lean, and then steers it right. Niebuhr could have turned toward a discussion of Christ's normativeness, as in *Christ and Culture* (pp. 11ff.), and then could have steered our understanding of Christ right. Niebuhr did not need to avoid his previous emphasis on Christ as the Rosetta stone that clues us to the workings of God in history (MR, 154). He could have pointed to the incarnate Jesus Christ's practices of breaking down barriers that exclude, and love of enemies (pp. 164 and 165 above) as the corrective. He could have affirmed that our knowledge of God in Christ always calls for correction by the methods of validation described in *The Meaning of Revelation*. This he began to do in his very last writings.

Niebuhr offered a similar criticism of exclusivism in an unpublished 1957 essay criticizing ecumenical theology (1) for not being fully trinitarian, and (2) for making Christ the possession of the church:[92]

(1) We interpret "Creator and Spirit only through Christ and not Christ also through Creator and Spirit. . . . We do not in this limited perspective take much note of the work of Jesus Christ outside the church or of the obedience rendered to him on the part of those who do not explicitly call him Lord. . . ."

(2) "We tend to define Jesus Christ by his relation to the church only. . . . We are in peril of worshipping the principle of our Christian unity, not the principle of the unity of being."

To correct these problems, Niebuhr leans toward the Christ of the New Testament: "Jesus' observations about the losing and finding of life, about seeking first the Kingdom, and about those who say, 'Lord, Lord' ring in one's ears at such a moment." And he emphasizes that Christ's orientation is toward God and the world, not simply toward the church: "We are not that part of the world to which Jesus Christ has come in human form, but we are that part of it which recognizes him as sent from God to redeem the world. . . . We are not Christ. But we identify ourselves with the Christ who had identified himself with" humankind.

These corrections do not suggest turning away from Christ, but defining Christ rightly. We should define Christ as the incarnation of God the Father and Holy Spirit who is active in the world outside the church. This is the first principle of the sovereignty of God, God's rule in all. Christian ethics is not only for the church but for the world as well. We should define Christ not as the church's possession, but as pointing toward the living, dynamic God, who is far more than the church's idea of God. This is the second principle of the sovereignty of God, the dynamic independence of the living God from possession by any human system.

We learn from Niebuhr a method of validation and correction that engages us in a process of continuous reformation. It is not a process of downplaying the particularity of the revelation in Christ. The eight steps of validation that Niebuhr developed are based on the core of who Jesus is and what Jesus taught: repentance, faith, God-centered disclosure within history, inclusive reconciliation and love of enemies, rule over all. Christ is not our possession. Christ calls us to repentance based on the good news of the rule of God.

Those who assume that the way to be inclusive is to speak only in universal categories want to de-emphasize Christ and specific Christian teachings. The resultant abstract language, however, lacks particularity and piety; it fails to move many persons; it lacks the transforming power of those times of prophetic faith that Niebuhr studied; and it produces churches lacking in converts and commitment. Furthermore, it often causes a fundamentalist backlash against God-denying modernity—in Christian, Muslim, Jewish, and Hindu communities.

Niebuhr's method of communitarian validation accepts the limits of our historical situatedness and the gifts we are given there. Christian inclusion and Christian opposition to jingoism, racism, classism, and sexism are based not on being ashamed of the particularity of the concrete life and teachings of Jesus, but on loyalty to that historically particular Lord who calls us to practice forgiveness, justice, inclusiveness, transforming initiatives, love of enemies, prayerful acknowledgment of our own sin, and sharing the good news with others while listening to their deeper concerns and acknowledging God's presence among them. We do not become open to others by renouncing Christian particularity and expecting others to renounce their particularity, thus limiting our conversation only to thin and abstract universal principles; we meet one another far more deeply when we affirm each other's own peculiar particularity.

So it was Dietrich Bonhoeffer, whose understanding of God was strikingly Christ-centered, who first and most clearly opposed Hitler and defended justice for Jews. He based his resistance on the Jewish humanity of the incarnate Christ, and on what Christ teaches in the Sermon on the Mount. And so Adolfo Pèrez Esquivel, Nobel Peace Prize winner for his work in Latin America, writes:

> We cannot agree with those of our brothers and sisters who seek to reduce the gospel to a message of false universality—bland tidings to all in the same tone that blissfully washes out the differences between rich and poor and speaks as if there is no difference between a rich Christian and a poor Christian. Such an insipid gospel can never be the leaven of resolute action for justice and the liberation of our people.
>
> We cannot resign ourselves to a church unity based on an abstract universality, on a colorless, odorless, and tasteless gospel of equality among all human beings that takes no account of social, economic, and cultural differences. Our love for the unity of the church must drive us forward together in search of a full gospel, a gospel read in its totality—not a mawkish message in which all differences vanish into thin air. . . . This kind of unity would be the very contrary of the eschatological unity in fullness for which Jesus prayed.[93]

We can reach a similar conclusion by reexamining Niebuhr's definition of idolatry. He saw idolatry as a violation of God's universality, as treating the finite and particular as if it were absolute and universal. This led him to shy away from historical concreteness, in spite of the powerful logic of his historical realism. By contrast, the biblical prophets and the Torah speak of God very concretely. God sees with compassion and hears the cries of the oppressed in particular historical situations, entering into covenant to deliver them, and performing specific deeds of deliverance. God becomes particular, historical, limited, and relative in these actions of deliverance. God gives specific covenant stipulations for our actions. The prophets declare, "Thus says the Lord"—and what the Lord says is not vague and abstract. Jesus speaks and acts in the prophetic tradition, concretely. He points out specific sins, heals specific people, breaks down exclusive barriers, forgives particular sinners, and teaches a concrete way of life, with authority.

Gerhard von Rad explains that the point of the prohibition against idols cannot be merely that God transcends finite representations; the other religions knew that. "The pagan religions knew as well as Israel did that deity . . . transcends all human ability to comprehend it, and that it cannot be captured by or comprised in a material object." Rather, the point is how, where, and when God and God's character are revealed. What the image is about is how God chooses to be revealed, "for the image is first and foremost the bearer of a revelation." The key is that Yahweh is disclosed not by an idol but by a word, the word of the promise to deliver and the word of the covenant at Sinai.[94] Idolatry is to claim that God, God's character, and God's will are revealed in some image rather than the way God has chosen.

Similarly, the *Anchor Bible Dictionary* defines idolatry by referring to Deuteronomy 4:12–18, which

> declares that because at Sinai the people saw no shape (*temuna*) but only heard a voice, they were not to make an image (*pesel*) in the shape (*temunat*) of any idol (*kol samel*). Since the context has to do with the way God chooses to manifest himself, the point of the passage seems to be that God makes himself known to his people through words rather than through a form. . . . His self-disclosure came through a revelation in words, and the Sinai experience constituted a paradigm of God's self-disclosure to Israel; thus images were prohibited.[95]

The biblical polarity is not the abstract absolute One versus the relative many, but the particular character and will of Yahweh manifested in God's word in the Exodus and at Sinai versus God's character as portrayed in an image fashioned by human hands. The way to avoid idolatry is not to be vague and avoid concreteness; it is to be faithful to God who hears the cries and sees the needs of the oppressed, delivers them, and enters into covenant with the people. And it is to refuse some other depiction of the character of God. *The prophetic faith corrects idolatry by speaking of God and justice concretely, in order to guard against idolatrous accommodation of God to cultural corruptions of greed and injustice.* The prophets and Jesus corrected idolatry not by insisting on God's abstractness, but by speaking so concretely and specifically of God's will and God's actions that the hypocrisy of idolatry stood naked in God's presence. They emphasized the plumb line of God's covenant, the content of God's delivering justice, the shape of God's merciful compassion. The interests of greed, injustice, and domination always try to silence the prophets: the more abstract and vague God's will is made to seem, the better. The way to correct the greedy idolatry of our time is not to drain Christ's teaching of concreteness, but, as Wyatt Tee Walker says, "to make it plain."[96]

In spite of all Niebuhr's corrections of Kant's detached universal rationality and agnosticism, a Kantian residue still remained in his assumption that the antidote to idolatry was to speak of God as the Absolute Universal Infinite One over against the historical, particular, and finite demonstration of the shape of God's faithfulness. That assumption hindered him from the concreteness in ethics that the historical realism of his method required.

Incarnational Correction Fits Historical Realism

We can learn a similar lesson from an important essay by Niebuhr's mentor in historical realism, Ernst Troeltsch. In "The Significance of the Historicity of Jesus for the Faith,"[97] Troeltsch argues that the history of religions shows that vital and healthy religion needs community; it cannot be simply individualistic. Furthermore, religion can be strong only if it worships "God in a community whose concrete form is determined by God." That requires a central figure, which for Christianity means Jesus. Therefore the effort of Kant and Hegel to define faith as an idea based on rationality and held by individuals, abstracted from its historical basis, "renounces whether consciously or unconsciously *all* forms of community," and is bound to fail.

185

"One perfectly clear result of the history and psychology of religion is that in all religion what really counts is not dogma and idea but worship and community." A law of social psychology is that individuals need communities and "these need a concrete focus. . . . In the religions of spirit it is the prophets and founder personalities who serve as archetypes, authorities, sources of power and rallying-points. . . . That is why all the great religions of spirit consist in reverence of their founders and prophets." The Christian faith

> must therefore always centre upon gathering the congregation around its head, nourishing and strengthening it by immersion in the revelation of God contained in the image of Christ, spreading it not by dogmas, doctrines and philosophies but by handing on and keeping alive the image of Christ, the adoration of God in Christ. So long as Christianity survives in any form it will always be connected with the central position of Christ in worship. It will either exist in this form or not at all. That rests on social-psychological laws which have produced exactly the same phenomena in other religious areas and recur a thousand times over on a smaller scale up to the present. . . . Lectures on religious philosophy will never produce or replace a real religion.[98]

And because in our time people think with "a fundamentally historical mode of thought," the understanding of Jesus and Jesus' teaching must be able to be validated by

> historical critical research. . . . Not all the details . . . are at issue here, but the basic facts—the decisive significance of Jesus' personality for the origin and formation of faith in Christ, the basic religious and ethical character of Jesus' teaching and the transformation of his teaching in the earliest Christian congregations. . . . [99]

Recovery of Theocentric
Incarnational Discipleship in the 1960s

What Niebuhr wrote in the 1950s was not his last word. His last writings took a new turn, pointing toward a more incarnationally concrete way to begin to resolve some of the problems.

In his Earl Lectures at Riverside Church in New York City in the winter of 1962, his final writing before his death, Niebuhr leaned back toward Christ as "symbolic form with the aid of which men tell each other what life and death, God and man, are *like*; but even more he is a form which they employ as an a priori, an image, a scheme or pattern in the mind which gives form and meaning to their experience" (RS,

154ff.). He quotes and interprets "the story Christ told which ended in the well-known statement, 'Inasmuch as you have done it to one of the least of these my brethren you have done it unto me.' The needy companion . . . is a Christo-morphic being, apprehended as in the form of Christ." He interprets life through the cross. He commends "Christians who think of and, in part, conduct their lives as imitations of Christ, as conformities to his mind; who follow him, are his disciples, live, suffer, and die with him."

He still criticizes the exclusiveness of Barth's theology, but reinterprets the meaning of responsibility with "the symbolic form of Jesus Christ—that is what makes them Christians" (RS, 162ff.). The incarnation becomes once again, not merely the incarnation of faith, but the incarnation of God (RS, 163). He interprets God's actions through Jesus' statement, "It is not the will of the Father that one of these little ones should perish"; and through Jesus' peacemaking teaching about God causing the sun to shine on "criminals, delinquents, hypocrites, honest men, good Samaritans, and VIP's without discrimination," and the rain to fall "on the fields of the diligent and the lazy." He writes of Pilate, Judas, and "the ethos of Jesus," understood not via Platonic, Aristotelian, Kantian, or universal utilitarian ethics, but through the Hebrew Scriptures, the prophets and the Psalms—and also Stoic ethics—as ethics of response to God. Christ is the one who reconciles us with God, enables us to call God "Father," and rejects fatalistic, deterministic understandings of God (RS, 173 and 176ff.).

Reflecting his struggle with God's power and evil, he states flatly that without Jesus Christ "the Christian can no longer imagine, or know, or believe in the Determiner of Destiny." He emphasizes that in the story of Joseph in Genesis, in the account of the Assyrians in the tenth chapter of Isaiah, and in the role of Pilate in the Gospels, we learn that we must reject a fatalistic understanding of God as all-determining. These other powers intend to do evil that God does not intend (RS, 155, 164–6, 168–9, and 173). He returns to the more personal and Christ-disclosed character of God.

He also suggests the resolution of the tension between the universality of God and particular revelation. The universality of God is not an abstract concept. It is God's character as seen in the reconciling action in Jesus Christ, working for the reconciliation of all. God's character is not abstract, universal transcendence, but active creation of universal, inclusive community (RS, 86–89). Niebuhr speaks of the oneness of God less as the One beyond the many and more as "the One who acts in all the many" (RS, 173). God's universality is neither determinism nor disparagement of the relative. The universality of God means that the ruler of all being is working in all events to create universal community, to reconcile us to God, to the world-community God is creating, and to all persons. Our distrustful understanding of the character of God's power is changed by Christ. "This one is our physician, this one is our reconciler to the Determiner of our Destiny. To whom else shall we go for words of eternal life, to whom else for the franchise in the universal community?" (RS, 177–78—the concluding words of Niebuhr's last public lecture).

In the same year, Niebuhr published his last essay: "The Illusions of Power."[100] Its text is Isaiah 10, the text he had just cited in the Earl Lectures to clarify that the evil the Assyrians and other wielders of power intend to do is not what God intends to do. "Through all the tragic story of the nations, including the story of our times, including the central, wonderfully symbolic history of the Cross of Christ, this word of God, this word about God, resounds: 'You thought to do evil, but I thought to do good. . . .'"

Niebuhr becomes concrete again about peace and war. He attacks our self-righteousness in the Cold War: Isaiah is saying God uses our enemy no less than us to do good, in spite of their sin and ours. God uses the pressure of our enemy to coerce us into "trying to overcome the deep injustice of discrimination against the Negro, an injustice by our own standards. . . . The covenant of equality lies at the basis of our national existence, though we have violated it from the beginning." God uses the pressure of our enemy to deliver us from our isolationism and to reconcile us to other nations. "Under the pressure of that inconvenient instrument—communism—in the hands of the Almighty, we have even learned to practice some love of other enemies and have not been permitted to maintain long hatred against Japan or Germany, or even against those so-called neutrals."

He sees God working in history to create a more united humankind, an international community. The Sovereign is working to reconcile, and this is our hope. Niebuhr follows Isaiah as he interprets the Cold War: the Russians are humans, not gods; they are a powerful threat now, but their power will pass as all powers do. He calls for a strategy of self-reformation in accordance with our own laws and promises, as well as for self-defense against the enemy. He calls for trust in "the one who makes us whole, who heals our diseases, who makes right our iniquities, who saves our lives from destruction."

Here is Niebuhr's last word. He returns to the more concrete understanding of God as revealed in the prophets, especially Isaiah, and in the Jesus Christ of the New Testament, who quotes Isaiah more frequently than any other prophet. He begins again to speak prophetically, concretely, of power structures and peacemaking. Here is the direction we should go in speaking of the "Christ" of Christ and culture.

We can learn from this that Niebuhr was right in his tower experience, in his historical research into the characteristics of transformationist faith, in his criteria for assessing the different ways of relating Christ and culture, and in his analysis of the meaning of revelation within history: prophetic Christian faith affirms God's rule over all, affirms the dynamic, living God who cannot be possessed by our systems, and affirms the concrete disclosure of God's character in Christ within our history and experience. This should be the basis for our description and assessment of different ways of relating Christ and culture. As John Howard Yoder has argued, to abstract from Christ is to produce an abstract Christian ethics.[101]

CHAPTER 4

A New Vision

Glen H. Stassen

1. Authentic Transformation

We owe a very large debt of gratitude to H. Richard Niebuhr for provoking us to clarify our own constructive proposals. Although what we have learned has pointed us sometimes in somewhat divergent directions, nevertheless we have learned far more from him and from each other than we can say. We hope that this process has been of benefit to you, our reader, as well.

Now the question is: what are the implications for an authentically transformationist relation between Christ and culture? Clearly *Christ and Culture* is not simply an impartial description. The three of us agree that Niebuhr wrote an argument for transformationism. He evaluates the types that he describes, and only the transformationist type passes his criteria. We, too, want to be authentic transformationists. But what does that mean?

In what follows, I shall weave together insights and parameters that have emerged from all three of us, as well as from Niebuhr.

The Transformation of Faith

First, authentic transformation means *conversion*. It begins with faith. It means *the transformation of faith* from distrust and idolatry to integrative faith in God. Faith is central for Niebuhr, as Diane Yeager shows—as the sovereignty of God is central.

In many different ways in several of his books, Niebuhr shows that faith is not solely a "religious" phenomenon, but is pivotal for human knowing, for science and politics, and for the formation of selfhood. Faith of some kind is crucial to all human knowing and selfhood. It is certainly crucial for Christians.

In the Gospels, Jesus comes proclaiming that "the reign of God is at hand; *repent and believe* the good news." Therefore, to speak of authentic transformation, one must begin with *repentance and faith*, not with ethics. To teach simply obedience to God's command, or to Jesus' teachings, or to the obligation to bring about social change, is a serious mistake. If Christian ethics is rooted only in conscience and obligation, it becomes a heavy duty, a guilt trip, or a self-righteous habit of judging and blaming. Yet this is how Christian ethics is often understood—as rooted in conscience and duty. Authentic transformation begins with the transformation of faith.

Yet in our individualistic culture, the transformation of faith is usually taken to mean much less than what authentic loyalty to God means. Faith is the response to God whose character is revealed in Christ, in God's covenanting with us. It includes faithfulness not to a vague God in general, but to God whose character is revealed. But our individualistic culture reduces faith to something vague, lacking in real content. Cut off from the discipleship that is embodied in the whole of life, faith becomes the choice of a consumer, not the commitment of a follower.

In the short space that I have, I want to build a case step by step for a much more integrative, wholistic understanding of faith.

1. In his posthumously published book *Faith on Earth* (hereafter referred to simply as *Faith*), Niebuhr shows that faith is a response to another person's demonstration of faithfulness, and hence *faith in God is a response to God's demonstration of faithfulness. That gives it specific ethical content*: loyalty to the character of God in whom it trusts. Furthermore, faith includes our response of faithfulness, loyalty, covenant: "To be a self is to be the kind of being which can and must bind itself by promises to other selves; which must keep faith with others; which in this I-Thou relationship of loyal-disloyal promise-makers trusts and distrusts" (*Faith*, 63). So faith is not merely an inner attitude, but a phenomenon of interpersonal covenant loyalty. It is commitment to a God who covenants, and to the covenant that God is committed to.

2. But our faith is normally distorted and distrustful; *it needs*

192

conversion. Our usual kind of faith is negative faith, distrust. It is the faith of someone fleeing God's presence, fleeing God's judgment. In a sensitive and strikingly insightful analysis, Niebuhr describes how distrust in God is present in us as *hostility, fear and evasion.*

"Overt expression of *hostility* by the self toward the Transcendent, the Determiner of Destiny, is relatively rare." Whenever hostility toward God arises, it is usually repressed (*Faith*, 68). It arises as disillusionment, as the sense that God is manipulating us, not caring about us, disloyal to us. It is often a protest "against Omnipotence on behalf of others" to whom we are loyal and who are being tragically mistreated (p. 70).

Niebuhr was highly reticent about making explicit references to his own experience or his own struggles in his writing. Yet to one who is, like Niebuhr, the loyal father of a handicapped child, there is a subtle poignancy and a directness in Niebuhr's words in *Faith on Earth* beyond what he had written previously. It cries out for notice. His writing of protest against Omnipotence on behalf of others we care about who are being tragically mistreated makes one think of Niebuhr's own handicapped child and his description of the sovereignty of God, which at times insisted that God causes all that is.

If the sovereignty of God as universal Ruler means God causes everything, does this mean that God causes the tragic suffering of the handicapped? Niebuhr's writings show signs of a continuing struggle with the relation of God's sovereignty to the suffering and evil that he experienced.[1] His own struggle enabled him to empathize with the protest he is here describing.

If, on the other hand, God's character is truly revealed in Christ, then God's will is very different from much that happens. God does not cause all the evil that happens; God does not cause all that the powers and authorities do; the character of God's causing is disclosed in Christ's mercy and love, and not in what causes the cruel handicaps of children. Then the sovereignty of God needs to be defined in terms of the character of God as disclosed in Christ, not in terms of a fatalistic belief that whatever happens is God's will.

The fatalism that believes God causes all that happens drives many persons to the hostility toward God that Niebuhr here describes. He writes: "Let the parent think of his child, involved in tragedy . . ." (p. 66). Niebuhr the parent is surely thinking of his own child. Although he chooses Bertrand Russell as spokesperson for the response of hostility, he describes the feeling of rebellion in his own words:

193

If the nature of things is the creation of a transcendent God, then that God is our enemy, and if it is not then the world itself is our enemy, and must be resisted though the fight may be carried on without personal hatred. What we are up against is not something neutral but something that is against us. Hence our proper attitude toward the Transcendent is defiance in the name of humane feeling or of spiritual values (p. 72).

Surely Niebuhr the sensitive theologian is writing of a defiance he can identify with. He seems to be thinking "If my child's tragically debilitating handicap is the creation of a sovereign God . . ."

When Niebuhr turns to the second form of distrust toward God, *fear* and *appeasement*, he speaks of God as the "all-powerful," "the Omnificent" (p. 73). Before "that Transcendent, that Nature of Things," we fearfully ask if our sin or our parents' sin caused our bodily or psychological illness. These are terms for God Niebuhr had affirmed earlier, and inner agonizing he had hinted at but had not previously expressed so forcefully:

> The terrors of conscience which haunt our solitude are to a large extent the terrors of those who confront an angry Otherness in the world which hunts out every secret fault, not with the love of a Master who undertakes to make his work perfect but with the animosity of a defender of personal glory, the vindictiveness of a finite being who can be deprived of power by other finite beings (p. 74).

One's conscience "contemplates with horror the implacableness of an enemy who visits the transgression of the fathers on the children, and it seeks to avoid by appeasement not only the destruction of the self but of those companions in and with whom it has its existence" (p. 75). I know I have sought, by prayer, good deeds, and acts of penance not adequately explained by my own rational theology, to ward off the blows rained on my own child. I think Niebuhr has too. One develops a defensive relation to God in spite of one's conscious theology of grace.

The most frequent of the three forms of distrust is *defensive evasion*, which Niebuhr also calls *flight* or *escape*, and which leads to *isolation* and *forgetfulness* (pp. 50, 76–77, and 99): "And perhaps still more frequently the effort is made to put all thought of that Other out of the mind while the self devotes itself to the little struggles and victories of life" (p. 68). This is

> the defensive mechanism whereby selves try to forget the presence of the ultimate reality while they construct for themselves an imagi-

nary world in which they can pretend to be at peace. . . . The flight from the other is accompanied by the flight from the self. . . . One flees from the ultimate . . . and tries to live among the things that are close at hand with such peace of mind and such pleasure as one can extract from them (pp. 76–77).

In a secular society this evasion of God appears as a religious devotion to getting and spending, a consumerism and materialism that threaten to destroy the very planet our lives depend on, while denying our dependence on what is wasting away. In Christendom it appears "in spiritualism and in Jesus-pietism, or in a worship of the Virgin and saints, and of a kind heavenly Father . . . , which regards death as an illusion, evil as mere appearance," and life as escape (pp. 76–77).

So distrust comes in three forms: it is "manifest in *fear, hostility, and evasion*" (p. 99). Therefore, in our seeking to live lives of authentic transformation, and to correct our misperceptions, distortions, disloyalties and betrayals, we must watch for these manifestations of faith as distrust. The most frequent form is defensive evasion of God's presence. To be authentic transformationists, we must search out the errors we make unknowingly because of the distortions of our defensiveness, and correct them. We must remove the log in our eye. We must acknowledge our own complicity in vicious cycles of defensiveness and projection. *We must repent continuously for our own defensive evasions* and the errors they cause.

3. *The shape of authentic faith comes from Jesus Christ.* Authentic transformation must include transformation of *faith*, repentance at the core of our basic trust/distrust relation to God and our basic loyalty/disloyalty to God.[2] That transformation is not a minor correction of course, but a reversal, a metamorphosis, a turning around, a repentance, a new birth, a death and resurrection.

What Niebuhr called "the reconstruction of faith" comes in "the interpersonal movement of faith that centers in the person of Jesus Christ . . ." (p. 87). "There is a prospect of salvation from diseased faith" (p. 85). But this salvation comes not by having faith in Christianity or the church, nor by believing neutral historical facts about Jesus, nor by faith in Jesus as the founder of a religion or as the object about whom doctrines are taught. Rather, it comes via Jesus Christ who "is personally present as Master and Lord. He is the personal companion who by his loyalty to the self and by his trust in the Transcendent One reconstructs the broken interpersonal life of faith" (p. 87).

Jesus enters into our experience of distrust and disloyalty. Jesus has

195

more faith than we have; he trusts "the Lord of heaven and earth who had thrown him into existence in such a manner that he could be the object of Joseph's and his people's distrust." He trusts God as One who has covenanted to care for the least valued beings, the lepers, the outcasts, the birds of the air and lilies of the field. He is completely loyal and faithful to his neighbors. "He seeks and saves the lost. He spends himself for others—and always with trust in God." Jesus is loyal to others as God is loyal to others (pp. 94–95).

Yet Jesus "was the subject of betrayal." Jesus' inclusive "loyalty to all—Samaritans and Romans, as well as Jews, to sinners as well as righteous, to the despised as well as the esteemed" was distrusted, betrayed, and crucified. His loyalty to God resulted in a suffering death, just as the Suffering Servant Song in Isaiah had predicted (pp. 95–96). "The faith of Jesus Christ came to the end of its historic existence with the cry: 'My God, my God, why hast thou forsaken me?'" Jesus identified with us in our distrust and disillusionment, and we identify with him in his and our deepest struggle and severest despair (p. 96).

And then comes resurrection. The faithfulness of God is yet manifest, in the midst of his and our dark night of despair. "In and through his betrayal, denial and forsakenness, we are given the assurance that God keeps his promises" (p. 97). This is the demonstration of God's faithful character, in which we can trust.

4. *We must not define the structure of faith individualistically—as subjective and passive—but wholistically and participatively as trust, faithfulness, and loyalty.* As Yeager makes clear, if Niebuhr's emphasis on faith turns us inward, away from social change, if it is individualistic, subjectivistic, or quietistic, so that it becomes evasion of God's call of participation in making justice flow down like a river, then it is in fact the evasion of authentic transformation. It is the evasion of the God of the prophets and Jesus.

Niebuhr's understanding of faith, the faith of authentic transformation, must not be understood as inward retreat away from God's dynamic change-making in the world. Faith should be understood as prophetic faith, as calling forth a church that lives in the presence of the living God who is dynamically sovereign.

Niebuhr offers a phenomenological analysis of the structure of faith in human experience that resembles the analysis of the structure of love in human experience by his friend and dialogue partner, Daniel Day Williams.[3] Both made similar criticisms of individualism and subjectivism. Both advocated a social, interactive, relational understanding of faith and love. Both grounded faith and love in God's demonstration of loyalty. Both saw faith and love as embodied in active participation as well as passive reception.

Faith for Niebuhr is not passive individualistic subjectivism, but triadic trust, faithfulness, and loyalty toward God and God's cause.

A. Faith is a response to *a Thou who is trusted, who covenants to be faithful.* "Trust is a response to and an acknowledgment of fidelity. . . . One cannot speak of faith simply as the trust which appears but must speak of it also as the fidelity to which trust is the response" (p. 47; cf. pp. 46–48). He criticizes Kant, Schleiermacher, and Tillich, arguing that the Thou (God in Christ) is personally present, and is not merely an inference from a subjective human experience (pp. 64–65 and 103–104). When Niebuhr writes of the fidelity to which trust is the response, he means the fidelity of Jesus Christ to God, and in turn God's fidelity to Jesus. Elsewhere he speaks of our trustful knowing of a Thou as a friend, a person in our acquaintance; and our trustful knowing of God. In each case, our trust is a response to the Thou's demonstration of loyalty, covenanting to be faithful (pp. 47ff., 50–51, 56–57, 63, et passim). Demonstrating loyalty and covenanting to be faithful include ethical content. They depend on a disclosure of what the loyalty is loyal to, what the content of the covenant faithfulness is. This gives covenant content, specific ways of faithfulness, ethical criteria, to faith. Niebuhr writes of specific ways in which Jesus is faithful to God (see below, pp. 207f.), and writes repeatedly of God's making covenant, binding God to be faithful in the ways the covenant indicates (pp. 41f., 47ff., 50f., 54–57, 103f.). Faith is not merely subjective and empty of content. Niebuhr criticizes Bultmann for seeking "to disjoin existential faith from beliefs about history, nature, and the ethical life." Contrary to Bultmann, faith has the content of "beliefs in the historical actuality of Jesus Christ, as presented in the New Testament" (pp. 10–11).

B. Faith involves *the I who trusts and is faithful, or who betrays that trust.* "As I trust and distrust the other loyal-disloyal self I become aware of myself as one trusted or distrusted by the other in my loyalty and disloyalty" (p. 49). Faith includes my commitment to be loyal and faithful. Almost as soon as Niebuhr introduces the question of religious faith, he contrasts dead faith with living faith. Dead faith "is not relevant to action"; it makes no difference in how people act. Living faith makes a great difference in how we act. It involves "the redirection of the will." It is not only belief in supernatural realities or dispassionate rationalism, but involves "emotion or human impulses toward affection, compassion and justice." Living faith is not only assent to a concept; the whole self—"feeling, seeing, contemplating, acting"—is directed toward the real God "vividly imagined, felt and loved" (pp. 6–8). One senses the influence of Jonathan Edwards, but Niebuhr quotes John Calvin: "Saving faith is that faith 'by which the children of God are distinguished from unbelievers, by which we invoke God as our Father, by which we pass from death to life, and by which Christ, our eternal life and salvation, dwells in us'" (p. 9). It is personal. We must believe the Lord's promises of mercy not only "as true to others . . . ; but rather make them our own, by embracing them in our hearts" (p. 10).

C. Faith *binds us to serve the cause that God is loyal to and that is revealed in God's faithfulness.* Faith in another involves "the objects of loyalty, that is, the causes to which I's and Thou's bind themselves to be faithful at the same time that they bind themselves to each other by acts of loyalty and trust" (p. 58; cf. p. 51). This, too is reciprocal: we do not simply bind ourselves to God's will, but God's will makes claims upon us (p. 59). The structures of faith "point beyond themselves to a cause beyond all causes, to an object of loyalty beyond all concrete persons and abstract values, to the Being or the Ground of Being which obligates and demands trust, which unites us in universal community." (p. 60). In other words, faith in God is commitment to serve God's will.

D. The *community of faith* is present, too, in the faith relationship, as corrector or encourager of continuous repentance. Our faith is faith in God, not faith in the church. But the church nurtures our faith, and it calls us to repentance when we err (pp. 85ff.). Lonnie Kliever first proposed that Niebuhr's understanding of faith and revelation should be diagrammed not merely as a triad, but as a tetrahedron, with God, Christ, self, *and the community of neighbors* present to one another in the faith relationship.[4] Similarly, I emphasized communal verification in Niebuhr's method (above, pp. 159ff.). Faith is not a subjective retreat from community, but a covenant relationship that is confirmed and

198

corrected by a community of co-believers, and by other communities of nonbelievers. Nonbelievers live in other communities with their own kinds of faith—faith in social science, in economics, in Marxism, in positivism, in other religions, etc. From the perspective of their faiths, they see aspects of what the Christian community does that Christians do not notice. We need to listen to the voice of God in their criticisms, too.

In these several ways, faith must not be understood as an inward retreat from God's dynamic change-making in the world. Faith is response to the covenant character of God; it commits the believer to a life faithful to God's character; it calls for continuous correction by communities of diverse faith.

For example, when Jonathan Edwards, Niebuhr's favorite theologian, described the Great Awakening of the eighteenth century as he observed it among his church members,[5] he did not describe faith as merely an inward disposition or subjective feeling in individuals. It began in community, when the youth changed their ways and started spending their Sunday evenings not in frolicking but in worshiping. It began in small groups: the youth "divided themselves into several companies to meet in various parts of the town . . . and those meetings have been since continued, and the example imitated by elder people." Sermons were preached on God's judgment and God's grace, and how to come to be accepted by God and be saved. In December "the Spirit of God began extraordinarily to set in, and wonderfully to work amongst us; and there were very suddenly, one after another, five or six persons, who were to all appearances savingly converted. . . ."

It was a response to God's faithfulness:

Here was a remarkable instance of an aged woman, of about seventy years. . . . Reading in the New Testament concerning *Christ's* sufferings for sinners, she seemed to be astonished at what she read, as what was *real* and *wonderful*, but quite *new* to her. . . . She then cast in her mind how *wonderful* this was, that the Son of God should undergo such things for sinners, and how she had spent her time in ungratefully sinning against so good a God, and such a Saviour; though she was a person, apparently, of a very blameless and inoffensive life.

Edwards says this transformation of faith comes not from the force of "mere legal terrors, but rather from a high exercise of grace, in saving repentance, and evangelical humiliation."

Then comes "some comfortable and sweet view of a merciful God, of a sufficient Redeemer, or of some great and joyful things of the gospel." It comes in various ways: "more frequently, Christ is distinctly made the object of the mind, in his all-sufficiency and willingness to save sinners; but some have their thoughts more especially fixed on God, in some of his sweet and glorious attributes manifested in the gospel, and shining forth in the face of Christ. Some view the all-sufficiency of the mercy and grace of God; some, chiefly the infinite power of God, and his ability to save them, and to do all things for them; and some look most at the truth and faithfulness of God." Some respond to the demonstration of God's faithfulness in the dying love of Christ, or the sufficiency of his blood as atonement, or his obedience and righteousness, or his being the Son of the living God, or the way of salvation by Christ meeting their needs.

It is a conversion from fear and evasion. "As they are gradually more and more convinced of the corruption and wickedness of their hearts, they seem to themselves to grow worse and worse, harder and blinder, and more desperately wicked, instead of growing better. They are ready to be discouraged by it, and oftentimes never think themselves so far off from good as when they are nearest."

And Edwards emphasizes on almost every page that the conversions are the gift of God's dynamic, present action—God's Holy Spirit. Niebuhr's description of Edwards' faith[6] never mentions the Holy Spirit, except once in a quote of Edwards' words, but Edwards speaks of the Holy Spirit on almost every other page. Perhaps Niebuhr is reacting against tendencies in our time to reduce the work of the Holy Spirit to subjective feelings divorced from the faithful character of God, from the sovereignty of God in the world, and from the prophetic dimensions of faith. We forget that it is the prophets of justice and covenant faithfulness in the Old Testament who witness most clearly to the inspiration of the Holy Spirit. But Edwards, and transformative faith, restore the centrality of the dynamic, present action of the Holy Spirit as God's gracious act of bringing us into a participation of faith and faithfulness, love and justice, in what God is doing. This is not a faith that is merely human effort, a faith without God's causing. It is a faith that *participates* in God's gracious giving, God's initiating, the pouring out of God's Holy Spirit. "Conversion is a great and glorious work of God's power, at once changing the heart, and infusing life into the dead soul."

"The Spirit of God has so much extended not only his *awakening*, but *regenerating* influences. . . . These awakenings when they have first seized on persons, have had two effects; one was, that they have

200

brought them immediately to quit their sinful practices; and the looser sort have been brought to forsake and dread their former vices and extravagances. When once the Spirit of God began to be so wonderfully poured out in a general way through the town, people had soon done with their old quarrels, backbitings, and intermeddling with other men's matters. The tavern was soon left empty. . . ." It involved a commitment to a changed way of living, a faithfulness to God's will.

As Niebuhr says, Edwards insisted that "it is necessary to test the authenticity of emotions, to distinguish between what is 'spiritual' and what is merely imaginary. . . . His test was fundamentally a moral one. Emotional experience is specious if it does not issue in genuine love of God and neighbor."[7] Edwards writes: "I have abundantly insisted, that a manifestation of sincerity in *fruits brought forth*, is better than any manifestation they can make of it in *words* alone: and that without this, all pretenses to spiritual experiences are vain. This all my congregation can witness." (He appeals to community verification by his congregation).

At the end of the second awakening, Edwards wrote a covenant for church members to sign, specifying the fruits that are the test of authentic transformation. Its content comes from Jesus Christ, and particularly from the Sermon on the Mount. It begins by saying we repent for our past backslidings and ungrateful departures from God, and humbly beg God for forgiveness and salvation through Christ, and for more gloriously pouring out God's blessed Spirit upon us.

Then, in summary form, it says we covenant to:
- act with justice and righteousness in all we say and do.
- avoid violating justice for private gain.
- avoid doing anything to our neighbor from a spirit of revenge.
- refrain from judging, or speaking ridicule or contempt of others.
- refrain from acting with enmity, ill will, or revenge in our hearts against any of our neighbors.
- be strictly searching and examining our own hearts with respect to enmity or revengeful desires.
- pray for help in rooting out any secret grudge against anyone, that we may all be united in peace and love.
- avoid engaging in freedoms and familiarities in company that stir up lust that we—(especially the youth)—cannot in our consciences think will be approved by the infinitely pure and holy eye of God.

Let me further illustrate this point by telling a little piece of my own experience. My own form of evasive faith has been resentment. I am a person of unusually strong drive, and want to do far too much for my own good or the good of others who live with me. Offered the opportunity to choose whether to do this or that, I try to figure out how to do both. I am always running to catch up, and am resentful that I can not get it all done. I score a one on the enneagram, and a J on the Myers Briggs, which means I want things to be right and I resent it when they are not right. Others may not see the resentment in me, but underneath it is there. My seminary, where I have taught for twenty years, has recently been experiencing wrenching changes in the middle of the culture wars that are polarizing evangelical church life in our nation; many of my friends on the faculty have left or been forced to leave, and many of us have been feeling abandoned, bereaved, angry, despairing. We have been accustomed to being appreciated by our students, and suddenly ideological attacks on all the seminaries in the Southern Baptist Convention have made us feel unappreciated and even resented. I had been grateful to teach there, and it had turned to resentment. My drive, my overcommitment, and my resentment have also hurt my marriage and my parenting. My Christian discipleship has not been what it needs to be in my family, and I have resisted changing. And that has caused yet more resentment.

Friends and family members tell me this is overstated: there is a nicer, friendlier, happier, more grateful side to me, and they are right. But I know there is also this underlying resentment. And I have to confess my resentment has sometimes dried up my relation with God and my life of meditation and prayer.

I wrote my part of this book in New York City, on a sabbatical leave to study Niebuhr, Bonhoeffer, Walzer, the New Testament, and peacemaking. There Rick Carson introduced me to Canaan Baptist Church of Christ in Harlem. Soon my wife and son David were going with me, and we became members. I learned more there that has stayed with me than what I have learned from any scholar.

The worship began with testimonies of gratitude, led by lay members. In fact, gratitude for God's providence, gratitude for the essential gifts of life, gratitude for being able to get up this morning, and for having food on the table, gratitude for God's love and gratitude for Jesus flowed throughout the whole worship service. There I sat newly aware of my own resentment, wondering why I was not more grateful, called to repentance by the gratitude of my fellow church members, knowing I should be grateful but not released to feel grateful as others were. I was evading God's presence because of my own resentment, and underneath that my own lack of Christian discipleship.

I was impressed by people's strong faith in God's providence. We sang "God will carry you through," and the choirs spoke powerfully of God's guidance and protection day by day. "God will take care of you. God will go with you to the end."

The faith is strongly Christ-centered. One favorite song that we still sing in our family, goes:

I want to be a follower of Christ;
I want to be one of his disciples.
I want to walk in the newness of life.
Oh, let me be a follower of Christ.
What do I have to do?
What do I have to say?
How do I have to walk, each and every day?
Tell me what does it cost,
if I carry the cross?
I want to be a follower of Christ.

There is a sense of the presence of the Holy Spirit in the worship, and especially in the singing of the choir, as well as the congregation, and in the feeling dimension of worship. The worship is wholistic and incarnational: head, heart, body, feelings, hands, and togetherness as a community.

Sermons (by Pastor Wyatt Tee Walker) are accurately and concretely exegetical. And they are concrete in confronting the powers and authorities, as well as confronting us church members concretely—our resentments, our daily relationships, our sexual faithfulness, our ministry to those with AIDS or those on drugs, our engagement for justice. In a sermon on tithing, Pastor Walker told us he had just gone through the computer record of our giving. "And I need to tell you, a lot of you deacons on the front row are not giving as you should. I went down some of the letters in the alphabet, and there are members who are not carrying their share." (I was wondering if he would say he had gone down the S's, and noticed the Stassens.... I can imagine others were wondering similarly.) Over 60 percent of the members have pledged to give 10 percent of their income or more. The church has eighty-one employees, most of them serving in the church's housing for the elderly or the poor, or in work with drug addicts, persons with AIDS, and people with other needs. There is a sense of genuineness, not evasion—in proclaiming Jesus' message of justice for the poor and outcast, mercy for the sinner, inclusion and welcome for the outcast, and in actually doing something about it.

When we had participated in several weeks of instruction for new members, and sat up front with the other new members about to be inducted into the church, Pastor Walker was very concrete in welcoming us into the church from the pulpit, calling on the whole congregation to try to remember that "the Stassens may not be like other whites you have known; they may have something different in their hearts; try to treat them accordingly. It may be hard for some of you who have had bad experiences from people who look like them. But the Stassens may be different. Not all people are the same. And these are our members now. Try to treat them accordingly. Make them feel welcome." And they did, in ways that now call forth powerful emotions of gratitude in me.

One day in late January I was walking home from Columbia University Library toward our apartment. A young, slight, Asian American man walked in front of me and turned to go in the same direction, right in my path. I had to slow my step and change my course in order not to walk into him. A very small shift of gait and direction, but it interrupted my drive to get where I was going. Such a small interruption called forth my under-the-surface resentment. I walked faster. I passed him. I showed him my speed and determination (and resentment). I looked left and started to cross the street. I saw the pile of snow and ice in the middle of the street, still there, unmelted, from last week's snow storm, and looked at it, thinking how I had passed him, how I had showed him. Suddenly, he called out: "Look out!" I stopped. A car came speeding through the intersection from the right, one or two steps in front of me. After it sped by, I finished crossing the street, stopped at the curb, turned and thanked my rival for calling out and stopping me. A block later, at Reinhold Niebuhr Place, I stopped and waited for him and thanked him three times, saying, "I don't know if you realize what you just did for me." He said, "I know." By then, I had had a block to think and realize I would surely have been killed or at least seriously maimed for life.

In the next few days, I had time to think gratitude to God, whose providence had given me another half to my life. I prayed: "You have given me this life for a purpose. Dear God, help me to do something worthwhile for you with it." Canaan was surely influencing my prayer life and my sense of gratitude.

In the next weeks, worshiping at Canaan, hearing so many people give their testimonies of gratitude who seemingly had so much less to be grateful for than I had, while I sat there with resentment still in my heart, the disparity became clearer and clearer.

I talked with a wise and confrontive counselor. He surprised me by telling me I am greedy. Not greedy for money but for trying to drive too many directions at once, for not being able to decide to do this one thing rather than several things. I asked my wife, my sister, and my spiritual guide. My sister was more confrontive and my wife more supportive, but I knew my counselor was right. I knew and confessed I had not been the caring husband I should have been, and my wife gave me surprising affirmation and even gratitude far more than I expected or thought I deserved. It felt good.

I was confronted by the concrete, nonevasive preaching and teaching of Pastor Walker, especially as he explained the meaning of Jesus' parables and teachings for our life-discipline. My life in quite specific ways was evading the point in Jesus' teachings. And worship in Canaan was putting me in the presence of God and calling me to repentance.

I finally realized that what almost killed me was that I was being moved down that sidewalk and across that street as if by a strange power—my greed, my drive, my resentment. How else could such a small matter as a man walking into my path cause me to be so resentful, so preoccupied with rivalry, and so careless in crossing a busy street in New York? A deeper awareness and confession of sin ensued.

The story goes on. It is too much to tell. It includes a specific confrontation by Joyce Hollyday at the Baptist Peace Fellowship conference the following summer, some very specific meditation, a concrete repentance and decision to new obedience recorded in writing, a deeply felt prayer for a heart released from resentment and freed to be grateful, immediately followed by a wonderfully thoughtful, funny, and overwhelmingly meaningful gift of gratitude and affirmation from Kevin and Holly Rainwater and other members of our Baptist Peacemaker group that brought forth a pouring of emotion, a movement of the Spirit, a change of heart, and an inward turning from underlying resentment to genuine gratitude that has proved remarkably real and lasting.

Now I carry some of Canaan Baptist Church with me, as do my wife and my son. We still sing Canaan's songs in our family. And we are all enormously grateful for it.

Niebuhr wrote *The Kingdom of God in America* in search of a prophetic faith that does not merely adapt to social forces, but transforms society and culture so they are more faithful to God's intent. When Niebuhr wrote of faith, he was not retreating inwardly; he was looking for a prophetic faith that transforms. That is what we mean by the transformation of faith.

Jesus Christ as Normative for Christian Discipleship

Niebuhr emphasizes Jesus Christ's faithfulness and loyalty as a disclosure of God's faithfulness and loyalty toward all of God's creatures, and he emphasizes God's claim on our response. He also emphasizes our defensive evasion: because of our shame and guilt, we hide from God, we cover up, we pretend God has not taught us what is right (Gen. 2:8ff.). The history of the church, and the history of humankind, are marked by defensiveness and evasion as well as by forgiveness and faithfulness. In many imaginative and often unconscious ways, we have diluted, distorted, reshaped and revised the patterns of faithfulness that are God's will in order to conform them to our resistant practices, or at least to tame them so they do not confront our unfaithful practices so forcefully. We reduce Jesus to a name to be praised and ignore his identification with the teachings of the prophets.

I argued above that the logic of Niebuhr's historical realism and faith in the sovereignty of God, if carried out fully and not blocked by Enlightenment rationalism or our comfortable evasion, should lead to affirming at least seven concrete normative practices or processes of deliverance taught and practiced by the Jesus of the gospels. Authentic transformation should be faithful to norms like these if it is faithful to Christ and not engaged in defensive evasion.

It is interesting to notice that Niebuhr's *Faith on Earth* offers significant pointers in this direction. At the very heart of Niebuhr's description of the reconstruction of faith is Jesus' demonstration of trust in God's faithfulness and loyalty to God's cause. Jesus' trust and loyalty are shown by his deeds and teachings, his moral character shown in actions which reveal God's will and his own faithful obedience. Thus Jesus' deeds and teachings are of the essence of our salvation, of the reconstruction of our faith, and of the faithfulness to which we are called. In two brief passages (pp. 94–95 and 98–100), not at all intended as a comprehensive description, Niebuhr mentions several ways Jesus demonstrates obedience to the shape of God's grace.

Several of them parallel the seven normative practices in intriguing ways:

1. Niebuhr has much to say about **Jesus' love,** seen as loyalty and caring: "By his loyalty to all to whom he trusts the Father to be loyal, . . . he makes himself known to us as one who has the character of a Son" (p. 100). Jesus "chastises them for their disloyalty to each other . . ." (p. 95). "This loyalty to all—Samaritans and Romans, as well as Jews, to sinners as well as righteous, to the despised as well as the esteemed" (p. 95). "His trust is in this Lord of heaven and earth as One who has bound himself to care for the apparently most despised beings, human and animal and vegetable in his creation" (p. 94). The community of faith "is the community in which Christ is the companion in every company, for which not a sparrow falls from the roof top without participation in the death and resurrection of Christ and in which what we seek to do in loyalty to our companion Christ is done in loyalty to the least of his brethren" (p. 109).

2. **Mutual servanthood:** Niebuhr writes that Jesus, "the faithful servant" (p. 100), "is forever warning us about our ambitions to be great" (p. 98). "He spends himself for others" (p. 95). "This forsaken and rejected Servant of God . . . is present with his wounds and in his rejection in all the companions whom in our great disloyalty we make the victims of our distrust of God and our diseased loyalties" (p. 98).

3. **Prayer:** Niebuhr writes that Jesus enables us to trust God enough "so that we pray to the mystery out of which we come and to which we return, 'Our Father who art in heaven'" (p. 99). "He is always here teaching us to pray" (p. 98). The cause to which he is loyal is the rule of the absolutely Transcendent One. His faith is first of all the faith of trust in the Lord of heaven and earth" (p. 94). Jesus directs all trust and loyalty away from himself to the Transcendent (p. 86).

4. **Evangelism:** Niebuhr says that Jesus "seeks and saves the lost" (p. 95). But more, his whole description of Jesus' reconstruction of faith is a proclamation of the good news of God's deliverance and a calling for conversion and commitment, for repentance and faith expressed in action.

5. **Forgiveness and inclusion:** Niebuhr does not mention forgive-

ness directly, but surely it is central to God's loyalty to us as demonstrated in Christ. He does mention inclusion several times in what he says about God's love: Jesus trusts in "this Lord of heaven and earth . . . who has covenanted to care for the apparently most despised beings, human and animal and vegetable in the creation. . . . This loyalty to all—Samaritans and Romans, as well as Jews, to sinners as well as righteous, to the despised as well as the esteemed . . ." (pp. 94–95).

6. **Delivering justice**: not hoarding money greedily, but almsgiving, forgiving debts, breaking bread together in the common meal, feeding the hungry, announcing good news for the poor, sharing goods, investing in God's reign and God's delivering justice, restoring economic justice—this was an essential mark of the coming reign of God in Isaiah 40–66, and Jesus saw God's rule already beginning in these practices. In the synoptic gospels, Jesus confronts others—especially the elite—for their injustice fifty-one times, not counting parallels, and they respond by plotting his death. Jesus' emphasis on delivering justice is a major reason why he died on the cross. Yet it is missing from Niebuhr's description, as it is missing from many other accounts of Jesus.

7. **Nonviolent transforming initiatives**: not returning evil for evil but taking initiatives of peacemaking, confronting injustice and hostility, being willing to suffer, asserting the dignity of the enemy—these themes of nonviolence and peacemaking initiatives are missing from Niebuhr's account, but the love for the enemy is present.

As I showed, Niebuhr does explicitly adopt some of these norms for measuring how truly some of the types of Christ-and-culture relationship reflect the ethics of Jesus—especially the first few types. He does so less clearly in the latter types, and least in transformationism. Perhaps by the time he described the latter types, he thought he had made the point. We want to make that point explicit for authentic transformationism. The logic of Niebuhr's description of the reconstruction of faith argues that he and we should see Jesus' moral, personal character as disclosing God's will for us: "In this coming of Jesus Christ to us the Son reveals the Father and the Father reveals the Son. The Son reveals himself as Son in his moral, personal character." And "by his resurrection from the dead, by his establishment as ruler of life," it is established that God's will is what Jesus trusted it to be, and that Jesus, the faithful servant, "is acknowledged by Reality itself" (pp. 99–100).

John Howard Yoder has adopted a different methodology in his book, *Body Politics*.[8] He has identified five practices of the early Christian churches as they seek to embody faithfulness to Jesus Christ and to be the church in their culture. These practices were normative for them and they are for us.

1. One is **reconciling dialogue**, with forgiveness and the discipline of conflict resolution.[9] "One objective . . . of this procedure is forgiveness, 'remitting' an offense, reconciliation, 'winning' the brother or sister, restoring to the community a person who had offended." But Jesus calls it "binding and loosing." This means it concerns not only conflict resolution but also the community's moral discernment, as it binds its members to a way of life. It does not create a legalism of rules (although there are some rules like truth-telling, promise-keeping, and caring for the needy), but a community process of discernment amidst trust and forgiveness. Much Christian debate about moral issues makes the mistake of concentrating on what the standards ought to be rather than on how they ought to be discerned and implemented. Instead we should emphasize the community's reconciling dialogue. We must clarify the process by which the community of faith can discuss issues and guide members in their discipleship. This needs to be a process that includes members who are often excluded. It needs to be a reconciling process.[10] This resembles the norm of nonviolent transforming initiatives above.)

2. Another practice Yoder identifies is the regular practice of **breaking bread together**—not a once-a-year Passover meal, but their regular common meal. It was a household practice with Jesus as head, having their common meal and celebrating with thanksgiving. It was linked with the Passover, the Exodus, and the entire Hebrew heritage—especially the memory of God feeding the crowds in the desert. It was the basic economic fact of economic sharing, and is a norm of justice relevant for the world. "It demands *some* kind of sharing, advocacy, and partisanship in which the poor are privileged, and in which considerations of merit and productivity are subjected to the rule of servanthood. In recent years Christian thought in many traditions has given

209

new attention to the needs or rights of the poor."[11] Surely this reflects Jesus' norm of justice as described above.

3. The third is **baptism and the new humanity**. This celebrates the effects of including Jew and Gentile, male and female, slave and free, in the same community. It is an egalitarianism and a new, unified humanity based not on an Enlightenment universalism but on the work of Christ. Here is the norm of inclusion identified above.

4. The fourth is the empowerment of every member based on grace and **calling forth the gifts of the Spirit**. It leads to an egalitarian understanding of authority in which everyone participates rather than an ordained clergy.

   There is not (i.e., there should not be) one "ministerial" role, of which then we could argue about whether it is gender specific. There are as many ministerial roles as there are members of the body of Christ, and that means that more than half of them belong to women. . . . The transformation that Paul's vision calls for would not be to let a few more especially gifted women share with a few men the rare roles of domination; it would be to reorient the notion of ministry so that there would be no one ungifted, no one not called, no one not empowered, and no one dominated.[12]

   This is surely close to the norm concerning mutual servanthood, rightly adding to it the emphasis on calling forth gifts from everyone.

5. Uncoerced consensus decision-making and mediation. "Everyone who has something to say, something given to him or her by the Holy Spirit, can have the floor." Priority is given to speech that encourages, improves, and consoles. Others must weigh what is said in an orderly way, and especially commit themselves to hear their adversaries and the underdogs in love.[13] This resembles the norm of love above, practiced in the process of decision-making.

Yoder does not claim these five practices exhaust the normative practices of the early Christian community. Surely he would include prayer and evangelism as major practices of that community.

Thus we see an intriguing convergence between Niebuhr's historically realist logic (in his early books and his brief summaries in *Faith on Earth*) and Yoder's biblically realist argument in *Body Politics*.

We should reiterate what was said earlier: these practices or processes of deliverance are based on grace, on God's redemptive actions in Jesus Christ and on God's dynamic grace acting presently among us. This fits Niebuhr's strong emphasis on grace. And we can participate in this grace, we can do these practices of Christ in the church and by analogy in different concrete and historically particular situations. This fits Yoder's emphasis on discipleship.

Norms like these are essential for a prophetic faith that emphasizes a historically concrete approach to Jesus in his historical continuity with the faith of Israel and the historical context of his day, and that seeks to correct our evasions and distortions (Stassen). Something like these norms is essential if we are to have a working church and a strategy for social change (Yeager). Something like them is essential if we are to have criteria for selecting which cultural practices we should affirm, reject, withdraw from, or transform, and if we are to follow Jesus as the New Testament calls us to do (Yoder).

Culture: Powers and Authorities

It is helpful to approach the question of Christ and culture via the biblical concept of *the powers and authorities*. This is the way the New Testament usually speaks of culture. John Yoder pioneered in calling our attention to this central biblical concept that was so long ignored when he translated and published Berkhof's *Christ and the Powers*,[14] and when he showed the fruitfulness of the concept in his own writings. It is receiving new attention by numerous New Testament specialists, and it provides a depth-perspective for understanding the culture that pervades our lives. To some readers this may seem odd, because most of us have regularly done kangaroo exegesis, hopping over this biblical concept wherever it occurred (on almost every page of the New Testament). But this kangaroo approach to what is a central concept in the biblical story has impoverished our understanding of culture and of our relationship to culture.

> When Jesus had called the Twelve together, he gave them **power and authority** to drive out all demons and to cure diseases, and he sent them out to preach the kingdom of God and to heal the sick (Luke 9:1; NIV).

> Keeping a close watch on him, they sent spies, who . . . hoped to catch Jesus in something he said so that they might hand him over to the **power and authority** of the governor. (Luke 20:20).

211

> Be strong in the Lord and in his mighty power. Put on the full armor of God. . . . For our struggle is not against flesh and blood, but **against the rulers, against the authorities, against the powers** of this dark world and against the spiritual forces of evil in the heavenly realms. Therefore put on the full armor of God . . . the belt of truth . . . , the breastplate of justice . . . , the gospel of peace . . . , the shield of faith . . . , the helmet of salvation and the sword of the Spirit, which is the word of God. And pray in the Spirit. . . . (Eph. 6:10–18).

> The ten kings . . . have one purpose and will give their **power and authority** to the beast. They will make war against the Lamb, but the Lamb will overcome them because he is Lord of lords and King of kings—and with him will be his called, chosen, and faithful followers (Rev. 17:12–14).

There are several advantages to recovering the biblical concept. I will try to make these clear as I explain the meaning of the concept. Walter Wink has studied the concept most systematically, and my explanation will follow his.[15]

The Terminology of Power

> It is amazing that this has been so consistently overlooked. On every page of the New Testament one finds the terminology of power: those incumbents, offices, structures, roles, institutions, ideologies, rituals, rules, agents, and spiritual influences by which power is established and exercised. The language and reality of power pervade the New Testament because power is one of the primary ways the world is organized and run. No human activity can be described without recourse to this language.[16]

Wink argues that the powers and authorities are not "some kind of invisible demonic beings flapping around in the sky, occasionally targeting some luckless mortal with their invisible payload of disease, lust, possession or death."[17] Nor are they accurately reduced to the categories of modern sociology, depth psychology, and general systems theory, and certainly not to our individualistic interpretation of everything as the free choice of private individuals. Rather, they are

> the inner and outer aspects of any given manifestation of power. As the inner aspect they are the spirituality of institutions, the "within" of corporate structures and systems, the inner essence of outer organizations of power. As the outer aspect they are political systems, appointed officials, the "chair" of an organization, laws—in short, all the tangible manifestations which power takes. Every Power tends to have a visible pole, an outer form—be it a church, a nation, or an

212

economy—and an invisible pole, an inner spirit or driving force that animates, legitimates, and regulates its physical manifestation in the world. . . . Both come into existence together and cease to exist together.[18]

The concept is fluid: A whole group of words is used, sometimes individually, but often in pairs or series, like principalities and powers, authorities and pharisees, rulers and elders, and many other combinations, to stand for the various dimensions of the powers and authorities. I prefer to use the terms, "powers and authorities" to stand for these concepts, which many others call the "principalities and powers," because "principalities" is an archaic term. We seldom experience princes and their principalities, but we do experience authorities every day. In any case, the terms point to the various kinds of power and authority that impact us regularly.

Within the fluidity of the terms, there are some clear patterns:

Archon, ruler = an incumbent-in-office.

Archē, rule = the office itself, or an incumbent, or the structure of power (government, realm, dominion).

Exousia, authority = legitimations and sanctions that maintain power.

Dynamis, power = the power or force that maintains rule.

Kyriotēs, dominion = the reign itself or its territory.

Thronos, throne = the seat of power, capital city, or headquarters.

Onoma, name = a person or power of celebrity or rank.[19]

Overcoming Dualism

"These Powers are both heavenly and earthly, divine and human, spiritual and political, invisible and structural. . . . [They] include human agents, social structures and systems, and also divine powers. . . . The vast preponderance of uses of the terms for power is for its human bearers or the social structures that manifest it."[20]

We notice that the passages from Luke, Ephesians, and the Book of Revelation with which we began this section speak of the power and authority Jesus gave the disciples to heal, the power and authority of the governor who could arrest and crucify Jesus, and the powers of both this world and the heavenly realms.

The normal, daily use of the terms [rule, ruler, or principality]

213

described the political, religious, and economic structures and functionaries with which people had to deal. . . . It is far from the case that these terms primarily referred to spiritual entities; to the contrary, these terms could be extended to take in spiritual powers because they were the normal terms for power in all its manifestations. . . . The vast majority of references are to human arrangements of power, with an occasional use to designate spiritual beings.[21]

The modern thought-world since the Enlightenment has split the realm of spirituality apart from the realm of political, economic, and military power. Furthermore it has identified the realm of spirituality as an individual matter, and the realm of power as a social matter. And it has spoken of what is individual as inner or internal, and what is social as outer or external, as H. Richard Niebuhr has sometimes been falsely understood to mean when he wrote of internal and external history.[22] The result is an extensive dualism, a compartmentalizing, in which we are blinded to the societal dimensions of the spiritual realm and the spiritual forces in societal matters. Furthermore, on the question of Christ and culture, Christ has tended to be relegated to the realm of inner spirituality, and culture is thought of as something social and external. The result is a powerless Christ, and a blindness to how culture powerfully shapes the inner lives of persons and churches. Christ is split off from culture.

The Modern Spirituality/Power Split

spirituality	power
individual	social
inner	outer
Christ	culture

Another result is that persons of faith often think of spirituality as concerned only with the lives of individuals, and as shunning work for justice and peace in society. Worse: they lack a vocabulary for understanding power structures, social conflict, and cultural formation. Therefore even when they want to work for justice and peace, they lack categories for understanding social forces and norms for guiding their actions. On the other side of the split, persons concerned for justice and peace think of spirituality as irrelevant or as a definite hindrance. Spirituality renders people either apathetic about what matters, or subject to takeover by authoritarian ideologies. Niebuhr noted this in his criticism of the dualist type, and Yeager noted it in her chapter on "The Social Self in the Working Church."

Recovering the language of the powers and authorities reintegrates our life-world. It cuts through our dualism. Thinking with the language of "powers and authorities" alerts us that the social world of power has an inner spirituality. It says that in combatting the powers and authorities, we must pay attention not only to their physical embodiments (a corporation headquarters, the White House, the NBC offices, Pantex), but also to their inner spirituality—their beliefs, myths, narratives, ideologies; their centers of value, trust, and loyalty—what has come to be known in recent years as their "corporate culture." Conversely, in seeking a faithful spiritual life, we need to name the impact that the powers and authorities have on our loyalties and perceptions. Otherwise we become unknowingly captive to the economic ideologies, the racial loyalties, the habitual lifestyles, the national pride, the received traditions and assumptions, the polytheisms and henotheisms promulgated by the powerful broadcasters of culture that penetrate our space. As Ephesians 6 says twice, we need the *full* armor of God: prayer and peace, faith and justice.

In Ephesians 6:14, *dikaiousune*, which means compassionate, reconciling justice, is frequently translated "righteousness." But the dualism of the modern thought-world immediately shunts "righteousness" into the individual-spiritual realm, and takes it to mean individual self-righteousness—almost the opposite of the biblical meaning. Therefore I have translated it "justice," as Wink also does. I do not mean punitive, authoritarian justice, but the compassionate justice that limits greed, reconciles enemies, feeds the hungry, and cares for the orphans. I mean the justice that the Holy Spirit inspired the prophets to proclaim, and Jesus to enact. It is spiritual, it is powerful, and it is social.

The Error of Gnosticism

One error in understanding culture is gnosticism—an ancient heresy that believed Jesus was only a spirit and not flesh; when Jesus walked, he left no footprints. Gnosticism also reduces the powers and authorities to spiritual forces and ignores their material manifestations. This heresy is still with us. Karl Barth said that some in Germany used talk of the demonic "to evade sociopolitical insight and responsibility. They treated demons as if they were disincarnate spiritual beings in the air, rather than *the actual spirituality of Naziism*. In fact, the demonic

215

was inseparable from its political forms: the Hitler Youth, the SS, the Gestapo, the cooperation of the churches, the ideology of Aryan racial purity. . . ." Standing firm against the powers and authorities meant standing firm against the spirit and the actions of Naziism. Similarly, priests in Brazil say that belief in demon possession reinforces the fatalism of people who blame disease on disembodied demons. Instead they need to see its causes in poverty and unhealthy practices that they can do something about.[23]

When the Powers are thought of individualistically, as demonic beings assaulting us from the sky, their institutional and systemic dimension is mystified, and belief in the demonic has no political consequences. "But once we recognize that these spiritual forces are *the interiority of earthly institutions or structures or systems*, then the social dimension of the gospel becomes immediately evident."[24]

The authorities and powers are the centers of power that order or manipulate our culture and our society so they fit their own interests or value commitments. These include business organizations, the media, labor organizations, peace organizations, churches, synagogues, mosques, governments, schools, universities, seminaries, economic systems, military organizations, professional societies, the A.M.A., and centers of technology. They also include the ideologies, legitimations, and sanctions that justify these centers of power.[25]

The Error of Materialism

So gnosticism is one error. It reduces the powers and authorities, and culture, to "spiritual" values or "spiritual" beings, and fails to pay attention to the material embodiment of power. The opposite error is materialism: reducing the powers and authorities to social systems, and omitting their spiritual dimensions. As a result, it fails to confront the inner or spiritual dimensions of power, and fails to achieve the changes it hopes for. It misperceives the full power of institutions.

Because the institution usually antedates and outlasts its employees, it develops and imposes a set of traditions, expectations, beliefs, and values on everyone in its employ. Usually unspoken, unacknowledged, and even unknown, this invisible, transcendent network of determinants constrains behavior far more rigidly than any printed set of rules could ever do. . . . This institutional momentum through time perpetuates a self-image, a corporate personality, and an institutional spirit which the more discerning are able to grasp as a totality and weigh for its relative sickness or health.[26]

Wink argues forcefully that we must not reduce the powers and authorities to a sociological description of institutions and social forces. If we fail to notice the spirit of an institution, the result "is always slavery to the unseen power behind the visible elements: the spirituality of the institution or state. . . ."[27] If we try to understand "the spreading terror of nuclear and ecological catastrophe" simply in terms of the personalities of individual leaders or the power of institutions, we miss the full reality. We miss the pervasive sense that there is no one in control, that the demonic has the national leaders in its grasp and "constrains them, against the best interests of humanity, toward rationalized suicide. The evil that grips us is simply too massive and intractable to face. Far easier to individualize it. . . ."[28] Furthermore, if we believe that we can achieve a good society just by changing institutions, as in communism, and ignore the spirit and the necessary personal transformation, soon the institutions will demand that people be forced, imprisoned, or killed in order to fit the institutions. The result is totalitarianism. "Reductionistic explanations are inadequate because they omit the one essential most unique to the New Testament understanding of power: its spiritual dimension."[29]

Created, Fallen, Being Redeemed:
God as Creator, Judge, and Redeemer

A third error is to see the culture—or the powers and authorities—as all bad or all good. The truth is that the powers are both good and evil. They are created in and through Christ for good purposes; and they are fallen. They plot against Christ and crucify him. But Christ triumphs over them, leading captivity captive and making a mockery of the powers. God's purpose is to redeem and transform them so that they serve peace for all under Christ's lordship (Col. 1 and 2). Therefore our response must be selective rejection and selective affirmation. Governments were created good, to do good things for people and for the world; but they are fallen and do evil; nevertheless, God is seeking to redeem their fallen spirits and use them as instruments of deliverance for people, as God used Cyrus and Assyria. The nations are under God's judgment, and yet have a vocation from God.[30] So the New Testament speaks of the *kosmos*, usually translated the *world*, but better translated as the *establishment* or the *system*. It is "the human sociological realm that exists in estrangement from God . . . the totality of human social existence." It is God's good creation, now estranged or fallen, and capable of redemption.[31]

Here we have a basis for bringing together Yoder's criticism of Niebuhr's monolithic understanding of culture and Niebuhr's three-fold criteria of the sovereignty of God. The biblical concept of the Powers provides an understanding of culture that is clearly not monolithic or homogeneous: culture is partly the good creation, partly evil, and partly being redeemed. Some parts are more good or more evil than other parts. Therefore our response must be selective and differentiated, just as Yoder argues.

As good creation, culture evidences the sovereign rule of God in and over all; as fallen and sinful, culture may not be identified with God's will but is rather judged by the living God; as being redeemed, culture evidences the redeeming work of God in Christ. Niebuhr insists that these not be merely bland affirmations, but dynamic experience, core faith; all our actions are to be response to God as Creator, Judge and Redeemer. The dynamism of the concepts of Powers and Authorities says this well.

The church's task is to see God's good creating action in all the Powers and Authorities that we encounter. Nothing is what it is apart from God's creating action, God's dynamic rule, God's sovereignty. Gratitude, appreciation, participation, creativity, and stewardship are our responses.

Here Wink offers an interesting perspective on "the elements" of nature, which he relates in part to modern physics and its attention to the elements of the nuclei and the forces that hold things together. He suggests we see the elements as revealers of God, or theophanies.

> They are, after all, created in and through and for Christ, along with everything else in creation (Col. 1:15–20). They exist solely for the service of the whole. They are essentially benign, not evil; it is primarily our idolatry or evil that turns them to destruction. They are essential as the basis for all that exists. We could not live for a moment without them. . . . If the heavens can tell the glory of God, why not the atoms?[32]

Yet at the same time he criticizes those scientists who have regarded matter as ultimate, rather than God, the soul, or persons. "You shall have no other gods before me," insists Wink.[33] Thus Niebuhr is surely right to see God revealed in the creation. And Yoder is surely right that we may not identify the creation as an autonomous and competing source of revelation in rivalry with God's revelation in Christ. The disclosure of God's will and ways in Christ is the criterion for interpreting God's intent as revealed in the creation. Otherwise, as Wink says, someone can use creation to validate a social Darwinism that justifies unjust privileges for the privileged and self-satisfied hardheartedness toward those who are suffering. Someone else can use creation to defend racism and segregation, or violence and war, as the will of God. Creation reveals God's dynamic activity, yes; but our astigmatic perception of its meaning must be straightened out by the lens of God's covenant justice and redeeming love.

This recovers yet one more dimension of wholeness beyond those in the table above. The "elements" point us to nature as a part of God's creation. Christ, through and for whom all is created, points us to a stewardship responsibility for the creation. Our culture includes a growing sense of respect for the environment: we are learning from biologists, chemists, physicists, ecologists, and many perceptive people that we need more simple and less consumptive life-styles, and we need economic incentives that encourage us to invest in energy-saving ways of life. Our culture also gives us a fallen relation to creation; we exploit God's good creation for our greed, our violence, or our comfort and temporary enjoyment; we let technology run amok in the fragile goodness of what we have been given. The nuclear bomb, the ozone hole, the poisoned air, land, and water are signs of our fallenness. "Your brother's blood cries out to me from the ground . . . which opened its mouth to receive your brother's blood from your hand. When you work the ground, it will no longer yield its crops for you" (Gen. 4:10–12). At the same time, our participation in God's redemptive action invites us to a more grateful, loving, just, and responsible relationship to nature, and to setting limits for those powers and authorities, and for you and me, who exploit nature with little or no attention to how the next generations will live. When we understand culture by means of the biblical concept of powers and authorities, we are reminded to pay attention to the powers that gobble up nature and consume it as if it were their own.

The church's task is to expose the falseness of the Powers by the witness of its pulpits, prayers, and public action, and to testify to God's redeeming action. Apostolic churches in the first century exposed the falsehood of Caesar-worship by refusing to pray to Caesar and instead praying for him, refusing to enter the army and instead befriending enemies, and refusing to be awed by Caesar's power and instead spreading the good news throughout the empire. During the time of Hitler, German churches failed to proclaim, pray, and act as they were called to do. Yet the churches have not always failed: "The march across the Selma bridge by black civil rights advocates was an act of exorcism. It exposed the demon of racism, stripping away the screen of legality and custom for the entire world to see."[34] And we add, many other marches less well known, which included, thank God, a goodly number of whites as well as blacks joining together in witnessing to the truth of God's judgment on the falsehood of the Powers and the truth of God's redemptive reconciliation.

The church's task, also, is to free persons for authentic struggle by replacing toxic ideas and images through the vision of a counter-reality capable of improving their lives.[35] Throughout his study of the biblical understanding of the Powers, Wink demonstrates that the church's task is to name the powers, to unmask them, and to engage them. We cannot fulfill our mission if we pretend they do not influence us and allow them to infiltrate our perceptions and our practices undetected, unnoticed, and unnamed. As Niebuhr says, our task includes our response to God as Judge.

And our task is to respond to God as Redeemer. The church's task is to preach to the Powers: "That through the church the manifold wisdom of God might now be made known to the dominions and powers in the heavenly places" (Eph. 3:10). Wink discusses this passage at length, explaining that God's lordship and redemption include the Powers, and the church's task is to proclaim the good news to them as well.[36] Wink disagrees with those who believe institutions are so hopelessly immoral that there is nothing we can do for them.[37]

Throughout the biblical drama, we are told that though the powers seem in control, God is yet lord; and we are called to be faithful to God's teachings. Again and again the biblical understanding of the Powers realistically acknowledges their power, but insists nevertheless on the sovereignty of God and the lordship of Christ. Much of biblical literature addresses a people oppressed by powerful empires, by beasts that symbolize one emperor or another, by powers and authorities of legalism, enmity, and greed. And the message is that God is still in charge; God rules; these powers were created in and through and for Christ, and Christ is lord over them. God is working to redeem.

This is the message of God as dynamic sovereign and active redeemer that is so central to Niebuhr's own faith, and to his research into transformative faith.[38] It also fits Yoder's emphasis—that if our response is to be selective, then we need clear norms to guide us in discerning what is good and what is fallen, what is being judged and what is being redeemed. The mysterious Book of Revelation, for example, which has been so badly misused for fanciful speculation about the timing of future events or, worse, to advocate militaristic or authoritarian actions, actually has a far less mysterious meaning. Again and again it repeats the message: God is Lord; God is judging the Beasts; God will redeem the followers of the Lamb; follow the teachings of the Lamb faithfully. The followers of the Lamb are distinguished by their doing the deeds Jesus teaches, doing God's will, keeping God's word, keeping God's commandments, holding faithful to the testimony of Jesus, doing the teachings of Jesus, following God's teachings as given through Jesus, obeying God's commands (Rev. 2:2; 2:23; 2:19; 2:26; 3:8, 10; 9:20–21; 12:17; 14:4; 14:12; 16:11; 20:12–13; 22:11). The message is so clear and so often repeated that one wonders at the hard work and imagination so many scholars and preachers have put forth to evade the message: do the teachings of Jesus; follow the way of the Lamb. The Book of Revelation often speaks of those who overcome, or those who are righteous, or those who are followers of the Lamb, versus those who lie and kill and steal, who are unrighteous, and who are followers of the Beast. The early Christian confession was "**Jesus Christ is Lord.**" Jesus the Lord gives us the criteria for relating Christ and culture.

Wink emphasizes repeatedly that the strategies the church is to follow in "preaching to the Powers," in combatting and seeking their transformation, are the strategies that Jesus teaches. They are the strategies of Jesus' teaching on peacemaking, and the strategies of justice, peace, prayer and faith.[39]

They are what Yoder has in mind when he writes of the need to specify the criteria that guide us in selectively relating to different aspects of the culture. We need criteria by which to discern which aspects of culture are more usable than others, or more in need of major transformation, or so evil as to require a strategy of refusal. Those criteria come from "the work and the words ... f that particular Palestinian populist, in all of his Jewishness and all of his patience."[40]

Therefore authentic transformation defines the "Christ" of "Christ and culture" with concrete ethical content from the Jesus of the New Testament, in continuity with the prophetic faith. It does not assume that Jesus' prophetic teachings cannot be obeyed. Rather, it assumes that the will of God may be known in the concrete and historically particular grace-based processes of deliverance that we see in Christ.

Yet our knowing is distorted by our unfaithfulness and idolatry. Therefore we need continuous repentance and community correction.

In that process the norms we have from Christ form an essential standard for our correction. Humility does not mean we should say we have no knowledge of the New Testament Jesus. It means our understanding of Jesus needs continuous correction. Jesus Christ is Lord—over the powers that infiltrate our living and our seeing.

2. The Transforming Church Embodied

How does the authentically transformationist church take shape in history? How is it embodied? What practices and structures characterize a transforming church?

Niebuhr argued that we are in history as the fish is in water; we cannot do theology or church from above time as if we were stars in the heavens rather than humans in history. He said history is the laboratory in which our faith is tested. Accordingly, he advocated the theology of the sovereignty of God not only because of his own faith experience but because it is the faith that has repeatedly produced authentic transformation in U.S. history. Furthermore, in *Christ and Culture*, Niebuhr also evaluated each type by its actual performance in transforming culture or being coopted by it. If we are to learn from Niebuhr's argument, what follows must be historically situated theology. It must pay attention to how churches embody authentic transformation in their practices and structures.

The Church Embodied in History, Not a Gnostic Idea Above History

What Niebuhr did not do was describe how his ideal types would be embodied in actual congregations. That created an ethical confusion noticed by Paul Ramsey and cited by John Yoder. All of Ramsey's students, regardless of the denomination or confessional tradition to which they belonged, or of the theology to which they held, concluded they were transformationists. My students respond a bit differently. They see parts of *each* type in their churches. For them, reading *Christ and Culture* is like taking an abnormal psychology course: each new disease studied feels like the one you have. They see withdrawal, accommodation, dualism, synthesis, and transformation in their churches. Like Ramsey's students, they finish the book convinced transformation is the route to health. But because Niebuhr does not prescribe any ingredients for the structure and practices of a church that wants to embody transformation, they think transformation in their heads while their bodies stay in churches whose structures and practices are accommodationist or dualist or anything but transformationist. Because actions speak louder than thoughts,[41] their thoughts communicate less effectively than their church structures, and eventually they, too, find themselves conforming to the shape of the church practices they are embedded in. Christians need to ask what kind of church embodies authentic transformation.

Otherwise we are in danger of teaching cheap transformationism or gnosticism. When the gospel is presented in such a way that everyone is convinced we are already saved and have nothing more to do, we have what Bonhoeffer calls cheap grace. When the problem of Christ and culture is presented in such a way that everyone is convinced we are already transformationists and nothing in the structure of our churches needs changing, we have cheap transformationism.

Gnosticism was a heresy the early church had to face, one from which present-day Christians are far from exempt. It taught that the gospel is about getting some ideas right and ignoring how they are embodied. If we think of authentic transformationism as ideas without embodiment in the structures and practices of churches, we are present-day gnostics.

Ernst Troeltsch, Niebuhr's mentor, in his classic *Social Teaching of the Christian Churches*, paid attention to the embodiment of each type of ethical teaching in church structures and practices that fit that type. He knew churches communicate their understanding of the shape of discipleship more by the way they live and relate than by their official declarations and proclamations. Words disclose—sometimes—but often they also cover up or divert attention. As Niebuhr wrote, the most prevalent form of unfaith is bad faith—defensive evasion. Therefore, people intuitively know to look for the practices that go with our words to assess what is real and what is not.

Accordingly, I want to ask what shape, what form, what structure, what practices, what actual visible embodiment authentic transformation is likely to take in a local congregation. Do some ways of being organized, some ways of walking the talk, fit an authentically transformative faith better than others do? We can focus this question concretely at the level of the local congregation. Carl S. Dudley points out that in the United States, people participate in

> more than 330,000 local congregations, which are found in every segment of society. There are more churches than schools, more

church members than people who belong to any other voluntary association, and more financial support for churches than for all other philanthropic causes combined.[42]

Similarly, James M. Washington argues that

the politics of black spirituality, which are inherently symbolic and psychological . . . must be embodied in church programs that recognize and resist the systemic nature of injustice lest they fall prey to the pitfalls of undisciplined subjectivism.[43]

Of course, our question is Christ and culture, not church and culture. To see churches as on the side of Christ, and culture as over against Christ, is just the kind of hypocrisy and self-righteous judging that caused Christ to sound strong warnings again and again. *Churches are part of the culture.* Churches are made of clay and spirit—or clay and air. Their members and their leaders spend most of their days in the world and only a few hours or less in the church, and when they come inside, they bring the smells of the fields and the malls with them. Or more accurately, the church is the people who spend most of their time in the world and are part of society, and while they are inside the church buildings, organized in church structures and processes, they are still in the world, still part of human society. Niebuhr insists that the church is a representative part of society, a cultural institution like any other and subject to the same temptations—trusting and distrusting, loyal and disloyal. *Society* is not simply over against Christ. It is created in and through Christ, it betrays and crucifies Christ, and it is continuously being recreated, rejudged, and redeemed. *Christ and culture* are not the same as *church and world.*

So when we ask about the incarnate shape of a church that is authentically transformationist, we are asking about an obedient/disobedient clump of historically and socially situated humanity organized in a set of institutional structures and practices. We are saying, "Let us show you the church in a handful of clay."

Nor do we ask about the church with its smells and its clay as if we individuals were somehow better than the church—moral individuals in immoral churches. In the process of our dialogue with one another as we wrote this book, we have learned a bit more about our limits, and about our need for grace and community. We know our own need for community. We do not believe in autonomous individuals detached from community embodiment. We have never seen one. Each of us knows we need churches that are transforming communities.

Many people are realizing that our society has allowed community to be fragmented by market-oriented measures of worth, cynical assessments of governmental leadership, and loss of faith in covenant responsibilities. We have become a fragmented people and a fragmented society. We need a new emphasis on covenant community and covenant faithfulness.[44]

How then shall we describe essential features of a congregation that embodies authentic transformation?

I want to suggest that we begin with the three essential features of prophetically transformative faith that Niebuhr found in his research for *The Kingdom of God in America*. The same three features form his criteria for evaluating the types in *Christ and Culture*, along with the criterion of transformative impact rather than accommodationist adaptation to social forces. Let us ask what these criteria imply about the way the church is embodied—its structure, processes, program, practices. Transformative faith as Niebuhr discovered it emphasizes: (1) the presently experienced shape of God's redemptive action in Christ, disclosing the normative pattern of God's faithfulness; (2) the living, dynamic character of God's rule and judgment that cannot be reduced to a static human possession or human value; (3) and the presently active rule of God over all, not part, of life. As I hope to show, these three themes correspond to Niebuhr's own definition of the church's responsibility as *Apostle, Pioneer,* and *Pastor.*[45] From that we may take our clue for the embodiment of authentic transformation.

The Embodiment of Authentic Transformation

Transformative Faith	*Church's Responsibility*
God as Redeemer whose character is disclosed in Christ	Apostle: announcing the gospel and making disciples
God as living, dynamic, always ahead of culture, never a static possession (Holy Spirit)	Pioneer: modeling the faith as alternative community ahead of society and culture
God as presently active Creator in all, including the culture	Pastor: caring for all, including sinners, outcasts, society

Prophet/Apostle: Announcing The Gospel and Making Disciples

First, *apostle*: "The Church is by nature and commandment an apostolic community which exists for the sake of announcing the

225

Gospel to all nations and of making them disciples of Christ." The church proclaims "that the center and heart of all things, the first and last Being, is utter goodness, complete love" and "that the goodness which appeared in history in the form of Jesus Christ was not defeated but rose triumphantly from death." To proclaim the love of God in Christ to all nations, the church must "discharge its apostolic responsibility by envisaging the needs of people in their societies as well as in their isolation before God." And it must call us to repentance for transgressions against what Jesus teaches, such as racist action, obliteration bombing, and "dealing with defeated nations in the spirit of retribution rather than of redemption"[46]

Thus an apostolic community *proclaims and teaches faith, repentance, and discipleship*—the mandate given by Jesus Christ in the Great Commission (Matt. 28:18–20). This is the logical implication of the historic-revelation dimension of the sovereignty of God—the presently experienced shape of God's redemptive action in Christ, disclosing the normative pattern of God's faithfulness. Hence the church teaches faith and grace not only as a doctrine, but as a present experience. It calls for commitment of basic loyalties to the cause God is loyal to, the particular way of God incarnated in Jesus. It calls for fundamental *metanoia*—i.e., transformation of mind, repentance, conversion, and commitment. It wants people to experience God's grace; God's faithful, merciful, redemptive action in Christ; love for enemies; justice for all persons; faith; repentance; and discipleship. Niebuhr's elegant New England language was shy about the language of passion, but surely the metanoia he often pointed to, and his identification with Jonathan Edwards, and especially his posthumously published *Faith on Earth*, point to *a fundamental reorientation of the basic faith at the core of our selfhood*, a reorientation that involves *passion, trust, and loyalty*.

Moreover, the reorientation is toward *discipleship, faithful following of the demonstration of God's way in Christ*. So Avery Dulles writes in the revised edition of his highly influential *Models of the Church*, advocating the model of "the community of disciples," as most adequate: "The way of Jesus is the way of the disciple, and discipleship consists in walking the way with Jesus." He points out that in the book of Acts, "all Christian believers are called disciples, and the Church itself is called the community of disciples (Acts 6:2, NAB). Here and elsewhere in the New Testament, Christianity is represented as a way of life by which one follows Jesus (Acts 9:2, 22:4), who is himself the Way (John 14:6)."[47]

And so Larry Rasmussen writes that the church is first the people of the way:

> The disabling and ultimately tragic development is that the focus soon shifts from Jesus and the particular way he incarnated with his community, the way of his God, to the metaphysical relationship of the individual figure, Jesus, to the church's God, now become also the empire's God. In the most un-Jewish of all possible moves, the Jew Jesus became a "detached" Jesus at the hands of the great ecumenical councils. He was detached from his own historic community and its way, and found himself metaphysically fused to God alone. So one searches in vain in the classic creeds, those pure distillations of the faith, for anything at all about Jesus as the way in any moral sense, or of his community's way.[48]

The apostolic Jesus identified with the tradition of the prophets of Israel, with their teachings, with their call to repentance, faith and justice, with them in the opposition they found and with their prophecies. The church as apostle, then, pointing to the particular way of the incarnate Jew, Jesus, needs to interpret him in that prophetic context. It needs to correct tendencies that ignore Jesus' concrete context and that reduce his teaching to a pale reflection of our culture. Hence, just as Niebuhr spoke often of the prophetic faith, I speak here of the church's responsibility as prophet/apostle.

In *Righteous Gentiles of the Holocaust*, David Gushee studies those Christians who rescued Jews from Adolf Hitler's incomprehensible war of extermination. He asks the same crucial question Niebuhr asked in *Kingdom of God in America*: What sort of faith led some Christians to refuse to accommodate to the racist culture and realistic fears of that time? What sort of faith led some Christians to act courageously, saving the lives of thousands of Jews whom they sheltered or helped escape?

Before he can answer these questions, however, Gushee has to confess on behalf of the church that most failed the test. Most Christians stood by passively or even helped the Nazis. "We let the church off too easily . . . if we do not remind ourselves that *one place many Christians learned to hate Jews was in church*." "The irrelevance of Christian faith for many self-identified Christian rescuers in so-called Christian Europe is an extraordinary finding. . . . Most painfully, these findings speak a word of judgment."[49]

Being religious was not what distinguished rescuers from nonrescuers. The same percentage of nonrescuers were religious as rescuers. What mattered was what kind of religion they had. Christians who were rescuers took Jesus' teachings on the way of love, justice, and inclusion concretely. They read the Bible concretely, seeing its teachings as directly normative, with rules and principles and virtues. They were not distinguished by the subtlety of their neoorthodox theology, but by their direct application of biblical teachings to their obedience when a hungry and desperate Jew knocked on their door. This

> serves as a reminder to Christian ministers and educators to return central biblical teachings on compassion and love to the forefront of Christian proclamation and education. Again and again, Christians need to hear the parable of the Good Samaritan, the commandment to love God and neighbor, the Golden Rule, the parable of the Sheep and the Goats, and related texts. . . . Our findings suggest that these texts form something of a biblical constitution for the Christian moral life. They should be the subject of regular reflection, proclamation, and application, with less central themes and texts falling into place around them.[50]

Many of the rescuers were distinguished by the norm of inclusion that Jesus taught: "Perhaps the religious resource most remarked upon in rescuer literature is a strong sense of religious kinship with Jews as a people."[51] Rescuer Germaine Bocquet said:

> The religious education I had received had instilled in me respect for the Jewish people, and gratitude that they had given us the prophets, the Virgin Mary, Christ, and the apostles. Jews were for me people of the Covenant, of God's promises. Jesus, the Messiah, was a faithful son of the Law, which he had come to bring to perfection, not to abolish.[52]

In his writing and teaching, Dietrich Bonhoeffer, whose brother-in-law was a Jew, emphasized again and again the incarnation of Jesus as a Jew and a human, and therefore the calling of Christians to stand in solidarity with Jews and all suffering humankind. Like many Dutch Reformed and French Huguenot families who carried out courageous deeds of rescue, the family of Corrie ten Boom read from their Bible daily—the whole Bible, including their Old Testament. Because of Calvin's emphasis on the normative value of the Old Testament for Christians and on God's sovereign faithfulness in keeping covenant with the Jewish people, "Jews in desperate need found among many Calvinist Christians a profound respect and solidarity precisely *because* they were Jews."[53] The same point is made by James Wm. McClendon about the Plymouth Brethren.[54]

Furthermore, the teaching that made a difference took place not only in churches, but in families.[55] To be transformative, the church cannot rely only on what it teaches inside the walls of its meeting house; it must teach parents to post teachings on the refrigerator, to tell of them in bedtime stories, to speak of them in conversations, and to embody them in their lives.

Another kind of evidence comes from sociologists of religion. During the recent decades of the civil rights movement and the movement for equality for women, the Vietnam War, the forced resignation of President Nixon, contentious Supreme Court decisions, and the decades of drugs, sex, and greed, the culture has become severely polarized.[56] Those churches that were "highest in socioeconomic status, those stressing individualism in belief, and those most affirming of American culture," declined dramatically. In the fifties, the faiths of established institutions "had become something of a 'culture-religion,' very much captive to middle-class values and somewhat lacking in their ability to sustain a strong transcendent vision." This is just what Niebuhr had seen prophetically in the early thirties: the axe was laid to the root of the tree; faith in our culture and institutions was dying, and we must turn instead to faith in the sovereignty of God.[57]

Sociologist Robert Wuthnow says a major reason why mainline churches are losing members is that in their reaction against legalism, their ethics have become too vague. Struggling, searching, and expressing doubt is the main message being communicated. Sermons often move from a simple structure to a more complex one, and the moral conclusion is hidden in many words. Churches with vitality are more concrete in their teaching and preaching.[58] James Hopewell reports that in the interviews he conducted, even in conservative Protestant congregations, he was surprised "by how infrequently . . . the name of Christ was mentioned in response to questions about crises such as death, family instability, or world catastrophes. Although the name of Christ is regularly used by church members in the intensive, self-identifying acts of worship and evangelism," people seem not to know how to speak of Christ when they confront life issues.[59] Dean R. Hoge writes that

> Ecclesiastical and creedal statements have been written abstractly enough, or with enough internal pluralism, to include all shades of theology in the denomination. . . . One problem with this policy in any denomination is lack of identity. The question Who are we? or What do we believe? is not satisfactorily answered by a recitation of diverse viewpoints current in the church. Evangelism is barely possi-

229

ble when the identity of the church and its gospel are difficult to state clearly. Today it is no accident that many middle-class Protestants are hesitant to discuss their own Christian beliefs with other persons.[60]

The lesson seems parallel to the lesson of the Holocaust. Churches need to be far more concrete in communicating the meaning of Christ's teachings for our life-context. The previous generation or two of theologically abstract ethics and ethically silent doctrine has left church members unable to articulate concrete guidance from Christ for their lives. Contextual ethics has been right in its emphasis on grace, but too vague on discipleship. To correct this, churches need to emphasize concrete incarnational discipleship.

By contrast with mainline churches, Roof and McKinney report, "almost all of the churches that retained distance from the culture by encouraging distinctive life-styles and belief grew." They "were 'identifiable' religiously and culturally, known for their distinctive beliefs and moral teachings; they offered an experiential faith centered around belief in salvation through personal commitment to Christ." Evangelicals, who describe themselves as born again, have encouraged others to believe in Jesus Christ, and have a high view of biblical authority, have grown significantly. Orthodox Judaism, with its concrete teachings, biblical authority, and sovereignty of God, also grew.[61] The same point could be made about Islam, with its concrete ethics, obedience to God, and sense of distinctive community and way of life.

Roof and McKinney report that evangelical churches are distinguished from mainline churches by having four times as high a percentage of their adults in religious education, twice the percentage of members in worship, twice the giving, and twice the likelihood to have grown 25 percent in membership in the past five years.[62] And they teach more concretely, less abstractly. This does not necessarily mean that they teach the full scope of discipleship as Jesus taught and embodied it. It does not mean that every church growing in numbers is growing in authentic transformation. But it does mean that vitality and strength of identification with the church community do seem to require more concrete, specific, and frequent teaching, with a sense of vision. Daniel Buttry's book describing the revitalization of a church advocates concrete teaching "directed toward shaping the life of discipleship and the community of the church," and "occasionally a national or global issue [cries] out for biblical challenge." He quotes Martin Luther King, Jr., who echoes Dietrich Bonhoeffer: "If you preach the gospel in all aspects with the exception of the issues which deal specifically with your time, you are not preaching the gospel at all."[63]

Michael Westmoreland-White points out that we are faced with a new degree of biblical illiteracy which undermines the churches' mission of incarnational discipleship. He cites George Lindbeck's claim that Yale Divinity School used to test incoming students for a level of biblical knowledge that would now surpass exiting graduates. In Roanoke College, a confessionally Christian institution, C. Freeman Sleeper regularly uses anonymous pre-tests of six simple questions for his introductory New Testament class. Less than five percent of students get all six questions. "Recovering a high level of biblical literacy in the churches is therefore an urgent priority for vital communities of faith."

Westmoreland-White suggests nine practices for such a recovery:[64]

- Mandatory new-member classes for basic catechetical instruction for all new Christians.

- Those who transfer membership from another congregation should be tested (gently) for biblical knowledge and basic grasp of the nature of Christian living and believing, and given education that fits their level.

- Churches must recover the practice of rigorous sustained Bible study in groups on a weekly basis for adults, not only children. Those churches that practice biblical study only for children leave their adults at a childrens' level of understanding, lack clear Christian identity, lack defenses against the infiltration of a secular culture, and decline in discipleship and membership.

- We must recover the practice of regular expository preaching. "This need not rule out creativity, such as the use of narrative style, monologues, and drama, but it must emphasize sustained attention to the content of the text, even as it is creatively applied to life. . . . Members should be encouraged to follow the text with open Bibles during the sermon. . . . Pew Bibles should be provided with pages marked in the bulletin for the benefit of visitors and new members."

- Churches should recover the practice of having "godparents" whose task is to help parents instruct their children in Christian living and believing, including the practice of regular Bible study.

231

- Singles, couples, and parents with children should be encouraged by the church to develop practices of regular family and personal devotion, including the practice of reading and discussing the Scriptures.
- Churches could also hold regular retreats that emphasize the Scriptures in spiritual formation and Christian living.
- Seminaries should reinstate Hebrew and Greek requirements, and more biblical courses than is often the case.
- Churches need to recover the practice of evangelism. Our privatistic culture encourages privatistic faith that is neither shared with others verbally nor enacted publicly in "'works of mercy,' and efforts at structural reform." We need to stop hiding our faith under a bushel, but to let God's light shine in our words and our deeds, both.

Westmoreland-White concludes: "I have urged these suggested practices at great length because the recovery of biblical literacy in North American Christianity is vital to any form of active discipleship and concrete Christocentric obedience. . . . Widespread biblical illiteracy did not become endemic among the American churches overnight. One cannot expect to erase this 'famine of the Word of God' (Amos 5:11) overnight, either."

In sum, the church is apostle: it proclaims and teaches fundamental reorientation of the basic faith at the core of our selfhood toward making disciples of all peoples, teaching them to obey everything Jesus has commanded us, baptizing them into the lordship of Father, the Son, and the Holy Spirit, as in the Great Commission (Matt. 28:19f.). It interprets Jesus in the tradition of the prophets of Israel, with their God-centered mercy, their concrete teachings, and their call to repentance, faithfulness, and justice. It reads the Bible concretely, seeing its teachings as pointing to concrete practices that are faithful in our historical context. It has distinctive beliefs and moral teachings, and an experiential faith with personal commitment to Christ. It emphasizes concrete incarnational discipleship, based on grace and repentance. It teaches not only inside the walls of the meeting house, but in families and in embodied practices.

Pioneer: Faithful Model for Human Community

Second, Niebuhr sees the church as *pioneer*, repenting and leading in following God's will on behalf of the whole society.

> The Church is that part of the human community which responds first to God-in-Christ and Christ-in-God. . . . It is that group which hears the Word of God, which sees God's judgments, which has the vision of the resurrection. In its relations with God it is the pioneer part of society that responds to God on behalf of the whole society, somewhat . . . as science is the pioneer in responding to pattern or rationality in experience and as artists are the pioneers in responding to beauty.[65]

Similarly, the Hebrew people and the prophetic remnant "pioneered in understanding the vanity of idol worship and in obeying the law of neighbor-love" and Jesus Christ represented humankind and pioneered for it in discerning, obeying, and relying on God's faithfulness.[66]

The pioneering mission of the church is the logical implication of the second dimension of the sovereignty of God: the living, dynamic character of God's rule and redemption that cannot be reduced to a human possession or human value—God as Holy Spirit. To respond to God is always to pioneer because God's will is always ahead of where society is. So Niebuhr speaks of God's judgments, of the vanity of idol worship, of obedience to God's law of neighbor-love, and of the hope of resurrection. God's rule cannot be reduced to the way things are; God's will includes judgment and change.

This is true of the church as of society. The church is part of society's vain idolatry, a recipient of God's judgment. So Yeager insists: "the church serves as a model precisely because it is representative of the larger culture, not distinct from it. As a representative of culture, 'it repents for the sin of the whole society and leads in the social act of repentance.'" In the wake of the many scandals that have rocked the churches, and in the light of the ideological captivity of much church teaching, the church can hardly be pioneer without leading in the act of repentance.

The mission of Christ and the church as representative of society parallels what Dietrich Bonhoeffer wrote of Christ and the church as representative or deputy (*Stellvertreter*—one who walks in the place of others).[67] It was Bonhoeffer who confessed his own sin powerfully during the Nazi period as a representative of German society, and thereby influenced German churches and the German nation to confess their sin publicly after the war.[68]

Furthermore, the church as pioneer or model points toward the theme that runs throughout John Howard Yoder's writings—the church as model and as *alternative community*. It points strongly toward the *koinonia* (community) nature of the church, a community of disciples obeying the particular ways of God revealed in Christ. A major way the church transforms society is by being a model, a pioneer, of what it means to live in love, justice, inclusiveness, servanthood, forgiveness—and confessing its own need for forgiveness.

And here Yoder brings a special insight that points precisely to the character of the church as pioneer community.

> Not only are there lessons for the outside world from the inner life of the Christian church as a society; a comparable creative impulse should radiate from the church's services to the larger community. The most obvious examples would be the institutions of the school and the hospital, both of which began in Christian history as services rendered by the church . . . to the entire society. . . .
>
> The witness of the church [to the state] must be consistent with her own behavior. . . . A racially segregated church has nothing to say to the state about integration. . . . Denominations with special experiences in overseas relief might speak of the distribution of surplus commodities in a way others could not. . . . Only a church doing something about prisoner rehabilitation would have any moral right to speak—or have any good ideas—about prison conditions or parole regulations. It would be quite normal for church agencies working in places of special social aid such as the inner city to have more specific things to say about abuses in the welfare administration, about urban renewal and ward politics.[69]

Furthermore, the church as community corrects the autonomous individualism that fragments our society. Larry Rasmussen works out the implications accurately:

> Even irrepressible dreamers know that nothing is ever real until it is embodied. . . . What counts with God and one another is not "opportunity," or even vision, but incarnation. What carries power and promise and generates conviction and courage is concrete community. So we must speak of moral leadership in the form of the church as a community of "pioneering creativity" (John Yoder). Very practical theological and technical attention must be given to what the churches do with their own institutional property and moneys. . . . It means attending to how governance happens in these ranks, the

quality of our treatment of one another within the household of faith, the mirroring of the vision of inclusive, egalitarian membership in each locale. It means attending to the way the earth and things of the earth are cared for in this open enclave of creation.[70]

Rasmussen continues: "'Pioneering creativity' must be broadened to speak of 'practices.'" He explains that practices "are those actions intrinsic to a way of life that center, sustain, and order that way of living. . . . They show the way. They perform the faith as a way of life. They are rites that embody what is right." He echoes what Yoder and I have written concerning practices of the Lord's Supper and baptism, delivering processes of forgiveness, inclusion, and delivering justice: The Supper of the Lamb is "the inclusion of the excluded in that decisive act of Jesus, his eating 'with outcasts and sinners' in a new table community that included all and dissolved their social differences." It is inclusion when "it breaks down the barriers between races, classes, gender, and culture [and shame and guilt] by welcoming all to the welcome table; when it connects with the many hungers of the world, including malnutrition and starvation, and moves people to alleviate them as best they can." Rasmussen continues with a historically rich description of baptismal practice; recovering baptism, as he describes it, in creative ways in our time could greatly enrich our membership in pioneering community.[71]

Rasmussen describes our need for community with sensitive moral perceptiveness. He diagnoses causes for modernity's fragmentation of community in "calculating market logic" and in interest-based association." We associate with people like we patronize department stores—based on calculated self-interest. The domination of market logic is seen in "divorce, distrust, suspicion, and general alienation."[72] And because we lack community, we lack moral formation. To resist and transform these powerful forces of fragmentation, we need pioneering community.[73] So long as churches are merely associations of autonomous individuals and not pioneering communities, we will be weak puffs of air against the winds of fragmentation and anomie.

What this means for church structure and practice seems clear: the assumption that church means one worship service a week is hopelessly inadequate. The need for pioneering community, combined with the prophetic/apostolic teaching of concrete, incarnational discipleship, clearly requires more time together. Churches need to emphasize the importance of *Sunday School classes, study groups, mission groups, action/reflection groups—for all members,* adults as well as children and youth. Nor can they do all the teaching themselves; they need to teach parents how to teach children.

They need *shared practices* that transform social experiences, moral formation and transformation, a meaningful sense of membership, and critical teaching of the difference between obedience to the subtle powers and authorities of our society and obedience to the rule of God. They need meals together with discussion and sharing, and meals for the hungry who would not otherwise be fed.

Many churches are forming mission groups with an inward journey of study and prayer and an outward journey of service or advocacy. Different church members may be called to specialize in children's advocacy or peacemaking or evangelism or feeding the hungry or mutual accountability for ethics on the job or divorce recovery. By beginning new groups as needs or gifts are identified, a church can empower diverse members, including visitors or very new members who are not yet sure they belong, to participate in spiritual growth and ministry. Buttry reported that when his church experienced a revival of revitalization and growth, 40 percent of the members belonged to small groups, and many others lived near each other and interacted regularly.[74]

Rasmussen proposes that two kinds of groups are essential. We need communitarian cell groups and also looser, task-oriented, associational groups. He calls this a cell-and-movement ecclesiology. We need mission groups within churches for mutual support and Christian teaching, and membership in association groups outside the church, where we can exchange insights, information, support, advocacy, and Christian witness with persons who have common interests. In a highly mobile world, a combination of both the intimacy of the cell group and the freedom to join or leave looser associations gives "the sense of personal presence and contribution." He identifies cell-and-movement ecclesiology with Dietrich Bonhoeffer's advocacy of the "arcane discipline" of prayer and action for justice.[75]

Robert Wuthnow's sociological research found that 45 percent of American adults, eighty million of them, "are engaged in some kind of voluntary caring activity. . . . Approximately thirty-one million people do volunteer work each year for their churches or synagogues. Twenty million provide free services to schools, tutoring programs, and other educational organizations. Sixteen million individuals donate time to some kind of hospital, nursing home, clinic, or health agency." Others staff hotlines and crisis intervention centers, organize fund-raising drives, and serve on the boards of nonprofit organizations. "When asked how important 'helping people in need' was to them, 73 percent . . . said it was absolutely essential or very important; another 24 percent said it was fairly important; only 2 percent said it was not very important."[76]

"The more often an individual claims to experience divine love, the more likely that person is to spend time on charitable activities," but only if he or she attends church regularly. For those who do not attend church much or at all, "how much or how little they feel God's love has no effect on the likelihood of their being involved in charitable work." Wuthnow interprets these and other data "to mean that religious inclinations make very little difference unless one becomes involved in some kind of organized religious community."[77] What makes a difference is participation plus seriously caring about God. This confirms the argument above for group participation combined with faith in the sovereignty of God. A church as pioneering community could call out the gifts of each member, helping each one find some kind of service or advocacy experience in church or society, and encouraging each one to share their experiences regularly during the church's Sunday School or small-group education program.

Wuthnow also reports that 20 percent of the U.S work force belong to a small religious group, and they "are significantly less likely to bend the rules at work or approve of those who do."[78] David Gushee's research on rescuers, people who performed acts of compassion in a radically different social context than the one Wuthnow studied, produced a similar conclusion. The straightforward sense of obedience to God that Niebuhr intends by the church as pioneer was a major factor. "For many devout Christians, if God wills something, the Christian has no choice but to obey." One Dutch rescuer said, "It's because I am an obedient Christian. I know that is the reason why I did it. I know it. . . . There was never any question about it. The Lord wanted us to rescue those people and we did it." Many rescuers had a vivid sense of God's providence, God's calling us to specific obedience, placing needy persons in our path, watching our actions, calling us to participate in or respond to what God is doing, judging us for our actions in the judgment day. "Even when a person is committed to an appropriately compassionate version of Christian faith (other versions do exist), that faith must be infused by the kind of religious commitment and spiritual vitality that makes it come alive in practice. Most of those Christian rescuers who explicitly cite biblical passages or other resources of faith simultaneously reveal a personal religious experience that proved empowering to them."[79]

Furthermore, group support was a crucial factor. "Rescuers had more friends, co-workers, and neighbors who were Jewish than did nonrescuers." And they often had friends, relatives, or a community collectively committed to rescue. "Nearly every rescuer was involved in some kind of supportive network." This leads Gushee to ask, "How many churches consist of people . . . who live in proximity to one another, share a common commitment to love, justice, and mercy, can be described as cohesive, associate with one another voluntarily, and have the skills to undertake a liberating action on behalf of people who are oppressed or persecuted?"[80]

Another crucial factor is *critical awareness* of the difference between obedience to God and obedience to the powers and authorities. The Christian community is shaped by its participation in society's practices, including the material conditions of work and domination, war and family structures, discrimination and marginalization, political and economic ideologies—the powers and authorities. If it is truly a pioneer, *faithful to God rather than accommodated to* the social forces that shape it and its members' character, then it needs critical analysis of those social forces. As the prophets pointed out practices of idolatry and injustice where they had infiltrated the community of Israel or other communities, and as Jesus confronted unjust practices fifty-one times in the synoptic gospels, so the church must develop skill with using the plumb line of the covenant to measure injustice and idolatry in the society and in itself. It must be able to name and assess the powers and authorities that seek, with great subtlety, to seduce it and its members. We cannot understand the good news of the gospel of Jesus Christ accurately unless we understand the captivities from which the gospel delivers us. In fact, if we do not become aware of the powers and authorities, we are likely to fall back into slavery to them. So Niebuhr's explanation of the church as apostle says the church calls us to repentance for transgressions against what Jesus teaches, such as racist action and obliteration bombing. And Yeager writes, "it repents for the sin of the whole society and leads in the social act of repentance." Yoder writes that *the church's task is to expose the falseness of the Powers* by the witness of its pulpits, prayers, and public action, and to testify to God's redeeming action.

David Gushee found that many Christian rescuers were helped to see through the false propaganda and unjust practices of the govern-

ment because their Christian community had experienced persecution—a memory kept alive in annual commemorations. This established a critical distance from the Christendom attitude of state-church,
establishment Christianity.

Furthermore, convictions about active nonviolence or about human rights gave many rescuers antibodies against the disease of Nazi
propaganda. Numerous pacifists were among the rescuers. Others had
learned from a kind of patriotism that contradicted the Nazi perver-
sions, a patriotism of human rights and democratic pluralism, and so
acted out of revulsion to the Nazi violations of human rights, "the
repugnance of Nazi racial doctrine positing Aryan racial superiority
and Jewish inferiority, and its embodiment in laws denying basic human
rights to Jews." Socialists and communists also "cited their universalist
and anti-fascist ideologies as a motive for rescue. They also sometimes
proved adept at analyzing the dynamics of Nazi oppression and sensing
the need for early, vigorous, militant opposition."[81]

The church must teach about the powers and authorities concretely—how they seek a lordship over us that denies the sovereignty
of God as revealed in Christ. In the time of the rescuers, that meant
teaching that the racism of the Nazis contradicted the apostolic faith.

> These findings imply that those who are tempted to consider patri-
> otism and any kind of political ideology outside the boundaries of
> the Christian moral life must rethink their stance. An inclusive,
> democratic, life- and justice-affirming patriotism and political orien-
> tation should instead be viewed as a potentially powerful force for
> sound personal behavior—even for Christians—as well as crucial for
> national character and conduct. Rather than withdraw from debate
> over the shape of national values and the responsibilities of citizens,
> the churches should weigh in for a particular kind of values and
> citizenship, beginning with their own membership.
>
> Moreover, the practice of habits of political discernment, resis-
> tance and solidarity should be highlighted. For the churches, so many
> of them wedded to a passive and unquestioning patriotism founded
> on cultural captivity and a misreading of Romans 13 and other
> biblical texts, this is a much-needed word. Churches need to be
> communities in which discernment of the political signs of the times
> is a well-refined art. Such discernment sometimes will lead to resis-
> tance in whatever form is both consistent with biblical norms and
> most appropriate to the situation and the faith-community's skills.[82]

The church needs her own structures of decision-making if she is to act faithfully, Yoder insists. He emphasizes the importance of the church as the locus of the process of decision. Significant decisions are too important to be made by autonomous individuals. We all have our blind spots, our defensive evasions. We need a community of account-ability. Pastors, too, need regular consultation with a community that is expected and encouraged to let them know when they are not aware of the effect of their actions, evading responsibility, or embodying other forms of distrust and disloyalty. Yoder points to the New Testament process of decision-making in the power of the Spirit called "the rule of Paul." Everyone who has something to say can have the floor. The other members are to weigh carefully what each person says. Consensus arises uncoerced out of open conversation. Anglo-Saxon democracy, freedom of assembly, freedom of speech, and freedom of the press arose out of Puritan demands based on this New Testament understanding and their experience with it in church communities.[83]

It is intriguing to notice the parallels at several points with the practical research of church growth specialists about factors in church vitality. Many Christian ethicists do not read the writings of church growth specialists, and vice versa. A major reason is that the best-known leaders of the church growth movement explicitly define discipleship in terms of a readily measurable marker: numbers of persons actively engaging in church fellowship. This is a drastic reduction and dilution of what Jesus' teachings mean by the discipleship of authentic transformation—and church-growth leaders admit that. This explicitly stated measure of what is right for churches to do literally means that if a church can increase the number of persons actively engaging in church fellowship by engaging in racist, militarist, or authoritarian activities that contradict what Jesus' teachings mean by discipleship, it should do so. The church growth specialists whom I know have other ethical principles about right and wrong that they hope guard against dominance by this narrow means-ends pragmatism, but the the guiding literature of the movement does not build in this correction explicitly. Another reason Christian ethicists do not often cite this literature could be that some have accommodated to the liberal individualistic belief that religious faith is an individual's own business, and thus they evade the clear norm of Jesus' ethic concerning evangelism. After all this is said, however, I think some important mutual learning could result from dialogue between the two specialties.

As Niebuhr says that history is the laboratory in which our faith is tested, so also church growth specialists test their methods by their practical results. Because they are seeking measures of church vitality, they find results that parallel in intriguing ways the church as apostle, pioneer, and pastor. Thom Rainer writes,

> There may be no greater evangelistic tool for developing relationships than small groups. Those churches that are proceeding deliberately and enthusiastically in this area will undoubtedly see the greatest evangelistic harvests in the years ahead. Our relationship-hungry society is willing to go into homes and other "neutral" sites as their first steps toward associating with Christians.[84]

He advocates many of the kinds of programs Yoder advocates for meeting people's needs in the church and in society outside the church as the best way to give new members a sense of participation in community, and to be the kind of authentic caring community that attracts new members. There is a "direct correlation between numerical growth of the church and significant ministry to the community. . . . The people of our society want to know that they can touch lives and make a difference if they are to be involved in our churches." He urges that we be willing to start something new if a handful of members sees a need:

> One of the most dynamic ministries with which I have been associated is the Food Bank Ministry of the Green Valley Baptist Church. It is now one of the largest food ministries in metropolitan Birmingham, but it began as a burden in the hearts of some of our laypersons. It was led by a layperson. Its staff includes about seventy lay volunteers.[85]

It is not easy to find a Christian ethicist who uses *statistics* to argue that a more active prayer life is essential to a church as pioneer. Rainer does: 71 percent of breakout churches reported an increased emphasis on prayer over the past several years as compared to only 40 percent of plateau churches.[86] Furthermore, Rainer places strong emphasis on active lay ministry, on discovering the gifts of every member, and on the pastor as equipper who empowers God's people to fullness of service.[87] Daniel Buttry and Ebbie Smith, with a somewhat different approach to church revitalization, make similar points.[88] Buttry emphasizes the importance of time for prayer open to all who are moved to pray, and the sense of the dynamic presence of Christ in the church.[89] He advocates spiritual warfare with the powers and authorities. And he argues it is crucial to have a pastor and other leaders with vision and persistence, who have a community of support and who encourage others in exercising their gifts.[90]

241

In sum, the church is pioneer, responding to God's judgment of idolatry and injustice in all of us and to God's always going before us in mercifully calling us to new and hopeful possibilities. To make that response of pioneering obedience it must have a process of discernment and a covenantal plumb line with which to tell the difference between idolatry and injustice on the one hand and faithful and loving hope on the other. It must be a community whose members can admonish and encourage one another. It must have practices that shape the community and form its members morally. It must have mission groups, or cells and movements, that its members participate in. It must have leaders with vision and persistence, and varieties of members with inclusiveness and participation, suited to their different gifts and callings. It must have an active prayer life as well as an active work life.

Yeager asks: But where is the visible church that does this? Not at 11:00 worship. Not even in active charitable activity. More than that is needed for church-as-repentant-community. She suggests perhaps "the traditional anabaptist understanding of Christian community is the necessary supplement here." She asks "what it would mean in late-twentieth-century America to try to be an independent community employing organizational structures different from those of the prevailing culture?" She reminds us that the church gets its mission from God's grace, and it is an error of idolatry to confuse this bit of human society with the rule of the living God. We cannot hope to put absolute or perfect structures in place.[91] Nor does pioneering mean self-righteous withdrawal from all of society; as Yoder says, it does mean shaking the dust off and withdrawing from some particularly hardhearted representatives of the powers and authorities, while participating in or seeking to transform others. Such selective pioneering is indeed happening already here and there, like mustard seeds that participate in God's grace.

Pastor: Caring for All Persons, Especially the Lost, the Outcast, the Needy

Third, Niebuhr sees the church's responsibility as *pastor*. He intends the New Testament meaning of pastor as shepherd who, in Jesus' teachings, is distinguished not by authority but by caring; caring not only for the sheep within the fold but especially *caring for the lost, the outcast, the needy*. He writes: The church "responds to Christ-in-

God by being a shepherd of the sheep, a seeker of the lost, the friend of publicans and sinners, of the poor and brokenhearted."

In this pastoral concern, the church comes to the aid of the needy *directly by itself giving aid, and indirectly by prodding other institutions to do justice to the needy.* Out of its pastoral concern for human beings in need, "the church has found itself forced to take an interest in political and economic measures or institutions." (p. 129). This too is the action of pastoral caring for those in need; often the needy are also the powerless, and they need caring communities to intervene for their rights. Both kinds of pastoral action, direct and indirect, are needed if the church is faithful to God who is universal sovereign, ruling not only in the church but in all of the world.

The pastoral mission of the church is thus the logical implication of the third dimension of the sovereignty of God: *the presently active rule of God over all things*—God as Creator and Ruler. All are included in God's rule and God's love, all of society, including members of the church and outcasts, friends and enemies, the powerless and the powerful, the orphans and the powers and authorities. God sends showers of rain and sunshine on the just and unjust alike. The response to God's universal mercy is universal caring.

For example, one church that I know, after one failed effort and a second lengthy discussion and discernment process, reluctantly reached consensus to invite the county Association for Retarded Persons to establish a weekday School of Hope for retarded adults in the church basement. This was direct aid, a caring service the church could help to provide. Gradually church members grew in awareness and openheartedness toward their new students' needs, their remarkable accomplishments, and their joy in finally having a school. Then an issue of city policy arose that would affect the mentally retarded. Members of the church who had never engaged in such civic action before gathered in the City Hall and spoke to the Mayor and City Council for the powerless whom they had come to know, and they won. Then some began to ask why these adults had never had any school when they were children; why had the right to a public education never been extended to these persons, who needed an education even more than others did? Without schooling, they were helpless, could not become personally independent, care for themselves, or be economically productive. With school they could. So one church member, a parent of a handicapped child, who had joined the Board of the County Association for Retarded Persons, joined with a few other parents in the state association to sue the state for the right to education for children of several varieties of handicaps, including mental retardation. Again they won. The state agreed for the first time to educate thousands of its citizens who had received no schooling before. This, too, was pastoral; it was action that grew out of the church's caring for people.

The parent who sued was a member of both the church's Liaison Committee responsible for the School of Hope, and of the County Association for Mentally Retarded Persons. That parent would not and could not have taken these actions alone, without the support of the church group and the county association. This illustrates the importance of church members joining groups—the church as pioneer. In fact, much that needs to be said about the church's mission as caring pastor has already been said in the description of the church as pioneer. One cannot describe the church's pioneering obedience without speaking of structures and practices of caring in response to God's universal, gracious sovereignty.

Yoder writes that "the powers are not merely defeated in their claim to sovereignty, and humbled; they are also reenlisted in the original creative purpose of the service of humanity and the praise of God."[92] This is a theme of grace. It means not only that we are *obligated* to care and to take action, but that as we do a simple action of caring, or a more complex action of confronting the authorities on behalf of the needy, we are likely to be *participating* in God's sovereign action of reenlisting the powers for God's creative purpose. "To know that the lamb who was slain was worthy to receive power not only enables his disciples to face martyrdom when they must; it also encourages them to go about their daily crafts and trades, to do their duties as parents and neighbors, without being driven to despair by cosmic doubt." Because Christ rules over the powers, his witnesses "are enabled to go on proleptically in the redemption of creation. Only this evangelical Christology can found a truly transformationist approach to culture." In that faith we may make "tactical alliances" with varieties of secular philosophies and movements without making them an opiate, because God in Christ has entered our secular world "in his ordinariness as villager, as rabbi, as king on a donkey, and as liberator on a cross."[93] God is not removed, outside the world; God is active sovereign here.

The ministry of *caring for the church's own members* seems so obviously essential for any church that one wonders at the need to emphasize it. But the grace dimension of the universal sovereignty of God requires special emphasis on God's caring for all diverse kinds of people within a church. Any gathering of sons and daughters of Adam and Eve is filled with people who sense that there is an inner circle from which they have been barred because of their particular faults, shortcomings, practices, vices, virtues, beliefs, inadequacies, history, class, race, gender, and for other unknown reasons. People try to present their acceptable frontside in the gathering and hide their backside. Membership, then, is only partial, and is partially alienating. In our culture, we especially need community. God's grace reemphasizes the need for transforming churches to become forgiving and including communities, to develop diverse mission groups, and to call out diverse gifts of every member. God's universal sovereignty is a call to imaginative inquiry about whose gifts are not being called out, what groups of people are not being encouraged to participate, what needs within the community could be included.

David Gushee's research on rescuers strongly supports the importance of teaching the universally inclusive caring and grace of God. The parents of rescuers modeled responding "to others' needs in a caring and giving fashion." Compared with the parents of nonrescuers, their disciplining of children relied less on physical punishment" and "more on reasoning with their children." They also held "very firm opinions on moral issues and on serving as a model of moral conduct."[94]

A full 76 percent of the rescuers themselves had "a self-conscious commitment to act with kindness, benevolence, mercy, and generosity to those in need, even the stranger." When rescuers cited Christian ethics as motivating them to take the risks they did, the largest number spoke of an ethics of care, kindness, benevolence, mercy, and generosity to those in need. Others "were moved to the depths of their emotions by the plight of suffering Jewish human beings and acted—often spontaneously—to alleviate that suffering. Once again, the moral importance of the emotions is demonstrated, as well as the enormous error in Western ethics of making reasoned moral convictions the single normative way of doing ethics and being moral."[95] Gushee quotes the broken but openhearted English of the Polish rescuer Alex Roslan:

> When I am going to the [Warsaw] ghetto. I felt stiff, I not believe, what was there, so many children was laid down, already dead. You walk blocks and blocks, dead children, dead and they covered by paper, just. They so skinny, the children, and the men stay and the women sit down, like ready to die, the fly eat from the nose, from

the mouth. I was there, I, I, I, I never believed it can be like that. . . . And the Jewish children tug at your jacket. "Hey mister give me something, give me something," then my friend say, "Hey, don't give nothing, because they no got a chance." But I say, "How can you not give?" How much money I had, I not remember, but I [give] everything. After I come home and I explain for my wife. My wife say, "You know, maybe me take a child from somebody."[96]

The church as pastor cares about all God's children. It participates in God's caring for the lost, the outcast, and the needy. It comes to the aid of the needy directly by itself giving aid, and indirectly by prodding other institutions to do justice. It becomes a forgiving and including community, developing diverse mission groups and calling out diverse gifts of every member. It teaches the universally inclusive caring and grace of God for all persons, even the stranger.

3. Evasive Tendencies

Jesus taught memorably by contrasting the way of deliverance with the errant paths that evade the way. In the Sermon on the Mount, he urged us not to continue in anger with someone, but to go and seek to be reconciled; not to love our neighbor and hate our enemy, but love our enemy as well; not to give alms with trumpet fanfare, seeking praise, but to give in secret, counting on God who sees in secret. The way of grace is clearer when it is contrasted with the way of bondage.

Niebuhr taught memorably by contrasting the way of transformation with four other types of Christ-and-culture relationship. Yoder's *Politics of Jesus* has had strong transforming impact by making clear how its interpretation of Jesus' ethics contrasts with "mainstream" or "Ivy League" ethics. If we learn from these models, surely we should conclude by indicating some ways of understanding the relation of Christ and culture that differ from our sketch of the way of transformation.

I do not imply, however, that there are only these five types and that persons or churches should conform to one type consistently. Consistency in relating to all culture the same way is not a virtue, because culture is not consistently good or bad. Some of the powers and authorities are more thoroughly fallen into idolatry and injustice while others are more amenable to good. The Book of Revelation depicts the government as an evil beast, and the Christian who teaches that we should obey the government as an especially evil beast (Rev.

12 and 13). The letter to the Romans depicts the government as ordained by God and to be obeyed by Christians, not revolted against (Rom. 13). We do not advocate relating to prostitution, drug-dealing, obliteration bombing, and a racist government the same way we relate to great art, family love, good parenting, and a government that pursues compassionate justice. The selective practices of *using* a bicycle, *withdrawing from using* drugs, and *participating in transforming* a complacent church or polluting corporation, are not signs of inconsistency. More likely they are signs of having clear ethical norms, and discerning how to relate to different dimensions of culture in a way consistent with those norms. This is a point we have learned most clearly from John Howard Yoder. Niebuhr also pointed in that direction when he suggested that St. Augustine and John Calvin did not conform neatly to the tranformationist type, and when he concluded that different types are appropriate to different historical situations.

Furthermore, it would be an error to think we could define types that characterize particular denominations, or even particular congregations, adequately. In an important book describing varieties of types of congregations, David Roozen, William McKinney, and Jackson W. Carroll define four different "orientations." But they caution that "most congregations give evidence of each orientation to varying degrees, with one or two orientations being dominant. . . . Four out of ten give strong emphasis to two or more orientations; and slightly more than 20 percent of congregations do not score high on any of the four."[97]

Perhaps I *can* describe some *tendencies*. If a church is to teach, for example, avoidance of drug abuse effectively and participation in making music worshipfully, it will need to develop practices and structures that embody those kinds of teaching. Some kind of embodiment is necessary.

I have been arguing for faith in God who is sovereign as our criterion for authentic transformation. Although Roozen, McKinney, and Carroll's study did not base their study on church leaders' understanding of God's action, or even include it consistently in the questionnaire on which they based their typology, they were led to conclude: "We believe it is impossible to read the congregational cases and fail to conclude that, in fundamental ways, each congregation's mission orientation is grounded in its understanding of the action of God in history."[98] Exactly. Transformative faith, if it is faith in the sovereign God and not idolatry, has at least these three dimensions: it is faithful to God who is universal ruler, who is independent judge, and who is concretely revealed. Accordingly, a faithful church will be caring pastor, repentant pioneer, and prophetic apostle. So the question is: Can we identify ways people, groups, and churches are likely to differ from or evade that kind of authentic faith? Most of us will probably recognize some of each tendency in ourselves and our communities.

This still leaves room for great variety in how to be authentically transformationist. It leaves room for us to confess that we embody such transformationist faith only very partially and under particular judgment. We all live only by grace. A significant experience in writing this book has been the unexpected extent to which we three have each come to an occasion—stimulated by our awareness of our own failures—to confess the tip of the iceberg of some of our own inadequacies as Christians. And each of us surely has blind spots that prevent us from seeing some of our inadequacies. The icebergs under the visible tip are bigger than we ourselves want to be aware of. Evasion, as Niebuhr says (and Genesis 3 and 4 said before him), is the most prevalent form of unfaithful faith. (It was this woman you gave to be with me, she gave me this fruit to eat—it was her fault or your fault. . . . How should I know where my brother Abel is—am I my brother's keeper?) None of us could join in signing this book if we were claiming to be paragons of authentic transformation.

Being openly normative in our argument, and confessing our own evasions, we believe that churches also evade full faithfulness to God who is Lord. Thus the tendencies I am about to describe seem to be ways of evading God's lordship. Within these earthen vessels, these Christian congregations, there is still grace, and there are still glimmers of authentic faith. But there are glimmers of evasion, too.[99]

The Living God as Independent Judge

One way to evade God's reality is to ignore or downplay the presence of God as Judge of our own loyalties. We avoid paying attention to the independence of the living God from all our human arrangements. We overlook the contrast between God's will and what we do, and assume that we ourselves, our group, our church, our movement, or our nation, are the embodiment of God's will. We treat the living God as the possession of our set of doctrines, our righteous actions, our community. The result is the accommodation of Christ to our culture. Christ is proclaimed as the mediator of God's loving forgiveness and acceptance, and as the model of loving affirmation, but the cross is not proclaimed as disclosure of our sin and of Christ's confrontation of our idolatry, injustice, and hardheartedness.

Niebuhr suggests two contrasting kinds of accommodation, the liberal individualist variety and the conservative authoritarian variety (C&C, 91ff. and 102f.). Martin Buber explains liberal individualism and conservative authoritarianism as reactions against each other. As a Jew, Buber experienced the fury of the authoritarian reaction.[100] Liberal individualism arose in the Enlightenment as a reaction against the authoritarianism of monarchy and state church. It insists on individual liberty and the development of individual character based on universal reason. But it erodes community and the richness of faith, and threatens to create anarchic permissiveness and chaos. Hence conservative authoritarianism arises in rebellion against liberal individualism. It insists on traditional authority and subservience to the powers and the authorities. But it imposes conformity, excludes the free decision of faith, and threatens liberty and creativity. Hence liberal individualism and conservative authoritarianism feed on rebellion against each other, and we are caught in a flip-flop, a pendulum swing, a vicious cycle of rebellion and backlash.

The alternative to this unstable process of reaction, Buber says, is to find an inclusive-participationist kind of community that provides a more stable grounding, and in which there is real covenant with the other as a respected other. Seyla Benhabib argues similarly, contrasting authoritarian integrative communitarianism with inclusive participative communitarianism.

Roof and McKinney, similarly, analyze present-day U.S. culture as pluralist-individualist, and revolt against pluralist individualism.[101] James Davison Hunter describes this individualist/authority polarization as more intense in the United States now than any time since the Civil War.[102] Bellah et al. write that "there are authoritarian groups in the United States, sometimes devoted to destructive ends. . . . A radically isolating individualism is not a defense against such coercive groups. On the contrary, the loneliness that results from isolation may precipitate the 'hunger for authority' on which such groups feed."[103]

In a time of postmodern polarization, we need to be especially alerted to both kinds of accommodation—accommodation to the individualism and to the authoritarianism in our culture.

1. Accommodation to Liberal Individualist Culture

First, let us look at the liberal individualist type. Robert Wuthnow, Robert Bellah et al., and Roof and McKinney describe a kind of individualism in our culture that dissolves questions of compassion, justice, and ethics into individual fulfillment or therapeutic expressiveness.[104] When churches lose their sense of God's otherness over against our culture, and do not clearly teach the difference between faith in God and the culture's individualistic ideology, the result is a church that is not a pioneering community but a temporary assembly of individuals. The church trusts individuals to be the embodiment of ethical principles, and to do the church's work of transforming society. Therefore it may teach some principles or virtues, but leaves the work of figuring out the concrete implications and working out the concrete transformation to the individuals. There is little sense of a community process of discernment. Nor is there much sense of the need for community encouragement and admonition of individuals. Individuals in the world are good enough to make love and justice happen. The insidiousness of the powers and authorities as they brainwash individuals is not much feared, respected, or combatted, and optimism about the effectiveness of individuals to transform their places of life and work is the rule. The church may sponsor some forums on "current issues," with different viewpoints being discussed, but it is naively unaware of the possibility that the church needs to work through a process of discernment to make a clear statement for guidance like the Catholic Church's pastoral letters on peace and on economic justice. The church loses its sense of being a pioneering community embodying a different way of life from the society. It loses its sense of the need to teach specific criticism of the powers and authorities that dominate the society. As a result, the society's ideologies infiltrate the church uncriticized, and shape the understanding of Christ without resistance.

In this kind of accommodationist church, the apostolic teaching of the church includes an ethic for individuals, but not an ethic for communities, corporations, or the society. The practice of evangelism withers, because religion is a private, individual matter, and people are embarrassed about asking others about their religion. Justice is reduced to individual liberty; justice as the right to basic needs of food, a home, a neighborhood, education, job training, a job, and healthcare drop out. Mutual servanthood becomes the mutual expectation that the other will serve my needs. Nonviolent initiatives of peacemaking are not taught as part of the apostolic mission of the church, since the gospel is read as an ethic for individuals and not for communities. Prayer may be emphasized as individual piety. Inclusion of diverse individuals is emphasized, in line with the emphasis on the freedom of individuals to be themselves. And while love is recognized as important for people in general, and desired for oneself in particular, Wuthnow and Gushee have shown that people tend to do acts of compassion less frequently when they are not members of groups that encourage such acts. Pastoral caring for individuals is likely to be emphasized, but not intervention for justice for others outside the church. God loves individuals, but God's active judgment within history is not perceived or proclaimed. As Niebuhr wrote, "A God without wrath brought men without sin into a kingdom without judgment through the ministrations of a Christ without a cross" (KGA, p. 192).

2. Accommodation to Authoritarian Reactionary Culture

In reaction against this individualism, reactionary accommodationism identifies with the pro-authority ideology in society. People grow angry at those who do not conform to the authoritative doctrine and to the authoritative way to live. They want to feel they belong to a community in which standards are enforced. Those who do not conform should be excluded or punished. The church needs a strong pastor, the family needs a strong father, the nation needs a strong ruler, and the world needs our nation's strong military. The temptation is to lord it over others as the Gentiles do, rather than to be a servant to others as Jesus teaches and models (Mark 10:35ff.). A certain hardheartedness rather than openheartedness creeps in. God's judgment is proclaimed—against others. But God is seen as on the side of our doctrine, our morality, our church, our nation, our authority. The tendency is to identify with the powers and authorities and emphasize their creation by God rather than their fallenness, except for those powers that are enemies of *our* authorities. The truth of God's dynamic, living, compassionate character, unable to be possessed by any human institution, is downplayed when it comes to our ideology. The authoritarian side of society is not criticized but championed. The vehicle for transforming society is support for "our" leaders, within the church and in the society outside the church. The need for open processes of discernment that correct, check, and balance the power of our leaders is overlooked and, indeed, those who suggest such open processes are resented. An authoritarian ideology infiltrates the church

251

and distorts its understanding of Christ. Christ is understood to teach the rules and understandings promulgated by a secular political ideology of conformity to authority. His teaching that we are not to lord it over one another as the secular Gentiles do, but to be servants of one another (Mark 10:42ff.), is replaced by a secular teaching that we are to serve the cause of authoritarian order and conformity.

In order to maintain the conforming community the leaders of such groups emphasize the apostolic function of teaching concreteness of doctrine and concreteness of ethics so that people can be sure that they fit in the community. They may emphasize evangelism in order to bring more people into our way for their good and for the strength of our community. But compassionate forgiveness and inclusion toward others who do not conform, and toward the hidden parts of ourselves that do not conform, may not be emphasized. Servanthood toward those in authority is emphasized, but not mutual servanthood. Justice tilts toward punishment of those who do not conform, rather than deliverance of the powerless, the outcasts, the aliens, the poor. Peacemaking initiatives are not much taught, since the way to peace is for those who are not under our authority to conform to our will. Prayer and love are values of the community, but their beneficiaries tend to be those who belong within the circle of authority and conformity. A God who sides with our authorities forgave us and brought us into His kingdom through the ministrations of a Christ who proclaims our traditional morality and judgment of others.

These tendencies follow from evading the living God's independence from our culture, values, beliefs, and institutions. They follow from the wish not to hear of God who judges our own practices. They are tendencies, not pure types. They are probably at least partially present in all of us and all of our churches. Roozen, McKinney, and Carroll, in their sociological study of different types of congregations, give several examples that may illustrate the liberal-individualist and conservative-authoritarian varieties of accommodation to the culture.

The liberal-individualist tendency is seen in what might be called *the individualistic, conflict-avoiding, civic type*. Congregations of this type encourage "members, as individuals, to become involved in social and political issues." They cooperate with other groups to achieve community improvements, and provide aid and services to those in need. They help individuals "to understand that they are 'agents' of God's hope, responsible for actualizing the good and humane as they share in the development of history and society."[105]

They are comfortable with, even affirming of, dominant social, political, and economic structures; indeed, many of their members are well placed in those structures. The congregations are pluralistic, tolerant of diversity, and embrace ecumenical involvements. They put a premium on civil harmony and religious peace.[106]

First Church of Christ, East Town, illustrates this type, according to Roozen, et al.[107] It "has few announced standards for membership and those it has are not applied rigorously." Members participate in town committees and civic affairs, but do not tend to see this clearly as a matter of Christian vocation. The level of commitment to the church and to teaching in church school is low. The committee meetings lack explicitly religious references, and members are unclear about any common theological self-understanding. A large percentage of the members' giving does go to denominational mission programs, and the minister does speak concretely to issues of social justice in church and in town meetings—for himself as an individual rather than for the church. The Board of Christian Concern occasionally informs the congregation about an issue like the Nestle boycott, but "there is no, even implicit, agreement at First Church about what issues are appropriate for the church to address, much less agreement on appropriate types of action." Church school on Sunday mornings runs through eighth grade, only. There are youth fellowship groups, but they provide primarily fellowship and have little education. In the fifteen years from 1965 to 1980, church school membership dropped from 668 to 175. Once a month after morning worship there is an adult forum on current issues. This is appreciated by members; their only criticism is that it meets too seldom. "Issue-related programs are chiefly informational rather than action-oriented." The church has started or participated in programs for refugee resettlement, assistance for youth from homes with conflict, outside aid for prison inmates, and support for people with alcohol problems. "It engages in service to needy persons in East Town while generally accepting and supporting the status quo. . . . Thus, while First Church is present in the community, it is also very much *of* the community."

Reactionary or pro-authority accommodationism may be illustrated by what Roozen, McKinney, and Carroll name the sanctuary type, but might be better called the *traditional authority type*. They define this type on the basis of four practices that their factor analysis singled out as characteristic of congregations in the type. They suggest that these congregations withdraw from society and are otherworldly.

The first two questions that define the type, however, do not actually mention withdrawal from society or otherworldliness, but advocate subservience to secular authorities; they have a this-worldly emphasis on submitting to the authorities of this world. The other two questions also advocate subservience to authorities—God and traditional ways of life. All four reject experimenting with new things; we should accept traditional authorities.[108] Alerted by the theological/ethical interpretation above, one notices a strain of accommodation to secular society's authoritarian ideology in all four identifying questions.

Furthermore, the four identifying questions say nothing about organized activity by the congregation or by groups. The congregation as pioneer, as community, is not in view, just as Martin Buber suggested. Insofar as they suggest identifying with a community, the community is a patriotic, civil society traditionally understood.

One example they give is Faith Episcopal Church.[109] In rebellion against the revised Episcopal prayerbooks, Faith Episcopal uses prayerbooks two generations older than what is officially sanctioned. The rector "has made clear his disapproval of women priests, the new Episcopal prayerbook, . . . divorce, and abortion. Communicants . . . are expected not to challenge openly the conservative liturgical and theological stance." The members are fairly wealthy, and see the church existing primarily to preserve their Anglo-American way of life in a community that has become Hispanic and Portuguese. They often speak of themselves and their church as American by contrast with nonAnglo citizens of the community. "The rector is clearly in charge. . . . He is the 'supreme commander'. . . . The role of the Vestry is primarily that of concurrence."

The full range of the apostolic teachings of Jesus is hardly taught. Although the church was originally founded as a Sunday School, which then grew into a church, the Sunday School no longer exists. There are almost no group meetings.

This is a fairly tame and probably dying form of authoritarian reaction. *Varieties of Religious Presence* does not include a more virulent authoritarian-reactionary congregation. But surely in Faith Episcopal we can see hints of accommodation to the reactionary authoritarian strain in our culture.

The Reign of God Over All

A second way to evade the sovereignty of God is to ignore or downplay the sense of the universal reign of God in history and the world. God may be seen as judging the world, or as distant and removed from the world, but not as actively present, ruling. The disclosure of God's will and character may be taught and proclaimed, but they are seen as obligatory guidelines for us to follow rather than as grace-filled, celebrative indicators of what God is actively doing. The result is an ethic of human effort, and maybe even sometimes heroic obedience, but not an ethic of participation in God's gracious initiatives. It may be an ethic of grateful response to God's forgiveness, or God's past revelation in Christ, but one does not find the joy of participation in deliverance that the first chapter of the gospel of Luke and much of the New Testament speak of, and that Niebuhr points to in his description of the sense of God's redemptive presence in *The Kingdom of God in America* and the presence of the living Christ in *Faith on Earth*.

In *The Consciousness Reformation*, Robert Wuthnow shows a shift among those whom he studied from belief in God's active rule to belief in nature mysticism and in a social-science interpretation of the determining forces of our existence.[110] His data show that whether and how people understand God to be actively ruling in their life-context powerfully affects their self-understanding and their ethics. This confirms the importance of Niebuhr's central insight in *The Kingdom of God in America*, and *Christ and Culture*. The sovereignty of God in all of creation, and radical faith in God as sovereign ruler, are the central theological discoveries of his career as theological ethicist and sentinel of transformationist faith. Many Christians, he contended, have lost that sense.

One result of a decline of belief in God's active rule in the world is that loyalty to Christ suggests withdrawal from the world. The church does not sense that God is active in the world. Therefore, loyalty to God as disclosed in Christ points toward withdrawal into a sanctuary, or withdrawal into individual solitude.

3. Withdrawal Into Sanctuary

In withdrawal into sanctuary, apostolic teachings are understood as applying to life within the church or within the community, but not to life outside. Prayer, love, and servanthood are likely to be emphasized as community practice. Nonviolence may be emphasized, but more as a rule that is faithful to the community than as an initiative that can be spread in the world—in contrast to Martin Luther King's sense of God's active providential rule and his hope for spreading nonviolent initiatives in the world of racial and international conflict. Justice is likely to be de-emphasized as an ethic for the world, except insofar as it contributes to safety for us and our community. Forgiveness may be emphasized in the community, but not inclusion of others who are different. Evangelism is likely to be limited to those who attend the church and its functions; the lack of hope for the world discourages hope for aggressive evangelism.

This "type" does emphasize community. It may be pioneering community as model for the world or as alternative to the world, or it may be simply defensive community with little hope for changing the world. Pastoral caring is emphasized, but is directed mostly to those within the community. The practices of the community and its members may be seen as obedient human efforts rather than as joyous participation in God's gracious initiatives. They are merely practices, not grace-based delivering processes.

Because this kind of withdrawal may see the community as a fortress against the world's threat, it has the danger of falling into the authoritarian type above. We have seen hints of this in Faith Episcopal Church above. It has very little sense of God's active rule in the surrounding community, or of being able to participate in that rule. "Faith Church has little confidence in its ability to relate to or work with the surrounding non-Anglo community; nor does the non-Anglo community express much interest in relating to Faith." One Vestry member said, "We are elderly Anglicans in the middle of a Hispanic and Portuguese neighborhood." Parishioners are frustrated and bewildered about what they can do for the area. Therefore they withdraw into their emphasis on tradition. "Communicants speak of themselves as a family, helping one another in times of sickness; joining in personal celebrations . . . ; and generally 'helping out.'"

St. Felix Roman Catholic Church is a similar example.[111] The Mass is the focus—thirteen of them a week. Almost no one takes part in any church activity besides the Mass. The church is one big square white-walled sanctuary and there is no educational space. The church "takes no stands on public issues. . . . The Church and its members seem to operate with the clear sense of separation between the religious and the public." The theology emphasizes personal knowledge of Jesus Christ, God our Father as a forgiving God, and the happy return of the sinner to God. Neither the theology of the leaders, nor the sermons, nor the almost nonexistent adult education program proclaim God's active rule outside the parish and the individual lives of the members. Nor is there a sense of obligation to donate to serve needs in the world; the annual giving is about $30 per member, which covers the expenses of the church, and the leadership does not see a major need to increase that. Nor did the discovery in a community religious survey that many newcomers in the neighborhood were unaware of the church cause the Parish Council to reach out with evangelism or any welcoming activity. The church has no sign on its property indicating that it is a church or what its name is. Sixty percent of the Catholics in the church's area are not active in the church. "Parishioners see the church as primarily responsible for the spiritual and physical needs of members." But the Pastor wants "to make them good citizens of the church, state, and country." This is God's plan for us, and if we would follow it, the "greatness that's in each of us would be developed and would bring good to ourselves, to the neighborhood, to the country, and to God."

Thus the withdrawal from a sense of God's active rule is combined with trust in the authorities that do rule in the world—and in the church. "The pastor is careful to observe the chain of episcopal authority." He says "the archbishop is the real leader of the diocese and we are just his extension in the parish." In the parish itself, "nothing happens without [the pastor's] approval, seldom without his participation." Furthermore, "the Finance Committee of the Parish Council is there to offer advice; the pastor determines most expenditures." The Parish formed a Parish Council only recently, over a decade after it was encouraged to do so, but the Pastor has veto power over the Council, which he does exercise. After the Christian Service Committee had worked several months polling members to develop support for the project of settling a refugee family, and making the complicated arrangements for the family, the following notice appeared in the parish bulletin:

> Because current financial income is less than current financial expenses the refugee resettlement family will not be coming to our parish at this time. Father Melley exercised his veto power over a seven to six acceptance vote by the parish council.

St. Felix does have a lay-led weekly prayer group, which has developed a deep commitment to studying the scripture, and especially the life and teachings of Christ, and to the needs of members. It has a food bank, a thrift shop, and an extremely weak Catholic Youth

Organization. Some members are involved as individuals in the prolife movement, or in programs for meeting needs of the poor in the city, but there is no energetic encouragement from the church leadership for members to find their niche in service or advocacy. Clearly St. Felix has many resemblances to Faith Episcopal, both of which Roozen, et al. call the sanctuary type. They are discussed separately here to illustrate two different dimensions of downplaying the sovereignty of God—the sense of God as Independent Judge, and God as Ruler in the world. Both dimensions are weak in the sanctuary churches.

Another kind of theology that does not see God actively ruling in the world now is the faith of Cristo Pentecostal Church.[112] God does rule, but that rule will not be manifest until The Second Coming—the end of the world—which is near, and expected before the year 2000. In the meantime, the world is ruled by evil powers and should be shunned. The signs that the end is near are catastrophes, wars, oppression, crime, drugs, prostitution, and disintegration of family life. One member explained, "The world outside, with its sin and carnal life, we cannot participate in once we become new creatures." Roozen, et al. report that "members consider themselves consecrated to the Lord, separated from the world although living in it." The members are Hispanic Protestants, while the neighborhood is constituted largely of Hispanic Catholics, which increases the sense of separation from the world. "Direct ministry to society, except through proselytizations, is not part of the congregation's understanding of its mission." Government programs are considered a waste. "Nothing will change until the heart of one changes and receives conversion. . . . In Christ is the solution."

Cristo has a strong sense of pioneering community. Only believers are baptized, they must be at least twelve years old, and must have shown a sincere change in their lifestyle for three to six months before baptism. Members are expected to participate in worship services four times a week, plus "on evenings where there are no services, active members are expected to meet together in their homes for prayer and study or to evangelize by making house calls." The church clearly emphasizes a strong change in life-style and supports members in their struggles with those changes. Members would like to develop their own school; it would help remove students from the bad language, stealing, dancing, and smoking in the world's schools.

God *is active*—in the faith community, if not in the world. God works genuine conversion in the lives of members, and the Holy Spirit

258

guides and inspires them in their living. A significant part of the life of the church is God's healing of persons with illnesses. Furthermore, we can participate in God's healing by prayer and fasting for healing or for solving a family problem. There are organized campaigns of prayer and fasting. "The Spirit is believed to manifest itself to any adult member or the pastor. . . . Consensus is understood as the action of the Spirit and a sign of God's presence." Although the pastor is the leader, the authority rests with congregational consensus. If the pastor proposes something that does not reach consensus, it is dropped. The pastor cannot spend more than $200 on his own. This is the practice Yoder writes of as "the rule of Paul," a democratic consensus process of discernment under the guidance of the Holy Spirit. It gives a strong sense of community cohesion, without authoritarianism in the hands of one leader.

With this belief in God's present ruling, it becomes important to study the scripture as well as pray and fast in order to know how to recognize God's delivering action and God's will. Much Bible study takes place. "Members speak knowledgeably about their beliefs, their moral code, and what is expected of them. They know the contents of the Bible and are in close agreement on theological issues and the implications of church membership." The sermons are expected to be long, filled with biblical teaching, and applied concretely to real life situations. The concrete application concerns the life of the members, and not what civic authorities or other powers and authorities in the world should do.

Thus much of Niebuhr's apostolic teaching and proclamation do take place, although Roozen, et al. do not try to summarize all the content of the teaching. We can see that the teaching is extensive, biblical, and concrete, but that it slights the public dimensions of delivering justice, peacemaking initiatives, and the public implications of Yoder's practices. Yoder's point, however, is that often these implications do have their influence simply because of their practice. For example, the democratic implications of the consensus process of decision-making are clearly having their impact on the members' understanding of authority, and must have carry-over implications on their citizenship. Roozen, et al. suggest that Cristo mediates between members and the wider society. It reinforces "values of personal discipline, family life, hard work, and patriotism—all of which serve Cristo members well in the very world the church devalues. Although the church is otherworldly in its theology, it encourages values and traits that often lead to worldly success."[113] Here the sociologists are speaking of accommodation to the world, but the church's leaders suggest that the changed lives of members actually transform the world more effectively than other means of change would. With their faith that God is actively present transforming lives, that God judges specific sins, and that they must study the scriptures extensively, they may be closer to authentic transformation than many other churches are.

4. Withdrawal Into the Individual

There is another kind of withdrawal: not into community but into the individual. This describes many persons who are only peripherally involved in churches, or who have withdrawn from them. "Radically individualistic religion presumes an autonomous believer, one who is on a spiritual journey, on his or her own quest, and often with little involvement in or connection with a particular religious community."[114]

Bellah, et al. argue that two kinds of individualism dominate our culture. One, utilitarian individualism, takes economic competitiveness in the free market as its model, competing to get what the consumer most wants for the least cost.[115] They describe the values of Ted Oster, a lawyer in the Silicon Valley, a member of no church or political organization, whose religion is "pinballism." He sees himself no more profoundly related to other persons or groups than a pinball is related to the bumpers that it bounces off of in a pinball machine. Ted is the consumer who puts the money in the slot and identifies with the pinball, a self-contained spheroid with a shiny, reflecting surface; relationships are merely bounces that get him toward his goal, merely external means to the ends of the consumer.

> He argues that "rigid" moral standards interfere with one's freedom and enjoyment of life, since "life is a big pinball game and you have to be able to move and adjust yourself to situations if you're going to enjoy it. You got to be able to realize that most things are not absolute. Very little is, other than life and death." If the self is to be free, it must also be fluid, moving easily from one social situation and role to another without trying to fit life into only one set of values and norms, even one's own. . . . Life conceived as a "pinball game" has its rules, but they are all instrumental, meaningful not in themselves but only as a means to the player's enjoyment. Bending the rules makes sense if it enhances the player's satisfaction. . . . "I guess I'm pretty result-oriented, and whatever produces a good result must be right, and whatever produces a bad result must be wrong."[116]

The other kind of individualism is therapeutic expressiveness, rebelling against authoritarian, heteronomous norms and advocating following and expressing one's own feelings.[117] Bellah et al. report an interview with Sheila Larson, a nurse whose religion is "Sheilaism."

> "I believe in God. I'm not a religious fanatic. I can't remember the last time I went to church. My faith has carried me a long way. It's Sheilaism. Just my own little voice." Sheila's faith has some tenets beyond her belief in God, though not many. In defining "my own Sheilaism," she said: "It's just try to love yourself and be gentle with yourself. You know, I guess, take care of each other. I think He would want us to take care of each other."[118]

Wuthnow describes a mystical kind of individualism. This emphasizes intense ecstatic experience as the primary way of constructing meaning. It is an intuitive perception of a larger whole of which one is a part, often expressing an affinity for nature, rural quietude, the sea, innocence, and simplicity. Mystics believe the force responsible for governing reality is their own mind-set, their own frame of mind. This is what mystical experience changes. Mysticism usually assumes human nature is basically good and can be made better.[119] Unlike the other types, mysticism has a sense of the presence of God or at least the Transcendent, but in the mystical relationship no moral laws are disclosed. The teachings of Jesus or the covenants of God are dissolved into openness to change or openness to the Transcendent; the individual intuits what is right along the way.

5. Dualist Split Between God Revealed in Christ and Realist Activism

There is also a realist/activist version of loss of faith in God's active rule in history. Here God as revealed in Christ may be seen as active in love and forgiveness for individuals and in the church, but the public arena is ruled by social forces best understood by the social sciences or by realist analysis of power and interests. In some ways this sounds like the sanctuary tendency, where God seems present only in the church and in individual lives, and not in the world, and where God's universal sovereignty is not experienced. The difference is that realist/activists urge members to be actively engaged in working for justice in the world. They do this, however, without a clear sense of participation in God's rule in history. God is not active in history; social forces and social change agents are. The forces described by the social sciences are not interpreted as related to God's present creating, judging, and redeeming action. Theology is split between God as revealed in Christ and a realist ethic based on social realities quite different from what is seen in Christ. Consequently, activism is not strongly supported by the apostolic gospel, but is based rather on experiences of injustice, or on social-scientific insights, or on a leap into avant-garde sophistication beyond childhood religion. Therefore, a split ethic supports social activism rather than deep transformation of faith, and a gospel of social analysis rather than Jesus Christ. The foundation of the pioneering community is not so much the gospel of Jesus Christ as the gospel of social analysis, or the gospel of a realistic God different from the God revealed in Christ. Something like this is seen in H. R. Niebuhr's criticisms of his brother, Reinhold, and of what H. Richard called the dualist or paradoxical type of Christ-and-culture relationship. Such a split has difficulty sustaining itself. Either it produces social action but not much Christ-centered gospel, and therefore lacks Christian converts; or its energy for social activism burns out and it retreats into one of the kinds of withdrawal.

At first glance, Downtown Baptist Church as described by Roozen, et al. appears to be authentically transformationist.[120] "'Justice,' for Downtown Baptist, is not an abstract or complicated theological concept. It is 'doing for others what you want for yourself.' Neither is 'justice' a theological 'option.' Rather, it is held to be the 'pilgrimage' by means of which one 'seeks and finds God.' The numerous vagrants and transients in the area know Downtown Baptist as a place where they can go for direct assistance."

Furthermore, there is a sense of community; the church is indeed the church as pioneer:

> The positive lay attitude has been promoted . . . by a carefully developed balance between social outreach and the nurture of the congregation itself. . . . The in-house ministry includes pastoral care, counseling, visitation, and other programs addressing the needs of the membership. The senior pastor has primary responsibility for this and does most of the preaching, parish calling, and development of care and counseling groups. This contrasts with a previous senior pastor, who gave less attention to pastoral concerns . . . the in-house/out-house strategy was devised through lay initiative.

The church polls members extensively before making a major decision, and is widely felt to be responsive to members' feelings. There is an active Sunday School for children and adult forum on social issues. "There are also several Bible study groups for adults meeting at various times throughout the week, one convening weekly to go over the next Sunday's scripture text with the senior minister. A half-dozen women's circles and other organizations combine study with fellowship and service projects." Furthermore, the church "has an active program of member visitation headed by the senior minister [who] has trained two dozen laypeople to visit regularly."

But when it comes to theological self-understanding, there is great diversity and not a clearly unified theological grounding for the church's action for justice. The pastor's theology is Tillichian, emphasizing a gospel of individual acceptance and inclusion but probably remaining quite abstract on grounding in God's delivering action for the church's social action. Nevertheless, there is widespread support for the pastor because of his ministry of pastoring, counseling, and visiting, and his very biblical teaching and preaching. This biblical emphasis is shared by the racial-minority members, most of whom "tend to be theologically conservative—not biblical fundamentalists—but evangelical in their stress on religious experience and personal salvation." Here there could be the basis for concrete connection between biblical faith and social action. But the staff and most members are "Social Gospel liberals emphasizing a commitment to justice, the expression of personal faith by active involvement in the world, and as much, if not more, concern for structural change as for individual transformation." The adult education "concentrates on pragmatic social issues rather than on abstract theological topics. It is the operative hermeneutic of most sermons, and it is the predominate 'language' laity use to express their faith and faith struggles." In the Sunday adult forum members did not feel that society had enough faith that invoking the name of the Lord in the cause of justice was an effective strategy toward change. "Matters of personal morality, discipline, and belief are left to the individual," thus threatening the church with a withdrawal into individualism. Roozen, McKinney, and Carroll note that Downtown Baptist has a large mixture of individualistic civic types.[121] In our individualistic culture, this raises the worry of a burnout or loss of community cohesion without a strong sense of theological grounding in God's redemptive action.

Downtown Baptist lacks an aggressive program of evangelism or membership growth. Its location is in the center of the city and the church is not attracting new members from nearby neighborhoods. The membership declined under the previous pastor's leadership, and readers cannot help but be curious about how it will do now. One wishes the minority members' evangelical sense of God's present rule as concretely outlined in the biblical story, with specific covenant content, in both private life and struggle for justice, could spread to the rest of the congregation and its staff—and to prospective members near and far.

One wishes that some of the biblical and evangelistic strengths of Mountainview Evangelical Baptist Church, which Roozen, et al. call an *evangelistic type*, could be combined with the strengths of Downtown Baptist. Both have a sense of being a pioneering and pastoring community—engaged proactively to transform the world, not only as individuals but together as a congregation. Both have a sense of being engaged biblically, and do extensive apostolic teaching to adults as well as children and youth. Both are clear that the world is in the grip of powers and authorities from which it needs to be redeemed, and both have hope, and evidence to back up that hope, that redemption is happening here and there. Both have some clarity in their sense of mission. Both have some evasive tendencies. Both could learn from each other. What Roozen, et al. call the activist type and the evangelistic type have much in common, when seen from the perspective of transformationist faith.

Mountainview's mission is "for a believer in Jesus Christ who is born again to receive biblically-based instruction and be strengthened in the vision to reach out to people in the name of Jesus."[122] The preaching is biblical and Christ-centered and the fellowship is warm, loving, and inclusively welcoming. The key is a personal relationship with Jesus Christ as both Savior and Lord; without that, we are lost. Like Cristo Pentecostal, membership is not automatic:

> The "new birth" must be evident in both motivation and behavior. . . . The applicant appears before the Board of Deacons to be tested on knowledge of and commitment to the theological precepts of Mountainview, on whether he or she intends to participate actively in worship and church work, and on the degree of seriousness about living "an exemplary life fittingly representing the Lord and His Church in the community." The applicant is expected to give a brief testimonial to a personal relationship with Jesus Christ.

There are extensive groups, classes, and communities for members. The four adult Sunday School classes are Bible-centered. Seventy-five percent of those baptized were drawn to the church through home Bible study groups. The style of leadership and administration is democratic, and initiatives and gifts of members are encouraged to come to expression.

Mountainview does not encourage withdrawal from the world. Yet it seldom teaches concretely what Christian faith, God's love, and God's justice and judgment mean for transformation in the midst of the powers and authorities in the world. One sermon, not typical of those usually preached, went this far: "God makes very clear in the Old Testament that his people are to make sure that other people do not get locked into abject poverty. . . . Let's face it, we need some changes. I am not going to tell you how to do it because that is a political statement, only that it must happen—that is a *Christian* statement." Social service projects are slow to develop, in spite of evidence that churches active in social service tend to grow more in successful evangelism. Mountainview is making its members more honest and conscientious in their places of responsibility in the world, and its active youth programs, home-based Bible study, and informal counseling for those facing life crises, all with a strong and clearly defined biblical base and sense of mission, are having a significant transformational impact on the lives of youth, families, and neighborhoods.[123] Yet it avoids the sense of God's commitment to justice and peacemaking. One wishes Mountainview could connect its biblical theology more clearly with the biblical sense of delivering justice in Downtown Baptist, and that Downtown Baptist could connect its justice ethic more clearly with the biblical evangelism of Mountainview. In many ways they are similar.

The Apostolic Teaching of God's Concrete Disclosure and Processes of Deliverance

The reader who has been following the sequence of discussion thus far, first describing evasion of God's judgment and then evasion of God's reign over all, might now expect a section on churches that evade God's concrete disclosure in Christ. These would be congregations that do not teach the full apostolic spectrum of normative processes of deliverance and discipleship. But we have already seen that. We have seen how churches that try to ignore the independent judgment of the living God on our way of doing things, or that do not sense God's present rule in all areas of life, inevitably ignore some parts of God's disclosure in Christ. We have seen how each of the tendencies described above distorts the apostolic teaching of the disclosure of God's character in Christ to fit its understanding of God's rule. Therefore, no additional section is really needed, although this dimension of evasion, the evasion of the full range of the disclosure of the way of God in Christ, may be the most crucial indicator of straying from the path of authentic transformation. It is so crucial that one dimension or another of this evasion has shown up in each of the churches we have examined.

The Living Presence of the Lord
in the Christian Community and in the World

The best way to conclude is by mentioning some highlights of Roozen's description of a transformationist church, St. Margaret's Roman Catholic Hispanic Church.[124]

St. Margaret's has a concrete theological center that supports its outreach and inreach ministries: life is centered in the Mass, and so is the theology. The pastor says "The eucharist is the living presence of Christ. In sharing that presence, the call is to go out to make that presence operational, living in the world. . . . It is an overflow of the Lord's presence. The Mass is part of the world and the world is part of the Lord." This understanding is widely shared by the laity. Members are encouraged to develop an active prayer life in response to the Mass. "A charismatic group exists within the parish. But under the influence of the priests' refusal to draw a distinction between the sacred and the secular, the group has made a conscious effort to keep its fellowship from becoming too introspective."

The staff "maintain that U.S. society is not conducive to spirituality in isolation from a religious community." They insist that "when Hispanics in the United States do not attend Mass and stay in touch with the faith community, they find few religious support mechanisms." They "are particularly sensitive to the erosion of faith that can take place in fast-moving, individualistic, and materialistic U.S. culture." They have organized extensive religious instruction, extending beyond First Communion through the teen years. To maintain a life of Christian discipleship in the midst of our secular society, people need more teaching in the church than can be found in many parishes, Catholic or Protestant. And in this there is a sense of participating in God's active presence. One teacher in the Learning Center remarked, "I help the youth under God's guidance, who gave me some gifts I am using to help them reach out to others." If the adults were as involved in education programs as the teenagers are, St. Margaret's could have an even more profound transformative impact. In their conclusion, Roozen, McKinney, and Carroll note that activism at St. Margaret's depends largely on the youth and the pastor, whereas at Downtown Baptist it is more firmly based in the lay leadership.[125]

> The youth program is perhaps the best example of St. Margaret's "wholistic" approach to ministry. The spiritual dimension of life is addressed through the Mass and discussions of the Gospel lessons and Sacraments. The intellectual dimension is considered by developing awareness of social reality and a sense of Christian responsibility for selves and others. An active concern for justice is fostered through personal involvement. The 'play' dimension is met by recreational activities after the sessions and at other times.

The Roberto Clemente Housing Corporation was started by the youth program. Like Habitat for Humanity, it rehabilitates housing and turns it into ownership by poor people. The pastor said: "The program is good because it is building something without the government's initiation. The work is done with the ingenuity of the people, their labor, and God's help. That power came from the Mass. The Lord gave the people talents and abilities and strengths to help themselves."

A staff member explained:

> The Mass is where life starts. If the church wants to teach values that are not paramount in the society, then the team of the parish must teach them to look at life as the Lord does and utilize their talents for more than themselves. Then they will have a real sense of the gifts they have been given, gifts being developed by the support system of St. Margaret's, so they will not only have happy lives as individuals but can also be of service to the Lord. This is countercultural, because it is not what the culture around us teaches.[126]

Here are all the dimensions of authentic transformation: The Mass is God's redemptive presence of grace with demonstration of the way—a grace-based practice of deliverance. The church must teach people to look at life as the Lord does—must teach the apostolic way. The congregation is a pioneering community in which members sense the gifts they have been given, and in which they have a support system. Servanthood—service to the Lord—is the objective. The church is doing its job of being a caring pastor in the inner community and the larger society. It has the sense of independence from the way of the world—it is countercultural. Could we ask for a more beautiful summary in one statement?

And that leads to an insight that was present here and there throughout our examination, but never noticed explicitly enough. H. Richard Niebuhr is trying to point to the universal rule of God not only as a doctrine, as an abstract principle, but as a sense of God's presence now. In *Faith on Earth*, he emphasizes that the Christ we know is first of all not the Christ of past documents or the Christ of the church, but the Christ who is present to us now, our living contemporary. St. Margaret's has that sense in the Mass. Where does that happen in Protestant churches and evangelical churches? The preached word alone is not enough; it can be too dry, too much declared from a distance. There needs to be the response of personal commitment, or the lifting of the spirit in the improvisation of African-American song, or the movement of the spirit in Pentecostal worship, or the open prayer of spontaneous participation in Daniel Buttry's church, or the calling forth of gifts that John Yoder advocates, or the sense of participating in God's redemptive work as taught and pioneered by Jesus Christ. That is surely what Niebuhr was pointing to when he described prophetic faith in *The Kingdom of God in America*. That is surely the gift of God's delivering grace. It is the gift of the experience of release into gratitude, the presence of God.

Thus our dialogue ends in gratitude. And with a challenge for each of us: to seek to participate in the grace of authentic transformation, and to give thanks. May we all share in that God-given experience.

BIBLIOGRAPHY

A. Selected full-length works on the thought of H. Richard Niebuhr

Cook, Martin. *The Open Circle: Confessional Method in Theology.* Minneapolis: Fortress, 1991.

Diefenthaler, Jon. *H. Richard Niebuhr: A Lifetime of Reflections on the Church and the World.* Macon: Mercer University Press, 1986.

Fadner, Donald S. *The Responsible God: A Study of the Christian Philosophy of H. Richard Niebuhr.* AAR Dissertation Series 13. Missoula: Scholars, 1975.

Folk, Jerry. *The Theological Development of Helmut Richard Niebuhr.* Ph.D. diss., Tübingen University, 1962.

Fowler, James W. *To See the Kingdom: The Theological Vision of H. Richard Niebuhr.* Nashville: Abingdon, 1974.

Godsey, John D. *The Promise of H. Richard Niebuhr.* Philadelphia: Lippincott, 1970.

Grant, C. David. *God, The Center of Value: Value Theory in the Theology of H. Richard Niebuhr.* Fort Worth.: Texas Christian University Press, 1984.

Hoedemaker, Libertus A. *The Theology of H. Richard Niebuhr.* Philadelphia and Boston: Pilgrim, 1970.

Irish, Jerry A. *The Religious Thought of H. Richard Niebuhr.* Atlanta: John Knox, 1983.

Keiser, Melvin. *Recovering the Personal: Religious Language and the Post-Critical Quest of H. Richard Niebuhr.* Atlanta: Scholars, 1988.

Kliever, Lonnie. *H. Richard Niebuhr.* Waco: Word, 1977.

McFaul, Thomas R. *A Comparison of the Ethics of H. Richard Niebuhr and Reinhold Niebuhr.* Ph.D. diss., Boston University, 1972.

Maeder, Michael William. *H. Richard Niebuhr's Doctrine of God and Critical Realism: An Attempt to Reconcile Orthodox Christianity with an Experiential View of God.* Ph.D. diss., Graduate Theological Union, 1976.

Molin, Lennart. *Hearts and Structures.* Ph.D. diss., University of Lund, 1978.

Ottati, Douglas P. *Meaning and Method in H. Richard Niebuhr's Theology.* Washington, D.C.: University Press at America, Inc.,1982.

Ramsey, Paul (ed.). *Faith and Ethics: The Theology of H. Richard Niebuhr.* New York: Harper, 1957.

Robbins, J. Wesley. *A Critical Analysis of the Christian Moral Philosophy of H. Richard Niebuhr.* Ph.D. diss., University at Chicago, 1970.

Stassen, Glen. *The Sovereignty of God in the Theological Ethics of H. Richard Niebuhr.* Ph.D. diss., Duke University, 1967.

Scriven, Charles. *The Transformation of Culture: Christian Social Ethics After H. Richard Niebuhr.* Scottdale, Pa.; Herald Press, 1988.

Tucker, Rexford Francis. *H. Richard Niebuhr and the Ethics of Responsibililty.* Ph.D. diss., Drew University, 1970.

B. Works of H. Richard Niebuhr frequently cited in the text

Christ and Culture. New York: Harper, 1951.

"The Christian Evangel and Social Culture." *Religion in Life* 8/1 (1939), pp. 44-48.

The Church Against the World, with Wilhelm Pauck and Francis P. Miller. Chicago and New York: Willett, Clark, 1935.

Faith on Earth. New Haven and London: Yale University Press, 1989.

"Faith, Works, and Social Salvation." *Religion in Life* 1 (1932), pp. 426-30.

"The Gift of Catholic Vision." *Theology Today* 4 (1948), pp. 507-521.

"The Grace of Doing Nothing." *Christian Century* 49 (1932), pp. 378–80.

"The Hidden Church and the Churches in Sight." *Religion in Life* 15 (winter 1945-46), pp. 106-116; reprinted *Religion in Life* 47 (Autumn 1978), pp. 371-80.

The Kingdom of God in America. New York: Harper, 1937.

The Meaning of Revelation. New York: Macmillan, 1941.

The Purpose of the Church and its Ministry: Reflections on the Aims of Theological Education, with Daniel Day Williams and James M. Gustafson. New York: Harper, 1956.

Radical Monotheism and Western Culture. New York: Harper, 1960

The Responsible Self: An Essay in Christian Moral Philosophy. New York: Harper, 1963.

"The Responsibility of the Church for Society." In *The Gospel, the Church and the World,* pp. 111-33. Edited by Kenneth Scott Latourette. Interseminary Series, book 3. New York: Harper, 1946.

"The Social Gospel and the Mind of Jesus." *Journal of Religious Ethics* 16/1 (1988), pp. 115-27.

The Social Sources of Denominationalism. New York: Holt, 1929; Meridian/World, 1957.

NOTES

Prologue

1. Though evidently not written for publication, Niebuhr's manuscript "Types of Christian Ethics" is a finished work and has required little editorial intervention. Punctuation and capitalization have been brought into conformity with current usage; syntax has occasionally been adjusted; where possible, citations have been provided for quoted passages; and the types discussed in the essay have been correlated with the variant descriptive terms Niebuhr uses to name the same types in *Christ and Culture*.

2. William James, *The Varieties of Religious Experience: A Study in Human Nature*, the Gifford Lectures 1901–1902 (New York: Random House, 1902), lectures 4–7.

3. Etienne Gilson, *Reason and Revelation in the Middle Ages* (New York: Scribner's, 1938), p. 5.

4. Count Lev N. Tolstoy, *My Religion*, in *The Complete Works of Count Tolstoy*, 24 vols. (New York: AMS Press, 1904), 16:105. The complete sentence reads, "Christ's teaching is the teaching about the son of man, common to all men, that is, about the striving after the good, common to all men, about the common reason, which enlightens man in this striving."

5. John Stuart Mill, *Utilitarianism*, ed. Oskar Piest, The Library of the Liberal Arts (Indianapolis: Bobbs-Merrill, 1957), p. 22.

Chapter 1

1. New York, Harper: 1951; Torch reprint series 1956.

2. It is striking that those who borrow Niebuhr's categories tend to extend them far beyond the realm of his original interest; e.g. with regard to the missionary challenge of nonChristian cosmologies and cult forms (Edmund Ilogu, "Indigenization in Nigeria," *International Review of Mission* Vol. XLIX/194, p. 176) or to the ways of responding to other religions (Geoffrey Wainwright, *Doxology*; New York: Oxford University Press, 1980, pp. 385ff.) or to the use of art in worship. One of the oddest ideological uses of the grid is in the preface written by Norman K. Gottwald to Daniel L. Smith, *The Religion of the Landless: The Social Context of the Babylonian Exile* (Bloomington: Meyer/Stone, 1989), p. xv.

3. Other such critical-inductive guides interpreted J. A. T. Robinson's *Honest to God* and Harvey Cox' *Secular City*. Pedagogically it can be claimed that to read a classic or a contemporary landmark text critically with students is more helpful than the teacher's simply expositing her/his own ("better") views.

4. I initially proposed to cross-reference this review to some of the later works (e.g. those by Diefenthaler, Fowler, Godsey, Hoedemaker, Irish, Kliever,

Stassen) at the points where those authors would round out an account or simplify a demonstration. Yet most of what I found helpful in them was not on this topic. The points at which they might open further dialog are not directly pertinent. I have thus had to resist particularly the temptation to pursue larger theological questions (e.g. the formula, "whatever is, is good," or the ambivalence of God as both slaying and saving) which these readers opened. The task of the present work is not to seek any kind of completeness in interpreting Niebuhr, to say nothing of contemporaneity.

5. In this sense this study differs from the texts by Glen Stassen in the same book.

6. Glen Stassen has discerned variations within *Christ and Culture* itself which can be illuminated by knowing more of the chronology of the drafting of its several chapters, and which may be correlated with other events in the author's intellectual life. This concerns Niebuhr's notion of the Kingdom of God, as well as nuances regarding Christology and violence. Of the other authors cited in note 4 above, Fowler especially, drawing substantially from Stassen, describes significant changes over time.

7. Niebuhr denies that the expectation of an early consummation of history is the *central* reason for the indifference of Jesus to culture, since he believes that the Schweitzerian line of Gospel interpretation misplaces the meaning of Jesus' hope (pp. 19–21).

8. Niebuhr cites with apparent approval (3f.) strong statements from Klausner according to which Jesus both ignored culture and abolished it; "He does not belong to civilization." We shall need to return to the question of whether this apparently uncritical citation represents agreement, or rather the first phase of an open-ended dialectic.

9. (C&C, 28, 15–19). Niebuhr identifies this argument as Jesus' own "theology," and sharpens its characterization by denouncing the views of Harnack and of Reinhold Niebuhr, for whom the image of God as "loving Father" is too soft. Jesus' view of "the transcendent power" of God, he says, seems "anything but fatherlike." Niebuhr expanded this theme in his later book, *Radical Monotheism and Western Culture* (New York: Harper, 1960). Fowler (in *To See the Kingdom: The Theological Vision of H. Richard Niebuhr*; Nashville: Abingdon, 1974, pp. 33ff) follows Stassen's demonstration of the importance for Niebuhr of his turn at this point toward a powerful vision of "divine sovereignty." Then on p. 28 Niebuhr goes on to counter-balance this "away from the world" thrust with what he calls "the other half" of "the meaning of Christ," namely a movement "toward men." Yet this "humanward" thrust is completely formal, conceptual, devoid of historical or cultural substance. I listed in my *Politics of Jesus* (2nd ed., Grand Rapids: Eerdmans, 1994; all further references will be to this edition), pp. 5–8, further strands of contemporary argument which in other parallel ways posit a dichotomy between Jesus and human reality.

10. Fifteen years earlier, in a lecture left unpublished for a half-century, Niebuhr presented a significantly fuller picture of Jesus: "The Social Gospel and the Mind of Jesus," edited by Diane Yeager, *Journal of Religious Ethics*, vol. 16/1 (Spring 1988), pp. 109ff. There he described Jesus in opposition to the vision of the "social Gospel" (including his brother Reinhold) and to that of Bultmann. His criticisms are such as I would by and large support, though it is astonishing to observe with what self-assuredness Niebuhr makes large generalizations about "the mind of Jesus" without reference to any particular Gospel texts, or to any New

Testament scholarship. His Jesus in this lecture is an apocalyptic and revolutionary Jew, interpreting history from God's perspective, and not a moralist pointing away from the world.

11. "The Mennonites have come to represent the attitude most purely, since they not only renounce all participation in politics . . . , but follow their own distinctive customs and regulations in economics and education." (p. 56). We shall need to return to this passage because of its odd logic. That conservative Mennonites want to have their own schools is taken as a proof that they reject culture. Yet if Catholics or Calvinists, Mormons or Jews want to run their own schools, that proves that they take "the cultural mandate" seriously. Mennonites also organize mental hospitals, health and fire insurance co-operatives, and overseas development agencies. Creating an alternative culture is hardly anticultural.

12. Even when they are socially effective (p. 66) he says that that is not because they want to be.

13. The critical reader will note that "nature" is used here in an ambivalent way; does it mean "selfishness" or "rebellious creatureliness" or "healthy self-regard" or merely "matter"? Or "reasonable insight"? Can either "nature" or "history" be spoken of as "fallen"? To this we may need to return.

14. (55, 69ff.) We shall return later to ask whether Tertullian's creative use of Latin language and Roman values indicates that he is inconsistent, or rather that Niebuhr's categories are questionable.

15. Niebuhr does not propose a better alternative for restructuring the Russian imperial economy or that of the Tolstoy family estate. One cannot tell whether Niebuhr thinks Tolstoy could have done better at what he had in mind, so that his failings were flaws in his person, or whether democratizing an estate is undesirable or impossible, so that the vision is what was wrong.

16. The examples Niebuhr gives (73ff.) do not tend to show that "radicals" are morally less worthy than people with other views of culture, but rather that it is by definition not possible within human experience to live up to his picture of what thorough (anticultural) radicality would call for.

17. C&C, 80.

18. "The Doctrine of the Trinity and the Unity of the Church" in *Theology Today* III (July, 1946), pp. 371-841948. Although published earlier than C&C, this article may well have been written later than some of the book's chapters. As a whole C&C was first presented as lectures in 1949. The editors of *Theology Today* paid Niebuhr the rare tribute of reprinting the 1946 article in volume 60/2 (July 1983), pp. 150–57.

19. Cf. my own attention to the claims of the "wider world views" of the first century, which the apostles challenged, in my *The Priestly Kingdom* (Notre Dame: University of Notre Dame Press, 1984), pp. 49ff.

20. It is much less clear to historians than it is to us that thinkers in early times had the same awareness we do of the problems of basic logical structure which we use to "illuminate" their positions. We assume a need to be "consistent" in proceeding from axioms to implications which may have bothered earlier believers (or earlier thinkers) less.

21. We think here of course (as was noted at the end of the previous chapter) not of the real Gnostics of history but of Niebuhr's ideal type.

22. The fact that his critique is only formal, centering on the danger of anachronism, lets Niebuhr avoid more substantial critical questions, such as why it was right, once the decision to "synthesize" was made, for Thomas to choose to

273

baptize Aristotle rather than the Cynics or the Stoics or Plato; or why Thomas was condemned by church authorities in his own day.

23. The reference to "preaching" fits the Lutheran mode. For the purposes of our present agenda Niebuhr would say that what "law" prepares for is the critique of "Christ," which is radical at the same time that it is not the last word.

24. A very fitting illustration of the way this works, which Niebuhr does not use, is the statement of the Lutheran Augsburg Confession (Art. 16), to the effect that killing in war is "without sin," whereas there might be other acts of civil obedience which the Christian should refuse (here Luther was different from later Lutherans) because they could not be committed without sinning. In this setting "sin" has to mean identifiable acts which one can and should avoid committing. Far more often and more broadly, in Luther as well as in Augustine and in the brothers Niebuhr, it is less possible to identify particular acts as more sinful than others, and still less possible to avoid them.

25. The fact that the pro-Hitler faction in German Protestantism used this name for themselves illustrates the principle we are talking about. They assumed that being "German" was a divinely binding assignment, whose claims on them were not challenged but rather ratified by their being Christian.

26. The debates within the German Protestant "Church Struggle" of the 1930s can fairly be used to illustrate this issue. Niebuhr does not refer specifically to the (then) contemporary German case, although he probably has it in mind. He does note the potential for cultural conservatism in Luther and Paul (188).

27. P. 195. It would appear that this state of things was initiated somehow by the work of Jesus Christ; how literally Niebuhr means this is not clear. He contrasts Paul's expectation of a future victory with John's "It is finished (19:30)," without being clear whether the "conversionist" view fuses the two or prefers John, or whether the Jesus of the Gospel accounts actually should be thought of as having achieved whatever this means.

28. This is shown tacitly by the shape of the text. There is no section in C&C criticizing this type, as there had been for each of the other four.

29. One of the quite odd characteristics of this vision of hopefulness within history is that Niebuhr seems to have no interest in concretizing it with a list of cultural achievements down through the centuries, which would not only illustrate the hope but also "prove" or even merely exemplify it.

30. Within English society of the late nineteenth century, it was important that Maurice was a very articulate socialist, and an Anglican. For Niebuhr in 1951 it is not evident that either of these traits of identity matters, although twenty years earlier Niebuhr himself had been somewhat of a socialist. Few Americans reading C&C in the late twentieth century would welcome the view that socialism illustrates "transformation," or would discern that as Niebuhr's intention. Niebuhr did not mention the fact.

31. Others will properly show that Niebuhr was not always in the same way equiprobabilistic; sometimes he made stronger claims for the rightness of one view. I grant that. I shall also be arguing later that his equiprobabilism, which he also sometimes clothed as "humility," is itself a kind of bias. What I am describing here is the surface impact of C&C, as a classic, on the average reader.

32. We noted the appeal to the doctrine of the Trinity and to "the Unity of the Church" in his *Theology Today* article (note 18 above). Properly absorbing diversity would seem to be his definition of unity; some critics would say that that is his criterion not only of unity but also of truth.

33. Rather than describing "humility" as a virtue, Niebuhr speaks more of "sovereignty" as the most important divine attribute. The functional meaning for us of God's sovereignty is precisely that no human wisdom is sure, leaving us before the risk of decision. Fowler (56ff., 69, 93) supports the interpretation of divine sovereignty as not so much a meaningful statement about God (since nothing verifiable can be said about God "as such") but rather a warrant for humans' being more confident in our own insights (Fowler, p. 93 calls it "overcoming inhibitions"). For more hebraic minds, God's sovereignty might have the opposite thrust.

34. Cf. in Paul Ramsey, ed., *Faith and Ethics* (New York, Harper, 1957). Hans Frei in this collection speaks of "the impact of historical consciousness and method." "Relativism" is one of the major categories in the index to the work. For a time Niebuhr rooted moral insight in the human activity of "valuing," in a way later readers might call phenomenological. He describes the complexity of how humans do in fact go about ethicizing, rather than prescribing how they should do it.

35. On the other hand Niebuhr would not espouse a principled notion of "value-freedom" such as has been projected in some sectors of the academic social science world. He would not claim that a generous and fairly descriptive pluralism is an alternative to avowing specific commitments.

36. Cf. Fowler, *To See the Kingdom*, pp. 263ff.

37. Illustrated above note 2, also note 57 below (Paul Ramsey).

38. The very thin concrete references to Augustine (214–15) and Maurice (227) provide nothing that anyone could argue against. Augustine is far more concrete on p. 212, where he sounds like a "radical."

39. This will be most visible when we return to what I call Niebuhr's "monolithic logic."

40. The same meaning held of course for the original, non-metaphorical usage of the term in the field of printing.

41. Cf. his *Christ and the Moral Life* (New York: Harper, 1968).

42. Just this once it was needful to insert this formal detour about method, in order to note consciously the problem Niebuhr raises without naming it, namely whether (and if so how) a typology is useful at all, as contrasted with a mere inventory of motifs. When listing motifs one does not suggest anything about how they naturally can or should interrelate.

Most of the rest of the present study shall operate on the assumption that at least initially, as well as in the public impact of the book, Niebuhr is using "type" in the standard strong sense, even though there are places where he qualifies this. The book as "classic" should therefore be dealt with on that basis.

43. Here I initially followed Roland Bainton, whose *Christian Attitudes to War and Peace* first gave wide currency to the distinction between "holy" and "just" wars; since then the use of types has been considerably refined. Cf. my *When War is Unjust* (Minneapolis: Augsburg, 1985), pp. 23ff. Cf. also my "The Credibility of Ecclesiastical Teaching on the Morality of War" in Leroy S. Rouner, ed., *Celebrating Peace* (Notre Dame: University of Notre Dame Press, 1990), pp. 33–51.

44. Cf. my *Nevertheless: The Varieties and Shortcomings of Religious Pacifism* (Scottdale: Herald, 2nd ed. 1992).

45. "The Church in the World," in James Leo Garrett, ed., *The Concept of the Believers' Church* (Scottdale: Herald, 1968).

46. The most striking image I know for the way the historian should seek to

275

let the real data back there contribute to how she retells the story is the bizarre suggestion of Paul Minear. Imagine an archaeologist trying to pry open a sarcophagus, using for the purpose a modern shovel. The mummy reaches out of the sarcophagus and bends the shovel, in order to make it more apt for the digging it was intended to do. Minear explained with this image the special creativity of his own work with the New Testament, illuminated by the predisposition to expect that the text might surprise us by telling us something unexpected about how to read it.

47. Although as I have indicated (above notes 43, 44) there may be many reasons for taking that negative stance, and many different answers to the question "if we refuse to kill, what do we do instead?"

48. To observe this is not at all to deny that with still closer, still more logical analysis or real life arguments one will also find additional sub-types, mixed-types, and off-the-wall crazy postures fitting none of the above. Logically "mixed" types may be most worthy of attention. As James Turner Johnson has shown, the "ideal" line between the "holy" and the "just" categories is not firm in history.

49. No attempt is made here to handle the many cases where passion or interest, rather than the reasons given, dictates what people say they think.

50. Cf. above note 44.

51. Or cf. my showing how a "Constantinian" social stance carries over to most of those who think they have overcome it, in "The Constantinian Sources of Western Social Ethics," *The Priestly Kingdom*, pp. 141 ff.

52. The Old Order Amish Mennonites, by changing as little as possible of the horse-drawn culture which their ancestors brought to Pennsylvania in the eighteenth century, while the world around them was transformed, have created something new.

53. Cf. bibliography. It is largely to his impact that we owe the subdiscipline of "sect cycle sociology."

54. I have often had to argue against the assumption that civil government is the prototype *par excellence* of social responsibilty: "Reformed versus Anabaptist Social Strategies: An Inadequate Typology," presented to a section of the American Academy of Religion November 1979, excerpted in *Theological Students' Fellowship Bulletin* 8 (May/June 1985), pp. 2ff., and reflected in Richard Mouw and J. Yoder, "Evangelical Ethics and the Anabaptist-Reformed Dialogue," *Journal of Religious Ethics* 17 (Fall 1989), pp. 121–37.

55. It is not too much to say that for Reinhold Niebuhr his parting of the ways with the pacifism of his earlier years was the hinge on which turned his entire social ethic, and thereby his entire theological anthropology, and thereby his entire reconstruction of theology. His majestic *Nature and Destiny of Man* is the *a posteriori* exposition of the foundations of his *Moral Man and Immoral Society* and his *Interpretation of Christian Ethics*, which in turn made sense of his breaking with the Fellowship of Reconciliation and *The World Tomorrow*. On the other hand, although in biographical reality the tragedy of WWII weighed most heavily on H. Richard Niebuhr, he does not accentuate the state as prototypical for culture as much as classical Lutheran or Reformed social thinkers have.

56. Cf. note 2 above.

57. Paul Ramsey, *War and the Christian Conscience* (Durham: Duke University Pres, 1961), pp. 112f.

58. One could distinguish the two orders. One could hold that the values of "culture" are in fact autonomous in what they call "good," but that we know about

them through Christ. Or one could hold that they are known independently of revelation, but are in substance identical with "Christ." (There are some who interpret the Roman Catholic tradition about "nature" in this latter way.) Only when both orders are dichotomized is the argument radical. In this setting both what we are called to do (namely to kill, or to accumulate wealth, or to seek self above others) and how we know we are thus called (namely through "nature" or "the state" or "reason" or "culture") stand in contrast with Jesus. Cf. the discussion of "other lights" in my *Original Revolution* (Scottdale: Herald, 1972), pp. 132ff.

59. The same would apply to Adventists and Mormons; there is nothing peculiar to Mennonites in this respect, except that Niebuhr chose to mention them.

60. *Christian Social Teachings* (Minneapolis: Augsburg, 1966), p. 41.

61. "Christ Against Culture: A Re-examination of the Political Ethics of Tertullian," *1978 Selected Papers* of the American Society of Christian Ethics (Newton Centre, MA: 1978), pp. 27–41.

62. This (66–69) might actually be one point at which, although as I said Niebuhr does not *generally* connect the typology of C&C with that of *The Kingdom of God in America*, he does assume a certain parallelism. Perhaps he thinks that the existence of the "sect cycle" would count as a backhanded argument against the radical position. What the radical reformers would call a sell-out Niebuhr would then call maturation into responsibility.

63. This is the point at which H. Richard Niebuhr, despite the difference just noted, is closest to his brother Reinhold, for whom the test case of war became the paradigm for all social ethics. Niebuhr was less thorough in this matter than Reinhold, and less accepting of war as an imperative prototypically representative of all of social responsibility. There was a time when Reinhold seemed to accuse him simply of quietistic pacifism. Nonetheless Niebuhr's treatment of the "radicals" in C&C, or his argument in "The Inconsistency of the Majority," *The World Tomorrow* 17 (January 18, 1934), lends itself to the same challenges.

64. The motto of Goshen College, the largest Mennonite institution where this kind of thinking was being done just after WWII, was "Culture for Service." I remind the reader that the original setting for this study was a campus ministries event. I have characterized the special intellectual challenge facing the children of enclave cultures when entering the intellectual "wider world" in my *The Priestly Kingdom*, pp. 48ff.

65. I have sought to describe this defensive response of modern midAmerican pacifists to the Niebuhrs, both in my *Nevertheless*, pp. 107–114, and in *Christian Attitudes to War, Peace, and Revolution* (Elkhart, Goshen Biblical Seminary, 1983; available from the Duke Div. School Bookstore, Durham NC 27706), pp. 372–420.

66. Although Reinhold Niebuhr's argument on this subject was the most widely noted and best remembered, H. Richard Niebuhr made the same point, perhaps even more directly and just as early: cf. his "The Inconsistency of the Majority" in *The World Tomorrow* 17 (January 18, 1934), pp. 43f., interpreted in Fowler, pp. 89ff. and Jon Diefenthaler, *H. Richard Niebuhr: A Lifetime of Reflections on the Church and the World* (Macon: Mercer University Press, 1986), p. 43.

67. Even in his 1933 Text "The Social Gospel and the Mind of Jesus," in which the Jesus of the Gospel narratives was interpreted in the most concrete terms, what mattered about Jesus for Niebuhr was his world view and his sense of mission, not the kind of concrete actions and impact which I studied in my *Politics of Jesus*.

68. Glen Stassen suggests that Niebuhr does not really identify with these

statements, even though he repeats them with no criticism. He uses overstatements or caricatures to set up a problem which he will later transcend with his own answer. On the level of Niebuhr's teaching style Stassen should know whereof he speaks. On that level I could accept his corrective. Yet here I am interpreting C&C in its own words, as a classic. Niebuhr sets aside with special vigor (p. 5) the notion that when Jesus' disciples understood him this way they were misunderstanding him.

69. The fuller, richer description of pp. 11–29 does not seem to me to contract this brief one at the salient points.

70. Radical Protestants would add that the disciples' confession of Christ's Lordship binds us to obedience, but this could not be called a "mainstream" accent.

71. Cf. in my *Politics of Jesus*, pp. 112-33.

72. In my essay "But We Do See Jesus" (*The Priestly Kingdom*, pp. 50–54; cf. below pp. 61f.), I point out that the "high christological" passages in the New Testament, when understood contextually and not as prooftexts, point toward, not away from, the human historical Jesus. J. Gustafson has suggested (in a personal letter, cited by permission) that "Niebuhr never was willing to commit himself to these texts as referring to anything that is objectively the case, historically or ontologically." I am currently not concerned to speculate about how in the twentieth century we might try to test whether the Lordship of Christ "is objectively the case," or what might count as either "historical" or "ontological." What matters here is whether this is what apostolic writers, whom I want to understand, thought then.

73. We shall further discuss the intention behind Niebuhr's use of the Trinity below pp. 61ff.

74. "While various New Testament writings evince something of this attitude, none presents it without qualification" (p. 45).

75. In the structure of the book, none of the later "type" descriptions begins with a New Testament section, although each chapter does reach back sporadically for biblical warrants.

76. A new caricature of the "against" position is used (e.g. on p. 106) as a foil to make the second position more attractive. Niebuhr says radicals say that "the whole world outside the sphere where Christ's Lordship is explicitly acknowledged is a realm of equal darkness," but can cite no such statement.

77. "The Doctrine of the Trinity and the Unity of the Church," pp. 371ff. In note 18 above I noted the rarity of its being reprinted thirty-seven years later in the same journal. If we did not have this text to enlarge the C&C references, the "modalist" implications of Niebuhr's appeal to the Trinity might be less transparent. Other unpublished texts from the same period could be cited to broaden this interpretation.

78. If we were concerned to argue with Niebuhr rather than to characterize him accurately, we might point out that under many constructions "nature" and "history" are also quite hard on culture. In the Bible grasshoppers and earthquakes, as part of nature, and Pharaoh and Assyria as parts of history, are destructive.

79. Others have spoken of the Spirit in yet other ways; as the way God acts within the "leadings" of the individual conscience, or in mystical insight, or in ecstatic "charismatic" worship, or in other religions. Niebuhr does not survey these alternatives, nor even explain why he does not. His concern is only to give God credit for the cumulative wisdom of the path taken by the (majority) churches in

the course of change over history. Invoking the Spirit is his warrant for such decisions being right when they differ from the ethic of Jesus.

80. Cf. the comment of J. Gustafson, note 72 above. Gustafson is most emphatic on pp. 27ff. of the introduction that he contributed to *The Responsible Self* (New York: Harper, 1963) in denying that Niebuhr based any claim on "the continuity of a pattern of ideas in the history of Christian thought." My study has been enriched at several points by the comments of students of Niebuhr, of whom Gustafson is only the most eminent. My gratitude to them for their help does not make them so responsible for my conclusions that I should try to name them all, or to acknowledge each borrowing. Particularly at this point there does however seem to be agreement on their part that Niebuhr's ostensible claim to be reading the doctrine of the Trinity as normative doctrinal history ought to be taken with a grain of salt. His concern is with the notion of balancing out competing considerations, to which end he uses numerous different triads; Trinity is merely one metaphor for that.

81. A notable example is the doctoral dissertation of Franklin Sherman, *The Problem of a Trinitarian Ethic* (University of Chicago, 1961). Sherman reinforces Niebuhr's categories by using them to interpret Dietrich Bonhoeffer and Werner Elert as well.

82. When Niebuhr is writing the most abstractly (e.g. p. 28) this "pointing away" is balanced by a movement toward humanity. Yet that "humanity" is so thoroughly self-emptying that it provides Jesus' hearers no commands to obey nor examples to follow.

83. It may very well be argued that this first "step" was already taken for Niebuhr by his teachers, idealists from Kant to Troeltsch, for whom Jesus taught noble principles but (by definition) could not and did not incarnate God's lordship in history. Their reason for that denial however was different from Niebuhr's. For them it is *by definition* or ontologically the case that the ideal cannot be incarnate. For Niebuhr however the impossibility of full incarnation is rather ethical. What Jesus calls us to do is not all we need or want to do.

84. Luther and Calvin had already done this with the State. The role of the prince, including the death penalty and war, is in Luther's catechism part of the created good order of the family. In the Decalog it comes under "Honor Father and Mother."

85. The same point is made still more strongly on pp. 44ff. in his *The Purpose of the Church and its Ministry* (New York: Harper, 1956). Overdoing Jesus is described here as "the most deceptive and *perhaps ultimately the most dangerous inconsistency* to which churches and schools are subject . . ." (italics added). It leads in turn to many other errors, like affirming the uniqueness of Christianity. Niebuhr also appeals here to "the long story of the Trinitarian debate in Christendom."

86. The mode of argument here is typical. The warrant for a classical doctrine is not that it is in classical sources, or that it is in some deep sense *true*, but that it stands for an issue which cannot be avoided.

87. In fact most of the theologians who (much later in history) did in fact seriously challenge the doctrine of the Trinity, and were called "unitarian," have not been at all radical about challenging culture. There were a few early unitarians among the Polish Anabaptists of the sixteenth century, but the main stream of unitarianism within the Protestantism of England and New England has been an upper-class movement.

88. It is not in my competence to decide whether the explanation for this tension should be in terms of change in Niebuhr's thought over time, as Stassen (followed by Fowler) might say, or of some other kind, but it does seem that the considerations just dealt with, the *Theology Today* article, and *The Purpose of the Church and its Ministry* make a stronger appeal to having orthodoxy on Niebuhr's side than do the interpreters cited in note 80 above.

89. There were thinkers in the sixteenth century, whom historians call "Spiritualists," who did argue thus.

90. Again here we encounter the strange mode of suggesting an argument without taking responsibility for making it, as if the course of intellectual history proves points on its own.

91. This is all the more striking when we remember that in *The Kingdom of God in America* Niebuhr had made much of the variety and the value of the free church alternatives within the American mix. Tertullian's position was "against" the world of his time but in terms of the surviving literature he is part of the main stream.

92. I have made elsewhere this point about the Reformed tradition (note 54 above). In this respect Niebuhr represents faithfully the German Reformed tradition of his family origins.

93. Especially in Fowler's account, following Stassen, it is visible that a special notion of divine sovereignty came in a unique way to have a particularly important meaning for Niebuhr in the early 1930's (Fowler, pp. 101ff.). Humility is not especially a virtue in itself; it is rather our side of the recognition of divine sovereignty. This is one of the places where I have had to resist the temptation to follow Fowler further in unfolding large theological issues.

94. Especially I have no interest in advocating the "radical" view to which he would assign me, as he defines it.

95. I have already made this use of his language in my own text "Sacrament as Social Ethics," *Theology Today* XLVIII/1 (April 1991), pp. 33–44.

96. Following earlier New Testament interpreters like Schmidt and Schlier, this Pauline testimony was first synthesized by Hendrik Berkhof, *Christ and the Powers* (Scottdale: Herald, 1962), from whom I borrowed freely in my *Politics of Jesus*, pp. 134–61. Since then creative social critics like Jacques Ellul and William Stringfellow have used the Pauline concepts; Walter Wink has done the most to exposit them systematically. For a synthesis of Ellul's use of the stance cf. Marva J. Dawn, "The Concept of 'the Principalities and Powers' in the Work of Jacques Ellul," (Ph.D. diss., University of Notre Dame, 1992).

97. This theme is exposited further on pp. 76–79 below. Here I have sketched it only enough to lay the basis for the point of the next paragraph. It is also used more fully in chapter 3 of this book.

98. We shall return to another, more classical form of the "autonomy" theme on pp. 77f. below.

99. The real Tolstoy was a quite quirky and inconsistent person, but he was not the antihistorical absolutist the categories of C&C make him look like. He was a plantation manager, an immensely popular storyteller and essayist, a commentator on current affairs, and a civilly disobedient agitator and fundraiser who helped the Doukhobors migrate to Canada. It seems not to have occurred to Niebuhr that to be the century's most famous writer is a cultural act.

100. The simply negative sense of *kosmos* which we are considering here is only fully at home in the Johannine letters. Wink calls it "the domination system."

101. All through this section "church" shall be used in the normative sense, as designating the shared fidelity to which believers are called. This usage makes no judgments affirmative or critical about empirical institutions within Christendom. Such judgments will be unavoidable, but only later in the argument.

102. The criteria listed at the beginning of the previous section, which we have seen to be operational for Niebuhr, are those which surfaced inductively as we watched the argument move. This is not to ignore that Niebuhr himself lists numerous other theological criteria: e.g. the goodness of creation, the imperative of obedience, the pervasiveness of sin, the primacy of grace, etc. (pp. 117ff.). There is no need further to treat such themes here because, although Niebuhr lists them as if they were arguments for the latter types against the first, they are all themes which all "radicals" would agree with, and they are in fact not specifiably operational in Niebuhr's text where the key differences are argued.

103. If there is to be concrete particular discernment, rather than seeking to solve problems deductively, by first defining a general stance and then "applying" it, we shall have to look at how a community thinks together. To look at the social shape of ethics is something Niebuhr taught us, though not so much in this book as in others.

104. This is a statement about how C&C deals with thinkers. Elsewhere in his work Niebuhr thinks of all of history, under the sovereignty of God who both chastises and heals, as an ethical laboratory. Yet that universal story does not tell us what to do. When we look at that story globally, the axiom is "whatever is, is good," and our role under God's sovereignty is that of patient, letting God act (Fowler 252ff., but also already 68–75). This is another of the points at which one would be tempted to pursue a dialogue with Niebuhr, beyond the limits of C&C, into other realms of theology.

105. The concluding evaluation by Fowler (pp. 265ff.) explains that this shortcoming is not adventitious. It follows from the way divine "sovereignty" (the counterpart of what I have been calling "humility") has to work. To concentrate on the claim that only God is ultimate does not help us to adjudicate among penultimate values. Especially it provides no criterion for measuring my values against yours. The higher view of the Jesus of the Gospels expressed by Niebuhr in 1933 correlated with the higher value of "doing nothing" (his code term for relativizing American responsibility for the New World Order) in the politics of the time; by the time of C&C this more culturally substantial Jesus had been left behind.

106. I make this point in a summary way in my *Politics of Jesus*, p. 226.

107. Glen Stassen reminds us at this point that the same Jesus who sweepingly rejected hoarding wealth still approved of splurging on ointment (Luke 7:36ff.).

108. Looking back, we can discern at this point yet another way in which the narrative of C&C was slanted. Niebuhr did not accuse F. D. Maurice and Augustine of not having it all together, as he did Tertullian or Tolstoy. Thomas or Calvin were not accused of inconsistency or of attempting the impossible, or of not bringing off a satisfactory synthesis; only the radicals.

109. I have descibed these processes in procedural and personal terms in my "The Hermeneutics of Peoplehood," in *The Priestly Kingdom*, pp. 28ff.

110. In my *Priestly Kingdom*, pp. 15–45, I describe the sociology of decision; in my *Fullness of Christ* (Elgin: Brethren Press, 1987), pp. 15–20; and in my *Body Politics* (Nashville: Discipleship Resources, 1992), pp. 47–70, I elaborate on the rootage of this social shape in the Gospel.

111. Those who survey chronologically the changes in Niebuhr's thought remind us that in the early 1930's Niebuhr wrote on *The Church against the World* (Chicago & New York: Willett, Clark, 1935).

112. One should not assume too cynically that idealism will have no attraction for nonbelievers, nor too sanguinely that most believers will live up to this normative vision of the church.

113. I previously yielded to dominant usage and accepted the term "distinctive." That is however deceptive, since in a post-JudaeoChristian world there are many moral values, derived from the biblical heritage, yet held to by all kinds of people. What matters for Christian fidelity is not to be **different** but to be **specific** i.e. true to one's kind.

114. Ever since I translated Hendrik Berkhof's *Christ and the Powers*, Pauline thought about the powers has seemed clearly to offer the clearest alternative to Niebuhr's "monolithic" logic. The very same "powers" are at one and the same time good creatures and rebellious, oppressive and claimed for redemption.

115. The place in Niebuhr's system where the pertinence of this problem perhaps shows the most clearly is his reading of the notion of divine sovereignty as englobing good and evil alike. "Whatever is, is good" (Fowler 79f., 87f., 167, 264). That God both slays and saves (Fowler 109ff., 133ff.) seems to me to be said with more careful, substantial, ethical discrimination in the biblical world view than by Niebuhr.

116. cf. above note 110

117. As explained above I do not write "distinctively (or "uniquely") Christian" because in a postChristian culture many Christian values are represented by persons who do not avow their rootage.

118. Fowler 164ff., 238, 264.

119. Cf. my text on "The Authority of the Canon" in Willard Swartley, ed., *Essays on Biblical Interpretation* (Elkhart: Institute of Mennonite Studies, 1984), pp. 265–290; and "The Authority of Tradition" in my *The Priestly Kingdom*, pp. 63–79.

120. Compare this with my treatment of "other lights" in the chapter "Christ the Light of the World" in my *The Original Revolution*, 1971, pp. 138 ff. Jesus says love your enemy; the vocation of hangman or soldier says kill him. Jesus says give your money to the needy; the vocation of banker says lend it at interest. This is the double dichotomy, in both form and substance, referred to on p. 55 note 58 above.

121. Cf. my paper on reformed typology referred to on pp. 51ff. note 54 above.

122. I reviewed this theme in the NT in my *Politics of Jesus*, pp. 162ff.

123. The reciprocity of subordination in the Pauline vision is one of the ways in which the apostle's use of the theme differs from that of their contemporaries. "Be subordinate *to one another* out of respect for Christ." (Eph. 5:21). I have called this redefinition "revolutionary" (cf. note 122 above). Some readers of my *Politics of Jesus* were too impressed by the oppressive use made of the same language in later Christian cultures to grant the presence of creative and liberating originality in the apostles' intent.

124. This was already Niebuhr's style in his *The Kingdom of God in America*. What he there called "a truly catholic Christianity" would remain invisible in order not to exclude anyone or any one stance by defining anything (New York: Harper, 1935; pp. xiiiff.).

125. Ibid.

126. A study program of the World Council of Churches around the theme "Gospel and Culture" runs the same risk of assuming in "culture" a univocality which only misleads.

127. This is what we saw in C&C; the picture differed in his earlier text on the Social Gospel, cf. note 10 above.

128. This was not only the case long ago. James Gustafson's glancing reaction to my writings is most fairly understood as transposing to me his response to the pietist biblicism of his Swedish Evangelical Covenant origins.

129. I have periodically been invited to speak on how the Bible serves in theological ethics. Only once has this kind of material been printed: "The Use of the Bible in Theology," in Robert K. Johnston ed., *The Use of the Bible in Theology: Evangelical Options* (Atlanta: John Knox, 1985), pp. 103–129.

130. *The Priestly Kingdom*, pp. 50ff.

131. The following paragraphs will add more cases to the initial five. I shall indicate that by marking each with a capital letter. The logical quality of this exercise in induction, accumulating texts which say formally the same thing in different settings with different words, is self-evidently quite different from conservative Protestant prooftexting.

132. There will be more to say on this text later.

133. Cf. *The Priestly Kingdom*, p. 53: (a) the writer appropriates the language of the host culture; (b) he places Jesus above the cosmos instead of inside it; (c) what makes Christ Lord is the Cross; (d) the reader is called not to glory but to discipleship; (e) in doing that Jesus reveals the Father; (e) the writer stands in that story and invites the reader into it.

134. Earlier sketchy statements by Berkhof, Caird, Rupp, MacGregor, and applied by Jacques Ellul, have now been followed up encyclopaedically in three volumes by Walter Wink.

135. A dozen texts are gathered and exposited in Berkhof. There are differences of nuance between early and late texts in the Pauline corpus, but that does not change the present point.

136. William Penn was original in many ways, having to do with religious liberty, penal institutions, education, the place of women, etc. His unique response to the Indians is mentioned here only as a segment of that creativity. He went against the current of the times; but that did not mean he was against culture. He was rather authentically transforming.

137. When I point out how much of Paul's message at Lystra and Athens was simply Jewish, this represents the tip of an iceberg. Most of the impact of Jesus was simply Jewish. Modern antisemitic biases have often assumed that Jesus is interesting to us (or revelatory for us) only at the points where he was "original." The opposite assumption should obtain. Maybe the entire *Gestalt* of Paul's style of preaching to Gentiles, or the whole cosmology of principalities and powers, was already there before, as part of the way missionary Judaism had already been addressing the Hellenistic world in its own terms.

138. Cf. note 133 above.

139. Since C. H. Dodd's *Apostolic Preaching* (New York: Harper, 1964) it has been traditional to designate speech marked by these dimensions of involvement as *kerygma*.

140. Cf. the characterization of Niebuhr by David H. Kelsey: "What makes this monotheism "radical" is its insistence that God is beyond all the many,

including the "many" through whom we apprehend God: Scripture, church, *even Jesus Christ himself*"; *Between Athens and Berlin* (Grand Rapids: Eerdmans, 1993), p. 72 (my italics). If all mediation is relativized, what this means epistemologically is that Niebuhr's own mind is sovereign. The name "God" has become a cipher for Niebuhr's rejecting any **concrete** value claims superior to our selves.

141. Cf. my exposition in *Politics of Jesus.* In pp. 158-61 I expand that survey with reference to the new work of Marva Dawn and Walter Wink. I limit my attention to this theme here because it also appears in the text by Glen Stassen.

142. Girard's lecture built on the foundation of his decades of interpreting violence and culture in the light of mimetic vengeance and scapegoating mechanisms. Yet he had not previously in such a brilliant way synthesized that analysis in terms of the figure of Satan in the Gospels and the role of Satan in the Gospel.

143. Cf. my fuller interpretation of this vision in "To Serve Our God and Rule the World," *Annual of the Society of Christian Ethics* 1988, pp. 3–14. Not only does this passage have the formal characteristics itemized above (note 133) but it adds the components of liturgy and of interpreting the meaning of history. It clearly did **not** mean that John's readers, or the church as a whole, would be violently threatening Caesar's control of the Empire. But neither did they ratify that control as a good thing, or say of it that "whatever is, is good," or identify its actions with the meaning of history.

Chapter 2

1. Friedrich Schleiermacher, *The Christian Faith*, 2nd edition, 2 vols., tr. and ed. by H. R. Mackintosh and J. S. Stewart (Edinburgh: T & T Clark, 1928; reprinted NewYork: Harper, 1963), 1:5–6.

2. Lisa Sowle Cahill, *Love Your Enemies: Discipleship, Pacifism, and Just War Theory* (Minneapolis: Fortress, 1994), p. 239.

3. Ibid., p. 34, quoting Martin Hengel, *Victory over Violence: Jesus and the Revolutionists* (Philadelphia: Fortress, 1973), pp. 47–48.

4. Vinay Samuel and Chris Sugden, "Theology of Development: A Guide to the Debate," in Ronald J. Sider, ed., *Evangelicals and Development: Towards a Theology of Social Change* (Philadelphia: Westminster, 1981), p. 20.

5. Ernst Troeltsch, *The Social Teaching of the Christian Churches*, 2 vols., tr. Olive Wyon (London: George Allen & Unwin, 1931; reprinted Chicago: University of Chicago Press, 1976), 1:88.

6. H. Richard Niebuhr, "The Social Gospel and the Mind of Jesus," *Journal of Religious Ethics* 16/ 1 (1988), p. 125. This posthumously published essay was read before the American Theological Society in 1933.

7. Lennart Molin, *Hearts and Structures* (Ph.D. diss., University of Lund, 1976), pp. 120-21.

8. H. Richard Niebuhr, *Christ and Culture* (New York: Harper, 1951), p. 256.

9. H. Richard Niebuhr, "The Hidden Church and the Churches in Sight," *Religion in Life* 15 (Winter 1945-46), p. 115. The article was reprinted in *Religion in Life* 47 (Autumn 1978); in the reprint, the quoted passage appears on p. 379.

10. H. Richard Niebuhr, "The Social Gospel and the Mind of Jesus," p. 122.

11. Justus D. Doenecke, "H. Richard Niebuhr: Critic of Political Theology," *Communio: International Catholic Review* 4 (1977), pp. 83–93.

12. C&C, p. 195.

13. Raymond L. Whitehead, "Christ and Cultural Imperialism," in Christopher Lind and Terry Brown, eds., *Justice as Mission: An Agenda for the Church* (Burlington: Trinity Press, 1985), p. 26.

14. Charles Scriven, *The Transformation of Culture* (Scottdale: Herald, 1988), p. 20.

15. See H. Richard Niebuhr, "The Hidden Church and the Churches in Sight," pp. 115-16: "Such conversion is antithetical to substitution. In the Christian life human *eros* is not supplanted by divine *agape* but the divine *agape* converts the human *eros* by directing it in gratitude toward God and toward the neighbor in God . . . . The gospel restores and converts and turns again; it does not destroy and rebuild by substituting one finite structure of life or thought for another."

16. H. Richard Niebuhr, "The Christian Evangel and Social Culture," *Religion in Life* 8/1 (1939), p. 46.

17. H. Richard Niebuhr in collaboration with Daniel Day Williams and James M. Gustafson, *The Purpose of the Church and Its Ministry* (New York: Harper, 1956), p. 19.

18. Ibid., p. 20.

19. H. Richard Niebuhr, "The Social Gospel and the Liberal Theology," *The Keryx* 22/8 (May 1931), 13.

20. H. Richard Niebuhr, "The Social Gospel and the Mind of Jesus," pp. 118–19.

21. H. Richard Niebuhr, "The Attack upon the Social Gospel," *Religion in Life* 5 (1936), p. 176.

22. H. Richard Niebuhr, "Faith, Works, and Social Salvation," *Religion in Life* 1 (1932), p. 428.

23. H. Richard Niebuhr, "The Grace of Doing Nothing," *Christian Century* 49 (1932), p. 380.

24. H. Richard Niebuhr, "The Only Way into the Kingdom of God" [response to Reinhold Niebuhr], *Christian Century* 49 (1932), p. 447.

25. Ibid. It is worth noting that Niebuhr uses this notion of emergent reality in several contexts. Here love is the emergent reality, and this coincides with his treatment of the kingdom as an emergent reality. His language here is instructive: "It ['love'] has created fellowship in atoms and organisms, at bitter cost to electrons and cells; and it is creating something better than human selfhood but at bitter cost to that selfhood." Niebuhr also treats suprapersonal social realities as emergent realities, comparing the social group to a physical organ which is dependent on but not reducible to its constituent cells. "The Hidden Church and the Churches in Sight" images the emergent reality of Christian life in a slightly different way: the church is "the society which is at the very edge of coming into existence, more real than all the communities that are passing away. . . . It is an emergent as mind was an emergent through the long ages when it was the most powerful thing in the world but had not yet become conscious of itself and was in that sense invisible, being confused and confounded with sense and the physical" (p. 114).

26. H. Richard Niebuhr, "The Christian Evangel and Social Culture," p. 48.

27. C&C, p. 216.

28. Ibid., p. 224.

29. H. Richard Niebuhr, "The Grace of Doing Nothing," p. 380.

30. H. Richard Niebuhr, Wilhelm Pauck, and Francis P. Miller, *The Church Against the World* (Chicago & New York: Willett, Clark, 1935), p. 1.

31. H. Richard Niebuhr, "The Responsibility of the Church for Society," in

Kenneth Scott Latourette, ed., *The Gospel, the Church and the World*, Interseminary Series, book 3 (New York: Harper, 1946), p. 114.

32. H. Richard Niebuhr, "Towards a New Otherworldliness," *Theology Today* 1 (1944): pp. 78–79.

33. Ibid., p. 81.

34. H. Richard Niebuhr, "The Responsibility of the Church for Society," p. 126.

35. H. Richard Niebuhr, *The Purpose of the Church and Its Ministry*, p. 26.

36. H. Richard Niebuhr, "The Gift of the Catholic Vision," *Theology Today* 4 (1948), p. 520.

37. C&C, p. 224.

38. This useful term is introduced in its adjectival form with a hint of apology ("if this term be allowable") in H. Richard Niebuhr, "Religious Realism and the Twentieth Century," in D. C. Macintosh, ed., *Religious Realism* (New York: Macmillan, 1931), p. 414.

39. C&C, p. 226.

40. H. Richard Niebuhr, *The Social Sources of Denominationalism* (New York: Meridian Books, 1929), p. 284.

41. Ernst Troeltsch, *The Social Teaching of the Christian Churches*, 1:126.

42. C&C, p. 227.

Chapter 3

1. Niebuhr, "Churches That Might Unite," *Christian Century* 44 (February 28, 1929), pp. 259–61.

2. Sidney E. Ahlstrom, "H. Richard Niebuhr's Place in American Thought," *Christianity and Crisis* 23 (November 25, 1963), p. 215, says Niebuhr called it "his own *Turmerlebnis* of justification by faith."

3. Niebuhr, "What Then Must We Do?" *Christian Century Pulpit* V (July, 1934), p. 145.

4. Niebuhr, "Reformation: Continuing Imperative," *Christian Century* 77 (March 2, 1960), p. 249.

5. "What Then Must We Do?", p. 146.

6. Niebuhr, "Evangelical and Protestant Ethics," in *The Heritage of the Reformation*, Elmer J. F. Arndt, ed. (New York: Richard R. Smith, 1950), pp. 218ff.

7. Niebuhr, "Toward the Independence of the Church," in *The Church Against the World*, H. R. Niebuhr, Wilhelm Pauck, and F. P. Miller (Chicago & New York: Willett, Clark, 1935), pp. 149–51.

8. "What Then Must We Do?", p. 146.

9. KGA, 193; "Toward the Independence of the Church," pp. 126–27. Niebuhr's writing manifests my point about historical concreteness, as his was an age not yet sensitive to the problems of gender-exclusive language. Following Susan Moller Okin's suggestion in *Justice, Gender, and the Family* (New York: Basic Books, 1989), pp. 10ff., I have quoted Niebuhr in his original language throughout. Niebuhr had a keen sense of ethical awareness, and did at times foreshadow the preference for gender-inclusive language.

10. Niebuhr, "Theology and Psychology: A Sterile Union," *The Christian Century* 44 (January 13, 1927), pp. 47–48; "Value-Theory and Theology," in *The Nature of Religious Experience*, J. S. Bixler, ed. (New York: Harper, 1937), pp. 95,

98, 102–104, and 112–13; *The Church Against the World*, pp. 9 and 137–38; KGA, 79 and 195; MR, 27–33; C&C, 15–17; RMWC, 24–37.

11. Niebuhr, "Religious Realism in the Twentieth Century," in *Religious Realism*, D. C. Macintosh, ed. (New York: MacMillan, 1931), p. 419.

12. He argued this point in four essays during the 1930s: "Value-Theory and Theology," "Theology and Psychology: A Sterile Union," "Can German and American Christians Understand Each Other?" and "Religious Realism and the Twentieth Century." Hence Niebuhr had to reject Kantian agnosticism, and instead developed his understanding of God as revealed in Christ. His attack on the Kantian beginning point began under the label of critical realism, then objective relativism, then historical relationism. Melvin Keiser, *Recovering the Personal: Religious Language and the Post-Critical Quest of H. Richard Niebuhr* (Atlanta: Scholars Press, 1988), shows how Niebuhr continued this theme through his last writings on faith and responsibility in dialogue with post-Kantians such as Polanyi, Wittgenstein, and Merleu-Ponty. Throughout it was crucial to affirm the knowable faithfulness of God, the character of God's action to which we respond.

13. I should clarify that there are two slightly different triads in the book. The most obvious is the triad of prophetic periods—Puritan, Great Awakening, and Social Gospel, and their respective emphases: the rule of God, the kingdom of Christ, and the dynamic hope. More subtly, there is the triad of themes that are essential to all three periods—the rule of God; the dynamic, living, non-possessable character of God; and the revelation in Christ. In the triad of **periods**, by far the least developed is the third theme: hope. In the triad of **themes** that are essential for all three periods, the theme of dynamic process, continuous metanoia, nonreducibility to static human possession, is Niebuhr's insight from Henri Bergson, the process philosopher. It is this theme of dynamic process, rather than hope, that became central for Niebuhr's other writings. Hope and dynamic process could be defined in such a way that they imply one another. See Daniel Day Williams, *God's Grace and Man's Hope* (New York: Harper, 1949); and James Wm. McClendon, Jr., *Ethics: Systematic Theology*, Volume I (Nashville: Abingdon, 1986), chapter 9; and *Doctrine: Systematic Theology*, Volume II (Nashville: Abingdon, 1994), Part III. Here is the beginning for a much-needed strengthening of Niebuhr's understanding of the Holy Spirit.

It is also interesting to notice how central another process philosopher, Alfred North Whitehead, was to Niebuhr's definition of the third theme, revelation in Christ, as transformation from God the void to God the enemy to God the companion. He refers repeatedly, in several essays and books, to this Whiteheadian terminology at the crucial turning point in his interpretations of revelation and faith. Combined with his perspectivalism in epistemology, his relational value-theory, his social selfhood, his contextual ethics of response (and anticipation), and his hope for universal inclusiveness, all this suggests how very close Niebuhr was to being a process theologian. Where he did not work consistently in a process direction was what I shall describe below as his Kantian residue and an unresolved tension in his speaking of the omnicausality or omnificence of God's power and rule. Niebuhr himself shunned explicit discussion of ontology. But everyone has ontological assumptions, whether explicit, or consistent, or not.

Bergson's process understanding, which so shaped Niebuhr's second theme, differs from Whitehead's process understanding. Like Heraclitus of ancient Greece, Bergson valued change, newness, rather than order. This influenced Niebuhr to shy away from commitment to concrete norms, from coalition with any social theory, philosophy or movement, and from the church as institution. It gave his ethics an indefinite character. Whitehead (and Niebuhr's mentor, Troeltsch, whose historicism resembles process philosophy) valued both the dimensions of change and continuity. So did Daniel Day Williams, the unusually Christocentric and biblically informed process theologian who was my teacher and enormously valued mentor, and who first pointed me to Niebuhr. Including the dimension of continuity in process allows greater concreteness, definiteness, and synthesis or coalition—a dialectic of definite order and relative newness—within the limits of historical continuity and change.

14. See "Our God is Able," in *Strength to Love* (New York: Harper, 1963). I owe much gratitude to Canaan Baptist Church of Christ, where Dr. Wyatt Tee Walker, Dr. King's chief of staff, has been Pastor for 26 years. The themes of God's providential care, the centrality of Christ, and a historically realistic perspective on our unjust culture and our own need for grace and forgiveness could hardly be clearer and more powerful than in Canaan Baptist, as well as in Martin Luther King, Jr.

15. Martin Luther King, Jr., "Pilgrimage to Nonviolence," in James Melvin Washington, ed., *A Testament of Hope: the Essential Writings and Speeches of Martin Luther King, Jr.* (San Francisco: HarperSanFrancisco, 1986), p. 38. See also King's fuller account in *Stride Toward Freedom: The Montgomery Story* (New York: Harper, 1958).

16. Martin Luther King, Jr., *Stride Toward Freedom*, pp. 78–79.

17. *Responsible Self*, p. 126. An accurate summary of this approach is presented by James Gustafson in his Introduction for *Responsible Self*, pp. 25–41; and by Clinton Gardner in the first half of *Biblical Ethics and Social Ethics* (New York: Harper, 1960). In the section on Christ, Gardner supplements Niebuhr with some material from George Thomas, *Christian Moral Philosophy*. See also its application by Waldo Beach in his "A Theological Analysis of Race Relations," in *Faith and Ethics*, Paul Ramsey, ed. (New York: Harper, 1957), pp. 205–224. I refer also to student copies of Niebuhr's ethics notes by George Parker, Robert Lynn, and James Gustafson, and to Niebuhr's own handwritten lecture notes, which may be read in the Harvard Divinity School Library.

18. See especially his two unpublished addresses, "Martin Luther and the Renewal of Human Confidence" (1959), and "The Anachronism of Jonathan Edwards" (1958), although the theme recurs in his published writings as well.

19. Niebuhr is strangely silent about the Holy Spirit. I believe the problem is that when he thinks of *persons* of the Trinity, he is thinking of independent centers of personality, rather than the Latin of the church fathers, where three *persons* means three characters of the one God's revelation to us (See *Faith*, 102–108; and compare McClendon, *Doctrine*, pp. 296–98 and 320, rightly quoting the clear and insightful contribution of Claude Welch). The doctrine of the Holy Spirit testifies that our experience of the dynamic presence of God is not reducible to our own ideals, institutions, or self-awareness, but is the experience of the living God—a central theme for Niebuhr. The Holy Spirit points to our sense of God's dynamic presence now—also a strong and central theme in Niebuhr's writings, which I wish he had connected explicitly with the Holy Spirit. Furthermore, it is the Holy Spirit who inspired the prophets in their proclamations of God's commitment to covenant justice and judgment on injustice, Jesus in his announcing the at-handness of God's rulership, and the disciples at Pentecost to be saved from this crooked generation, sell their goods and distribute to those who had need, form community

and practice effective evangelism. Had Niebuhr written directly of the Holy Spirit's empowerment of the struggle for justice and community, as in the inspiration of the prophets, Jesus' announcement of the reign of God, and the early disciples' practices, then his Christian ethics lectures on God as Governor and Judge would point not only to our experience of limitation and our restraining of others; they would also point to God's commitment to *justice* that flows like a mighty stream, and to the kingdom of God (God's rule), which emphasizes community-restoring covenant justice. See my essay in *Theology Without Foundations*, ed. Hauerwas, Murphy, and Nation (Abingdon: Nashville, 1994).

20. See above, p. 61.

21. See above, p. 40.

22. See above, p. 42.

23. See above, p. 59, citing C&C, 28 and 39.

24. See above, p. 60.

25. See above, p. 279, n. 82.

26. Lonnie Kliever, *H. Richard Niebuhr* (Waco: Word, 1977), pp. 145–50.

27. Joseph L. Allen, "A Decisive Influence on Protestant Ethics," *Christianity and Crisis* 23 (November 25, 1963), p. 217; John Bennett, "Ethical Principles and the Context," Presidential Address, *Yearbook of the American Society of Christian Social Ethics* (1960–1961), pp. 12ff.

28. Michael G. Cartwright, "The Practice and Performance of Scripture: Grounding Christian Ethics in a Communal Hermeneutic," *The Annual of the Society of Christian Ethics* (Knoxville: University of Tennessee Press, 1988), pp. 31ff.

29. Gerd Theissen, *Social Reality and the Early Christians* (Minneapolis: Fortress, 1992), pp. 10–13.

30. Immanuel Kant, *Religion Within the Limits of Reason Alone* (Chicago: Open Court, 1934), p. 163.

31. (MR, 28; See also 23–37). Niebuhr's analysis in the early 1930s and even the late 1920s of the dilemma Kant had bequeathed to theology and of its influence on subjectivism in theology parallels Barth's analysis in his *Protestant Thought: From Rousseau to Ritschl* (New York: Harper, 1959), especially chapter iv. His solution differs, of course. Some have misinterpreted Niebuhr by trying to fit him into Kantian categories; I am endeavoring to demonstrate that attempt to be an error.

32. Niebuhr, "Ernst Troeltsch's Philosophy of Religion," (Ph.D. diss., Yale University, 1924), p. 164. See also pp. 56–60, 74, 111–13, 163f., 218, 262–63, and 266–70.

Niebuhr said the problem in theology was that "Berkeley, Hume, and Kant succeeded in transferring the point of view. . . . Henceforth the subject displaced the object in the center of attention." This caused sterile subjectivism in religion, hollowness in belief, and formlessness and lack of precision in theology and ethics. He urged theology to "resolutely turn its back on all psychologism" and devote itself wholeheartedly to the study of its proper object, God, as "revealed in the ethical and spiritual life" (Niebuhr, "Theology and Psychology: A Sterile Union," p. 47). Niebuhr makes a similar point in *Faith*, 23, 40, 45–46, 64–65, 103.

33. "Ernst Troeltsch's Philosophy of Religion," pp. 172, and 169–86.

34. Ibid., p. 171. Niebuhr continued to commend William James's epistemology in *Faith*, 110.

35. Ibid., pp. 111–12, 163–64, 195–96, and 270.

36. (New York: Harper, 1931 and 1960), 2:1004 and 1006.

37. Ibid., p. 1004.

38. See also Troeltsch, *The Social Teachings of the Christian Churches*, p. 9; "The Dogmatics of the 'Religionsgeschichtliche Schule,'" *American Journal of Theology* XVII (January, 1913), pp. 14ff.; *Christian Thought: Its History and Application* (London: Univ. of London Press, 1923), pp. 67–68.

39. Genesis 11. For two highly insightful essays, see Jeffrey Stout, *Ethics After Babel: The Languages of Morals and their Discontents* (Boston: Beacon Press, 1988); and Michael Walzer, "Zwei Arten des Universalismus," *Babylon: Beiträge zur jüdischen Gegenwart* 7 (1990), pp. 7–25. See also Walzer's later development of this point in *Thick and Thin: Moral Argument at Home and Abroad* (Notre Dame: University of Notre Dame Press, 1994).

40. Hans Frei, "Niebuhr's Theological Background," in Paul Ramsey, ed., *Faith and Ethics* (New York: Harper, 1957), p. 49; C&C, 24–25; RS, 92–93.

41. C&C, 173–74, 179, 186–89; RS, 92. See Niebuhr's reviews of several of Emil Brunner's books in *The Westminster Bookman* 7 (Sept.-Oct., 1947), pp. 7–8; 9 (May-June, 1950), pp. 3–4; 12 (June, 1953), pp. 11–13; and *Theology Today* 3 (January, 1947), pp. 558–60.

Each of the criticisms in this paragraph of individualistic existentialism and its understanding of revelation is made by both Niebuhr and Frei. But surprisingly, Frei is aiming his criticisms at Niebuhr. His otherwise precise and perceptive discussion of Niebuhr's theological method does not mention Niebuhr's departure from Kierkegaardian existentialism.

Frei treats Niebuhr's concepts of inner history and outer history as a Kantian dualism with no interaction between the two. Niebuhr, however, specifies four ways in which they interact, as will be seen below—concerning Niebuhr's method of validation. And he states they are perspectives, not separate truths.

Frei then expresses surprise that such dualism does not occur in Niebuhr's other books. I think that is correct, and that Niebuhr is not a dualist in fact—in MR either, and certainly should not be read by importing Kant's dualism.

Frei shifts to warning against a dualistic interpretation of inner and outer history in his "H. Richard Niebuhr on History, Church and Nation," in *The Legacy of H. Richard Niebuhr*, Ronald F. Thiemann, ed. (Minneapolis: Fortress, 1991), p. 13. I emphasize my admiration for Frei's interpretation of Niebuhr; except on this point, which he corrected later, he is accurate and incisive.

42. Niebuhr, "The Triad of Faith," *Andover Newton Bulletin* 47 (October, 1954), p. 10.

43. Niebuhr, "On the Nature of Faith," in Hook, ed., p. 99. See also *Faith*, 47.

44. Ibid., p. 98.

45. MR, 71f., 99–101, 110, 123, 126, 129, 132f., 136f. Story appears ten times—pp. 46, 60, 64, 72, 90,125. As Niebuhr proceeds, he seems to shift from story to drama. To some, *story* connotes fiction to be read in private. *Drama* is embodied in deeds, enacted in community, and includes social conflict, history, and the patterns by which we interpret our lives and their struggles. Drama is more explicitly social and communal, not private or individualistic. See "dramatic history" below.

46. Hazen Foundation, (1949?), pp. 10–12.

47. Among many examples, see Stanley Hauerwas, *The Peaceable Kingdom* (Notre Dame: University of Notre Dame Press, 1983); Hauerwas and L. Gregory

Jones, *Why Narrative?* (Grand Rapids:Eerdmans, 1989); Paul Nelson, *Narrative and Morality* (University Park: The Pennsylvania State University Press, 1987); McClendon, *Ethics: Systematic Theology*, Volume I and *Doctrine: Systematic Theology*, Volume II.

48. (MR, 91; cf. 73f., 77, 80, 90, 92, 94, 103f., 106, 122).

49. Martin Cook has rightly noticed that Niebuhr's method is not fideist or "internalist," but does involve external validation. See his *The Open Circle* (Minneapolis: Fortress, 1991), pp. 74ff.

50. Frank Tupper, *A Scandalous Providence: The Jesus Story of the Compassion of God* (Macon: Mercer University Press, 1995), pp. 22ff.

51. Michael Walzer, *Company of Critics* (New York: Basic Books, 1988), pp. 67–68. For a fuller account, see Walzer, "Zwei Arten des Universalismus," pp. 7–25, as well as his *Thick and Thin*. Walzer's and Niebuhr's methods are intriguingly similar; a synthesis between them could provide a powerful ethic.

52. Walzer, "A Particularism of My Own," *Religious Studies Review* 16/3 (1990), pp. 196–97. His *Exodus and Revolution* (New York: Basic Books, 1985) is the story of such reiteration.

53. Bleicher, commenting on Gadamer and Habermas, argues that we need criticism not only by the idealism of inner history, but of the material conditions of work and domination: "The experience of half-truths, lies, propaganda, manipulation and oppression of thought, censorship, etc. provide a prima facie case. . . ." *Contemporary Hermeneutics: Hermeneutics as Method, Philosophy and Critique* (London, Boston, and Henley: Routledge and Kegan Paul, 1980), pp. 3–4, 143, 155, and 175.

54. E. P. Sanders, *The Historical Figure of Jesus* (London: Penguin, 1993), pp. 106, 147, 192–94, 197, 204, 226f., 237; W. D. Davies and Dale Allison, *A Critical and Exegetical Commentary on the Gospel According to Saint Matthew* (Edinburgh: T & T Clark, 1988), pp. 616f.; Richard Horsley, *Jesus and the Spiral of Violence* (Minneapolis: Fortress, 1993), pp. 181–84.

55. Wink, *Engaging the Powers* (Minneapolis: Fortress, 1992), chapter 7.

56. Richard Horsley, "Ethics and Exegesis: 'Love Your Enemies' and the Doctrine of Nonviolence," in Willard M. Swartley, ed., *The Love of Enemy and Nonretaliation in the New Testament* (Louisville: Westminster/John Knox, 1992), p. 91. Horsley engages in a debate with Theissen and Wink here and elsewhere, although their positions actually are close. Horsley locates the Jesus movement in Galilean villages and emphasizes that Jesus' peacemaking was not merely negative prohibitions (nonviolence or nonretaliation) but positive initiatives of reconciliation, and especially positive steps to alleviate the economic need and the economic injustice experienced in those villages. If we see Jesus' teachings as concrete practices which are relevant in other concrete situations, not by rote repetition but by concretely imaginative reiteration according to the faithful will of God in those contexts, then we can understand how specific peacemaking practices in the villages that Horsley describes become the peacemaking practices adapted to relations with Romans and other Gentiles that Theissen and Wink describe. This is Klassen's point in *The Love of Enemy and Nonretaliation*, pp. 11 and 28. My own interpretation in *Just Peacemaking: Transforming Initiatives for Justice and Peace* (Louisville: Westminster/John Knox, 1992) agrees with Horsley in placing greater emphasis on economic justice, and with Wink on transforming initiatives.

57. Theissen, *Sociology of Early Palestinian Christianity* (Philadelphia: Fortress, 1978), pp. 12ff. and 41–46.

58. Gerd Theissen, *Sociology of Early Palestinian Christianity*, p. 37; Richard Horsley, *Jesus and the Spiral of Violence*, pp. 193ff. and 246–55; Albert Nolan, *Jesus Before Christianity* (Maryknoll: Orbis, 1992), pp. 62ff.; Pinchas Lapide, *The Sermon on the Mount: Utopia or Program for Action?* (Maryknoll: Orbis, 1986), pp. 23, 79–82, 105ff.

59. Theissen, *Biblical Faith* (Philadelphia: Fortress Press, 1985), pp. 92 and 120; Sanders, *The Historical Figure of Jesus*, pp. 236ff.

60. Theissen, *Sociology of Early Palestinian Christianity*, pp. 49–50 and 61; Theissen, *Social Reality and the Early Christians* (Minneapolis: Fortress Press, 1992), pp. 136ff. John Dominic Crossan, *The Historical Jesus* (San Francisco: HarperSanFrancisco, 1991), pp. 218ff., taking into account Horsley's argument against an early Zealot movement.

61. Theissen, *Social Reality and the Early Christians*, pp. 150–54. Yoder made the same point in *Politics of Jesus* (2nd ed. Grand Rapids: Eerdmans, 1994), chapter 5. In that book, Yoder discusses manifold New Testament passages incisively; I shall not cite them here, but simply rely on his discussion. See also Pinchas Lapide, pp. 103–134.

62. Walter Wink, *Engaging the Powers*, chapter 9. Glen Stassen, *Just Peacemaking*, chapters 2–3.

63. William Klassen, "Reflections on the Current Status of Research," in Swartley, ed., *The Love of Enemy and Nonretaliation in the New Testament*, p. 4.

64. Gerd Theissen, *Biblical Faith: An Evolutionary Approach*, pp. 87 and 127.

65. Theissen, *Sociology of Early Palestinian Christianity*, pp. 55, 58, and 64.

66. This is the major theme of Elizabeth Schüssler Fiorenza, *In Memory of Her* (New York: Crossroad, 1983); See also Horsley, *Jesus and the Spiral of Violence*, chapter 8 and especially pp. 240ff. Yoder had already emphasized this theme in *The Politics of Jesus*, and he develops it in *Body Politics: Five Practices of the Christian Community Before the Watching World* (Nashville: Discipleship Resources, 1992), pp. 47–60.

67. Wink, *Engaging the Powers*, chapter 6.

68. Wink, *Engaging the Powers*, chapter 6; Sanders, *The Historical Figure of Jesus*, pp. 196ff.; David Garland, *Reading Matthew* (New York: Crossroad, 1993), pp. 66–70; This is at the heart of the argument of Allen Verhey, *The Great Reversal: Ethics and the New Testament* (Grand Rapids: Eerdmans, 1984).

69. Ibid., pp. 161ff. and chapter 16.

70. Ibid., pp. 304ff. Marcus Borg, *Jesus: A New Vision* (San Francisco: HarperSanFrancisco, 1987), pp. 43–45.

71. H. R. Niebuhr, "Introduction to Biblical Ethics," in Waldo Beach and H. R. Niebuhr, *Christian Ethics* (New York: Ronald Press, 1955), pp. 33–34.

72. Larry Rasmussen, *Moral Fragments and Moral Community* (Minneapolis: Fortress, 1993), pp. 138ff and 152ff.

73. Ibid., p. 160.

74. *The Social Teachings of the Christian Churches*, pp. 156–58, 231, 244, 252–54, 257–59, 280–83, 577–79, 622–25, 673–36, 688–91.

75. *The Priestly Kingdom* (Notre Dame: University of Notre Dame Press, 1984), pp. 61–62.

76. (Nashville: Discipleship Resources, 1992).

77. H. R. Niebuhr address, Monday Noon Forum, Union Theological Seminary (New York), February, 1960. The address is reported in articles by Douglas

John Hall and Stephen Rose in *The Grain of Salt*, 13/9 (Feb. 23, 1960), pp. 1–2; my description is based also on my own notes and conversation with Niebuhr.

78. PCM, 36; RMWC, 86, and scattered throughout his writings. In his unpublished essay, "A Christian Interpretation of War," p. 8, he calls idolatry "the worship of the finite as though it were infinite, the devotion to the relative as though it were absolute."

79. Niebuhr, review of *The Protestant Era*, in *Religion in Life* XVII (Spring, 1949), p. 292; review of *Systematic Theology*, in *Union Seminary Quarterly Review* VII (November, 1951), p. 49. See also *Faith*, 103–104, including footnote 4.

80. "Evangelical and Protestant Ethics," p. 224; see MR, 22–38.

81. "Reinhold Niebuhr's Interpretation of History," unpublished lecture, The Hazen Foundation, 1949.

82. H. R. Niebuhr, "The Grace of Doing Nothing," *The Christian Century* 44 (March 23, 1932), pp. 378–80. Reinhold Niebuhr, "Must We Do Nothing?", ibid. (March 30, 1932), pp. 415–17. H. R. Niebuhr, "The Only Way Into the Kingdom of God," ibid. (April 6, 1932), p. 447. Hans Frei interprets the debate, and Reinhold's misunderstanding, in his "H. Richard Niebuhr on History, Church, and Nation," pp. 15ff.

83. Reinhold's misinterpretion of his brother's argument has influenced several subsequent commentators on the debate. For example, Richard B. Miller's otherwise close and perceptive analysis, "H. R. Niebuhr's War Articles: A Transvaluation of Value," *Journal of Religion* 68 (1988), says HRN "argues for nonintervention by the United States in the Sino-Japanese conflict . . . thus implicitly allying himself with Christian pacifists" (p. 242). Miller gives no evidence or citation for this statement. But having assumed H. Richard was arguing for nonintervention and pacifism, Miller then concludes: "What is puzzling . . . is that he distanced himself from those positions to which he seemed allied. In [HRN's reply to Reinhold], "he retorted, 'To import pacifism of any sort into this struggle is only to weaken the weaker self-asserters'" (p. 243). Miller finds it puzzling that HRN explicitly rejected pacifism as relevant to the debate because he assumes HRN was arguing for pacifism. Nowhere in the debate does HRN argue either for nonintervention or for pacifism. It was widely agreed that the U.S. seemed powerless to do anything. The question was *how* to do nothing—resentfully, self-righteously, or expectantly.

84. "War as the Judgment of God," *The Christian Century* 59 (May 13, 1942), pp. 630–33; "Is God in the War?", ibid. (August 5, 1942), pp. 953–55; "War as Crucifixion," ibid. 60 (April 28, 1943), pp. 513–15; "A Christian Interpretation of War," unpublished (1943).

85. "The Responsibility of the Church for Society," in *The Gospel, the Church and the World* K. S. Latourette, ed. (New York and London: Harper, 1946), p. 128; see also "Utilitarian Christianity," *Christianity and Crisis* 6 (July 8, 1946), pp. 3–5.

86. *The Church Against the World*, p. 146.

87. "Why Have We Gathered in This Place?: A Critical Evaluation of Selected Theories of Community," (Ph.D. diss., New York: Union Theological Seminary, 1993), pp. 100ff.

88. KGA, 55–56. See RMWC, 47–48; "The Grace of Doing Nothing"; Jon Diefenthaler, *H. Richard Niebuhr: A Lifetime of Reflections on the Church and the World* (Macon: Mercer University Press, 1986), pp. 64ff.

89. In his *Engaging the Powers*, pp. 309, 311, and 314ff., Walter Wink argues

that the biblical concept of the principalities and powers makes clear that much evil happens which God does not will; blaming it on God creates problems of theodicy, fatalism, and misinformed prayer. This connects with Diane Yeager's perceptive call for a theory of principalities and powers in Niebuhr's thought. To know the difference between what God does and what the powers do, we need concrete norms indicating what God does and does not do or will. Frank Tupper's incisive and persuasive *Scandalous Providence* supplies the corrective that I want to argue for here.

90. "Religious Realism in the Twentieth Century," pp. 420–21.

91. H. Richard Niebuhr, "The Lord's Prayer," chapel meditation at Union Theological Seminary, New York, 1953 (typescript based on a tape recording, available in Harvard Divinity School Library).

92. "The Church Defines Itself in the World" (June, 1957).

93. Adolfo Pérez Esquivel, *Christ in a Poncho* (Maryknoll: Orbis, 1983), p. 134.

94. Gerhard von Rad, *Old Testament Theology*, 2 vols., tr. D. M. G. Stalker (New York: Harper, 1962), 1:214–18).

95. Edward M. Curtis, "Idol, Idolatry," *Anchor Bible Dictionary*, David Noel Freedman, ed. (Doubleday: New York, 1992), 3:379. I also owe thanks to Phyllis Trible for insights on this point.

96. Dr. Wyatt Tee Walker, my pastor at Canaan Baptist Church of Christ, often says this in his sermons, which are characterized by clear and memorable biblical exegesis, and concrete and prophetic application in our lives.

97. In *Ernst Troeltsch: Writings on Theology and Religion* (Atlanta: John Knox Press, 1977), pp. 182–207, translated by Robert Morgan and Michael Pye, to whom we owe a debt of gratitude. Troeltsch's German in this essay is complex, and the essay had not been read as widely as it deserves. Morgan and Pye perhaps reveal a widespread tendency to overlook the concrete content of Jesus' ethics when they translate the title, "Die Bedeutung der Geschichtlichkeit Jesu für den Glauben," as "The Significance of the Historical Existence of Jesus for Faith." By *Geschichtlichkeit* Troeltsch means to include the basic shape of Jesus' teachings and not merely that Jesus existed; and by *den Glauben* he means the faith of the Christian community, not only individuals.

98. "Significance," pp. 196–97. I have altered the translation of the German *Kultus* to *worship*, which is its meaning in contemporary English.

99. Ibid., p. 200.

100. *The Pulpit* 33 (April, 1962), pp. 4–7.

101. *The Politics of Jesus*, pp. 4ff.

Chapter 4

1. See evidence in my "Sovereignty of God," pp. 254-72.

2. "Since Niebuhr conceives of sin as false faith, salvation from sin means the transformation of natural faith into radical faith." Lonnie Kliever, *H. Richard Niebuhr* (Waco: Word, 1977), p. 93.

3. Daniel Day Williams, *The Spirit and the Forms of Love* (New York: Harper and Row, 1968), chapter VI and IX, as well as his earlier *God's Grace and Man's Hope* (New York: Harper, 1949) with its criticisms of individualistic existentialism.

4. Kliever, pp. 87, 93, 108, and p. 197, note 57. Kliever developed a triadic

interpretation and a tetrahedron model extensively in his 1963 dissertation. Glen Stassen and James Fowler both wrote dissertations on "The Sovereignty of God in the Theological Ethics of H. Richard Niebuhr," in 1967 and 1972, respectively. Fowler applied and thereby confirmed a number of Kliever's and Stassen's insights, and subsequently published a revised version as *To See The Kingdom: The Theological Vision of H. Richard Niebuhr* (Nashville: Abingdon, 1974).

5. Jonathan Edwards, *Select Works of Jonathan Edwards*, volume I (London: The Banner of Truth Trust, 1965), "Narrative of Surprising Conversions" and other writings.

6. H. R. Niebuhr, "Jonathan Edwards," in Waldo Beach and H. Richard Niebuhr, *Christian Ethics* (New York: The Ronald Press, 1955 and 1973), pp. 380–89.

7. Ibid., pp. 385–86.

8. Yoder, *Body Politics: Five Practices of the Christian Community Before the Watching World* (Nashville: Discipleship Resources, 1989).

9. Ibid., (pp. 4, 6, 9, 11–12, and 41–42).

10. Ibid., chapter 1.

11. Ibid., pp. 16–23.

12. Ibid., p. 60; and chapter 4.

13. Ibid., p. 61.

14. H. Berkhof, *Christ and the Powers*, translated from the Dutch by John H. Yoder (Scottdale: Herald, 1962).

15. Walter Wink, *Naming the Powers: The Language of Power in the New Testament* (Philadelphia: Fortress, 1984). See also Wink's other two volumes, *Unmasking the Powers: The Invisible Forces That Determine Human Existence* (Philadelphia: Fortress, 1986) and *Engaging the Powers: Discernment and Resistance in a World of Domination* (Minneapolis: Fortress, 1992). Since Yoder pioneered in bringing the concept to our attention, numerous other scholars have also developed the concept further, so that we now have a tool available for our use that H. R. Niebuhr did not have ready at hand.

16. *Naming the Powers*, p. 99.

17. Ibid., p. 4.

18. Ibid., p. 5.

19. Ibid., p. 10.

20. Ibid., pp. 11–12.

21. Ibid., pp. 14–15.

22. In *The Meaning of Revelation*. Niebuhr was misinterpreted by some as setting up a Kantian dualism between inner and outer history; his intention was much more interactionist.

23. *Unmasking the Powers*, p. 54.

24. *Engaging the Powers*, pp. 77–78.

25. *Naming the Powers*, p. 66; See also pp. 84 and 110.

26. Ibid., p. 110.

27. Ibid.

28. *Unmasking the Powers*, p. 55.

29. *Naming the Powers*, p. 103.

30. *Unmasking the Powers*, pp. 102–105.

31. *Engaging the Powers*, p. 61.

32. *Unmasking the Powers*, pp. 145 and 147.

33. Ibid., pp. 144 and 147–48.

34. *Unmasking the Powers*, p. 64.

35. *Naming the Powers*, p. 126.

36. Ibid., pp. 89–99 and elsewhere. See also Yoder, *Christian Witness to the State* (Newton: Faith and Life, 1964).

37. *Engaging the Powers*, pp. 82–83. Wink's point is strengthened when we realize that when he uses the word, "things," he is referring to English translations of Greek New Testament passages that never say "all *things*," "*things* on heaven and earth," etc. The Greek simply says "all," "all on heaven and earth," and the like. Paul is not thinking primarily of inanimate "things," like rocks and trees, as the English suggests, but of persons and powers which bear a spiritual reality and which need redeeming. The Greek, *ta panta* and *panton*, often refers to "all who believe" or "all who sin" etc.—clearly meaning not simply things, but persons or realities that have a spiritual-personal dimension (see Rom. 8:28 and 32; 11:36; 12:17 and 18; Gal. 3:22; I Cor. 8:6; 15:27–28; II Cor. 5:18; Eph. 3:9 and 4:10, and throughout Eph. 1 and Col. 1). Many of these passages express Pauline concern for overcoming the hostility between Jews and Gentiles, and their lack of faith, and the powers that keep them hostile and disbelieving; the passages are not primarily interested in inanimate "things" like stars, moons, mountains, or trees.

38. *Unmasking the Powers*, pp. 58, 64, 80–82, 126.

39. Ibid., pp. 84ff.; *Engaging the Powers*, p. 84, and the whole of part 2 and part 3.

40. John Howard Yoder, "To Serve our God and to Rule the World" (Presidential Address of the Society of Christian Ethics), *The Annual of the Society of Christian Ethics*, Diane M. Yeager, ed. (Washington: Georgetown University Press, 1988), p. 7.

41. See Eberhard Bethge, *Dietrich Bonhoeffer* (New York and London: Harper, 1977), p. 783: "The starting point of hermeneutics is not philosophy or translation but discipleship—the relationship of the interpreter to the Lord in prayer discipline and action for others." And p. 788: "The proclamation of Jesus in our world . . . will not be able to separate the preached word from the life of the preacher because this very life speaks more loudly than any words."

42. Carl S. Dudley, ed., *Building Effective Ministry: Theory and Practice in the Local Church* (San Francisco: Harper, 1983), p. xi.

43. Quoted in Wade Clark Roof and William McKinney, *American Mainline Religion: Its Changing Shape and Future* (New Brunswick and London: Rutgers University Press, 1987), p. 233.

44. See William Johnson Everett, *God's Federal Republic: Reconstructing our Governing Symbol* (New York: Paulist, 1988).

45. Niebuhr, "The Responsibility of the Church for Society," in K. S. Latourette, ed., *The Gospel, the Church and the World* (New York and London: Harper, 1946), pp. 111–33; See Diane Yeager's essay above.

46. Ibid., pp. 126–28.

47. Avery Dulles, S. J., *Models of the Church*, expanded edition (New York: Doubleday, 1987), pp. 210–11.

48. Larry Rasmussen, *Moral Fragments and Moral Community: A Proposal for Church in Society* (Minneapolis: Fortress, 1993), pp. 138–40.

49. David Gushee, *Righteous Gentiles of the Holocaust* (Minneapolis: Fortress, 1994), pp. 158 and 165).

50. Ibid., p. 171.

51. Ibid., p. 119.

52. Ibid., pp. 119–20.

53. Ibid., p. 123; cf. pp. 121–23.

54. James Wm. McClendon, Jr., *Doctrine: Systematic Theology*, Vol. II (Nashville: Abingdon, 1994). pp. 359–60.

55. Gushee, pp. 93–95.

56. Roof and McKinney, *American Mainline Religion*, pp. 19–22.

57. See above, pp. 130-31.

58. Wuthnow conversation with Glen Stassen after the Norton Lectures at Southern Baptist Theological Seminary, Louisville, November 1993.

59. James F. Hopewell, *Congregation: Stories and Structures*, edited by Barbara G. Wheeler (Philadelphia: Fortress, 1987), p. 165.

60. Dean R. Hoge, *Division in the Protestant House* (Philadelphia: Westminster, 1976), p. 126; see also pp. 46 and 115.

61. Roof and McKinney, *American Mainline Religion*, pp. 20–24.

62. Ibid., pp. 19–23 and 81–82; see also Hoge, pp. 43–44.

63. Daniel Buttry, *Bringing Your Church Back to Life: Beyond Survival Mentality* (Valley Forge: Judson, 1988 and 1990), p. 83.

64. Michael Westmoreland-White, "Incarnational Discipleship: The Ethics of Clarence Jordan, Martin Luther King, Jr., and Dorothy Day" (Ph.D. diss., The SOuthern Baptist Theological Seminary, 1995), pp. 299-304.

65. Niebuhr, "Responsibility of the Church for Society," p. 130.

66. Ibid., p. 130.

67. Dietrich Bonhoeffer, *Ethics* (New York: MacMillan, 1965), pp. 224ff. et passim.

68. Ibid., pp. 110ff.

69. Yoder, *Christian Witness to the State*, pp. 19–22.

70. Rasmussen, *Moral Fragments and Moral Community*, pp. 152–53.

71. Ibid., pp. 154–59.

72. Ibid., p. 53.

73. See Roof and McKinney, *American Mainline Religion*, pp. 99f. and 251.

74. Buttry, *Bringing Your Church Back to Life*, p. 67, and interview with Glen Stassen at the Baptist Peace Fellowship Conference, Birmingham, July, 1993.

75. Rasmussen, pp. 128 and 166. See Bethge, *Bonhoeffer*, pp. 783ff. on the arcane discipline. Cf. Stassen, *Journey into Peacemaking* (Memphis: Brotherhood Commission, 1983 and 1987).

76. Robert Wuthnow, *Acts of Compassion* (Princeton: Princeton University Press, 1991), pp. 5f. and 10.

77. Ibid., pp. 154–6.

78. Robert Wuthnow, *New York Times* (February 28, 1993), Midwest edition, p. 29, and Norton Lectures, November 1993.

79. Gushee, pp. 141ff.

80. Ibid., pp. 101f., 108–110.

81. Ibid., pp. 111, 113, 126ff., 134ff.

82. Ibid., pp. 111–12.

83. Yoder, *Body Politics*, pp. 61ff.

84. Thom S. Rainer, *The Book of Church Growth: History, Theology, and Principles* (Nashville: Broadman, 1993), pp. 198–200, 221, 282, and his chapter on small groups.

85. Ibid., pp. 75–84, 203, 222, 240, 260.

86. Ibid., p. 183. An ethicist would object that this makes prayer a means to

an end. Surely Rainer means statistics add yet one more argument to his other reasons for advocating prayer, reasons he knew long before he studied statistics. And surely prayer is not only a good in itself but also a means to seeking God's good purposes.

87. Rainer, pp. 195ff.

88. Ebbie Smith, *Balanced Church Growth: Church Growth Based on the Model of Servanthood* (Nashville: Broadman, 1984), says "discipleship means changing from the self-centered, worldly existence to the life-style exemplified by Jesus," and emphasizes a servant pattern of ministry as seen in the prophet Isaiah and the incarnate Christ.

89. Buttry, pp. 51–52, 28–29, 34f., 44ff., 96–99.

90. Ibid., pp. 36ff., 41ff., 61ff., 85ff., and 137ff.

91. See Jim Wallis, "Idols Closer to Home: Radical Christian Substitutes for Grace," *Sojourners* (May, 1979), 10–14.

92. John Howard Yoder, *The Priestly Kingdom: Social Ethics as Gospel* (Notre Dame: University of Notre Dame Press, 1984), pp. 61–62.

93. Ibid.

94. Gushee, pp. 93f.

95. Ibid., pp. 113–114.

96. Ibid., p. 114.

97. David Roozen, William McKinney, and Jackson Carroll, *Varieties of Religious Presence: Mission in Public Life* (New York: Pilgrim, 1984).

98. Pp. 262–63.

99. See the perceptive book by one who has learned much from Niebuhr, James Gustafson: *Treasure in Earthen Vessels: The Church as a Human Community* (Chicago & London: The University of Chicago Press, 1961 and 1976).

100. Martin Buber, *Between Man and Man* (New York: MacMillan, 1947), pp. 41, 70f., 199ff.

101. Roof and McKinney, *American Mainline Religion*, pp. 37–38 and 251.

102. James Davison Hunter, *Culture Wars: The Struggle to Define America* (United States: Culture Wars, 1991), p. 50.

103. Robert N. Bellah, William M. Sullivan, Ann Swidler, and Steven M. Tipton, *Habits of the Heart: Individualism and Commitment in American Life* (New York: Harper, 1985), p. 162.

104. Bellah, et al., *Habits of the Heart*; Roof and McKinney, *American Mainline Religion*; Robert Wuthnow, *The Consciousness Reformation* (Berkeley: University of California Press, 1976); Wuthnow, *Acts of Compassion: Caring for Others and Helping Ourselves* (Princeton: Princeton University Press, 1991).

105. This is a quote and paraphrase of the four defining items in the factor analysis carried out by Roozen, et al., pp. 84–86. Elsewhere they say this type relies on education of their members (pp. 35 and 100), but I have not included this because education is not mentioned in the four defining items that members affirmed in the questionnaire. What the authors mean is that this type avoids organized group action, and avoids conflict. The forfeit reliance, they assume, must be education. Our theological interpretation suggests rather that congregations that lack a sense of God's independence and judging of the culture, and that rely optimistically on individuals as their vehicle, do not see the need for much specific education of adults. They are weak in adult education. This is confirmed by the observation elsewhere by Roozen et al. that in their questionnaire about what issues congregations addressed during the previous year, "the most consistent

pattern in the analysis" of all four types was that the civic congregations did not address any of the twenty-one issues more or less than the average congregation. They "appear to have staked out the middle ground" (p. 92). They avoid conflict and rely on good individuals.

106. Roozen, et al., *Varieties of Religious Presence*, p. 100.

107. The following description summarizes Roozen, et al., *Varieties of Religious Presence*, pp. 101–116.

108. For the sanctuary type, which might be better called the individual traditional authority type, the distinguishing practices were:

> (1) Helping people accept that their condition and status in life is determined and controlled by God, and that therefore one has only to accept it and live the best life possible";
>
> (2) "Helping people resist the temptation to experiment with the new 'pleasures' and 'life-styles' so prominent in our secular society and media";
>
> (3) "Fostering a sense of patriotism among their congregation's members";
>
> (4) "Encouraging members to adhere faithfully to civil laws as they are mandated by governmental authorities" (see items 4, 6, 16, and 23 on pp. 84–86).

109. The following comes from Roozen, et al., *Varieties of Religious Presence*, pp. 192–204.

110. (Berkeley: University of California Press, 1976). Wuthnow studied residents of the San Francisco Bay Area, and contended trends he saw there were likely to be typical, or become typical, in the rest of U.S. society. This generalization was later criticized by other scholars, including Wuthnow himself.

111. Roozen, et al., *Varieties of Religious Presence*, pp. 178–92.

112. Ibid., pp. 204–216.

113. Ibid., p. 257, and footnotes 7 and 8.

114. Roof and McKinney, *American Mainline Religion*, p. 40.

115. Bellah, et al., *Habits of the Heart*, pp. 117ff., 124, 127, 130, 151f., 158, 171f., 175ff., 197, 251, 256.

116. Ibid., p. 78.

117. Ibid., pp. 126, 129ff., 235.

118. Ibid., p. 221.

119. *Consciousness Reformation*, pp. 123–33.

120. Roozen, et al., *Varieties of Religious Presence*, pp. 146–59.

121. Ibid., p. 251.

122. Ibid., pp. 230–46.

123. Ibid., p. 259.

124. Ibid., pp. 160–76.

125. Ibid., p. 248.

126. Ibid., p. 175.

261
ST 796

93759

LINCOLN CHRISTIAN UNIVERSITY

CPSIA information can be obtained at www.ICGtesting.com
Printed in the USA
LVOW11s1616150915

454264LV00003B/668/P

3 4711 00225 2809